Coding
for
kids

2nd Edition

by Camille McCue, PhD

for
dummies®
A Wiley Brand

Coding For Kids For Dummies®, 2nd Edition

Published by: **John Wiley & Sons, Inc.,** 111 River Street, Hoboken, NJ 07030-5774, www.wiley.com

Copyright © 2019 by John Wiley & Sons, Inc., Hoboken, New Jersey

Published simultaneously in Canada

For general information on our other products and services, please contact our Customer Care Department within the U.S. at 877-762-2974, outside the U.S. at 317-572-3993, or fax 317-572-4002. For technical support, please visit https://hub.wiley.com/community/support/dummies.

Wiley publishes in a variety of print and electronic formats and by print-on-demand. Some material included with standard print versions of this book may not be included in e-books or in print-on-demand. If this book refers to media such as a CD or DVD that is not included in the version you purchased, you may download this material at http://booksupport.wiley.com. For more information about Wiley products, visit www.wiley.com.

Library of Congress Control Number: 2019934591

ISBN 978-1-119-55516-2 (pbk); ISBN 978-1-119-55519-3 (ebk); ISBN 978-1-119-55522-3 (ebk)

Manufactured in the United States of America

V10009095_032919

Table of Contents

Part 3: Moving from Here to There, Again and Again... 107

Chapter 8: Emoji Explosion 109

Chapter 9: Smelephant.............................. 133

Part 4: Variables, Simple Conditionals, and I/O 163

Introduction

So you want to learn to *code* — awesome!
Coding — writing computer programs — has something for everyone: creativity, logic, art, math, storytelling, design, and problem solving. From games and simulations to helpful tools and electronic gadgets, this book coaches you step by step through coding *real programs* in *real programming languages* that you can share with family and friends.

About This Book

Many kids want to learn to code, but not every kid has computer programming classes at school or a camp he or she can attend during the summer. That's where this book comes in!

Coding for Kids For Dummies will help you learn all of the basic coding ideas and skills used by real computer programmers. Everything you do here will be useful in learning new skills and more advanced programming languages in the future. Best of all, the tools in this second edition are free, available online, and easy-to-use.

This edition of the book covers the following:

- **Scratch**, a learning language developed at MIT that has risen in prevalence to the point where it is arguably the most popular kid programing language available. As such, this book features numerous projects in the most recent version of Scratch — Scratch 3.0. Scratch is a block-based language that offers new coders an easy entry into computer programming. And it's fun!

⌲ **JavaScript,** which is used in everything from apps to websites to electronics. New programming environments have made JavaScript more accessible than ever through interfaces that allow you to switch between block-based and text-based formats. You can begin learning in block-based mode (as in Scratch), and then transition to text-based mode as you build skills and confidence in coding. In this book, JavaScript projects are presented through two different vehicles (officially called *IDEs* — integrated development environments): Code.org's App Lab, for building mobile device apps, and MakeCode, for coding instructions to operate a small electronics board called a micro:bit.

⌲ **Fundamental computer programming concepts,** which apply to both the projects in this book and additional coding (and, more generally, computer science) work you might pursue in the future.

Additionally, graphic design and animation are incredibly important skills that go hand-in-hand with coding to create great-looking and easy-to-understand digital tools. Although this book provides a little bit of guidance in these areas, the main focus of the content in these pages is coding.

Foolish Assumptions

Hello person buying this book and reading this intro! I assume you are a kid who wants to learn to code. Awesome! You are starting on an adventure that will take you from being a user of technology to being a maker of technology. And it's a lot easier than you might think.

Here are a few other assumptions I make about you (or your technology) as you get started:

⌲ You are comfortable typing on a tablet or a computer and using a mouse or touchpad. Your experience can be either on a Windows or Mac system because instructions for coding each project are platform-independent.

✔ You have an Internet connection and know how to open a web browser to access websites.

✔ For readers choosing to use the micro:bit electronics board, you have a USB port on your computer (via which you'll connect the micro:bit).

✔ You've played with a few apps, websites, or games on a computer, so you have some idea regarding how user interfaces (UI) look and how people interact with a computer via the UI.

✔ You're comfortable with basic math, math operations such as adding whole numbers, and logical operations such as comparing two whole numbers. I introduce algebraic variables in this book, but you don't need to have any prior knowledge of variables.

Lastly, if you struggle with spelling and punctuation — and you're operating in text-based mode — you may need to spend extra time troubleshooting your code for misspellings. The IDE for a programming language can give you clues about which commands it doesn't understand, but you will need to pay special attention to the details.

Icons Used in This Book

As you work through the projects in this book, you'll see four icons. These icons point out different things.

The Tip icon gives you a tip that you can use to make your work easier. You'll see some tips over and over again.

The Remember icon helps you remember and connect the coding concepts and skills you're working on with the big ideas of coding!

The Warning icon tells you to watch out! It marks important information that may save you headaches.

TECHNICAL STUFF

The Technical Stuff icon lets you know more about the nuts and bolts of technical details and hardware help.

Beyond the Book

On the Dummies.com website, I give you some extra goodies that you won't find in this book. Go online to www.dummies.com/cheatsheet/codingforkids for a cheat sheet of coding commands in Scratch and JavaScript. (You can also type **Coding for Kids cheat sheet** in the search bar at www.dummies.com.) Download the information, print it, and keep it with your computer!

Where to Go from Here

You can work on the projects in order, or you can jump around and work on any project you choose. After you gain a little experience coding, you can go in a bazillion new directions. Learn more advanced concepts in Scratch and JavaScript. Make up your own projects. Work on learning more advanced programming languages.

I hope this book inspires you to continue learning more about coding and making things with tech. Kudos on taking the first step! Now go get started!

Part 1
Getting Started

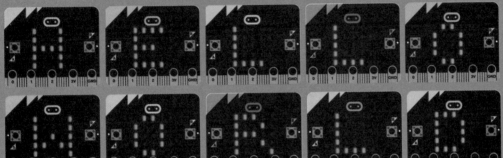

In this part you'll . . .

- Discover the ingredients in a computer program

- Explore the basics of using Scratch, App Lab, and MakeCode

- Gain strategies for fixing code when things go wrong

What Is Coding?

You know that *coding* has to do with building the apps you use and controlling the technology in your life, but what exactly is coding? *Coding,* also known as *computer programming,* is creating instructions for a computing device to do something. You use a language to communicate with other people, and computers use a coding language to communicate. And just as you can learn to write, speak, and understand languages different from the one you first learned as a toddler, you can learn to communicate in a coding language — so that you can "talk to" computers!

You're probably wondering whether coding is hard to learn. The answer is that it's easy to get started with coding, and easy to write real computer programs to perform all sorts of tasks! Unlike the early days of coding, when computer programmers talked to computers using long sequences of numbers (0s and 1s), you can now write code by using words and symbols that you can understand easily. For example, you can tell an app to play a sound three times ("boom boom boom!") with a command such as `repeat 3 (play sound boom)`. Neat, huh?

This type of human-friendly coding, which is called a *high-level language*, is what you will use when you're first learning to code. (Many professional programmers also use high-level languages.) Later, I talk more about high-level languages and the languages you'll use in this book.

You're probably also wondering whether you can make anything cool as a new coder. Yes, you can! In this book, you write code to build games, toys, and electronic gadgets. Everything you create you can play with and share with your friends and family.

What Languages Will I Use?

This book is filled with great projects you can do to learn the basics of coding and make real apps. You'll be using two programming languages to code: Scratch and JavaScript.

In the Scratch language, you build code with *blocks* (also called *tiles*) that snap together to make complete programs. Scratch is a learning language, created especially for kids, and has its own *integrated development environment (IDE)*, which is a fancy name for a place where you write and test code.

JavaScript is a professional programming language that real coders use to make all sorts of things from apps to websites. You will use two easy-peasy IDEs to code in JavaScript: App Lab and MakeCode. As with the Scratch IDE, these JavaScript IDEs let you work in block mode, snapping together your coding commands.

But when you feel ready to tackle text-based coding — typing your commands — you can switch to text mode in App Lab and MakeCode.

You can create your code in Scratch, App Lab, and MakeCode on any computer or tablet. Just be sure you have a good Internet connection, and you're ready to go! You learn more about the basics of working with each language and programming environment in Chapter 2.

What Does a Computer Program Look Like?

A *computer program* consists of the instructions you code to make a computer do something. A program looks like a list of steps, filled with words and symbols. Many words in the list will be familiar, such as for, if, and forever. Words in a computer program are called *commands* because you're commanding the computer to perform some sort of action. Some commands look like combinations of words you know, smushed together into new words. For example, JavaScript uses the onEvent command to find out whether a user has pressed a button.

You might also recognize many of the symbols in a computer program. These look like operators you use in math class (+, –, >. =) and also like punctuation marks you use in English class, such as a period (.) and a semicolon (;).

All of the commands and symbols in a computer program are organized in a special order so that the computer can understand what it is supposed to do. Planning that order and then coding it is a bit like writing an essay, solving a math problem, performing dance choreography, or running a play in football. You have to put together and *execute* (run) the program in a specific order — you can't just put the instructions anywhere and expect the program to work correctly.

A Hello World! Example

Historically, the first computer program a new coding student writes is one that prints the words *"Hello World!"* on the computer screen. Figure 1-1 shows an example of what that code looks like in Scratch, and its resulting *output* (what it displays onscreen).

Figure 1-1

Figure 1-2 shows the same code in JavaScript (in block mode and in text mode) using the App Lab IDE, and its resulting output.

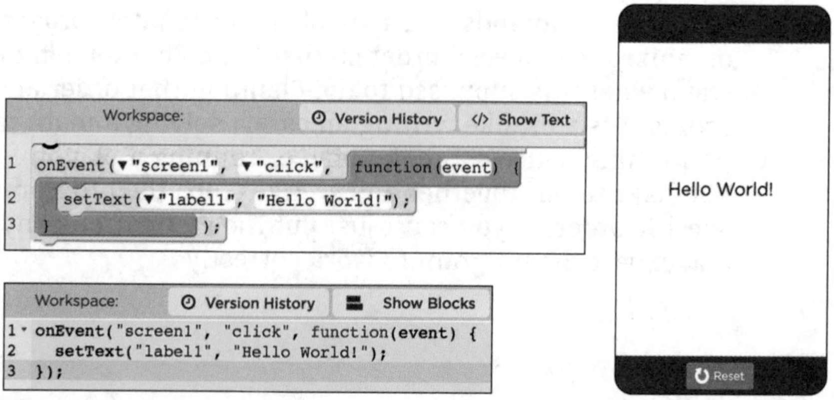

Figure 1-2

Figure 1-3 shows the same code in JavaScript (in block mode and in text mode) using the MakeCode IDE, and the output when displayed on the micro:bit electronics board. Because the micro:bit can scroll only one letter at a time, the figure displays only the letter *H* at the beginning of "Hello World!"

You'll be making little programs like this, and much bigger programs too, in no time!

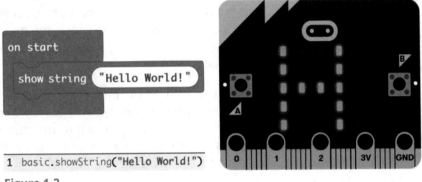

```
1 basic.showString("Hello World!")
```

Figure 1-3

Recipe for a Program

Many mornings, I cook chocolate chip pancakes for my family, following a recipe I created myself. A recipe is like a computer program, and following the recipe is like executing the program. The recipe has parts, including gathering and measuring ingredients, mixing the ingredients to make the pancake batter, and then dropping spoonfuls of the batter onto the griddle to cook it. Similarly, a computer program has parts such as asking the user for information, doing something with that information, and then telling the user the result.

Within each part of a program, you write small chunks of code to perform different processes. A chunk of code that performs a task is called an *algorithm*. For example, one algorithm I perform when making pancakes is testing the surface temperature of the griddle: I plug in the griddle, set it to a certain temperature, and drip a few droplets of water onto the surface to see how quickly they evaporate.

Constructing algorithms is important in coding programs to run on a computer. Think about the types of algorithms you might make in a favorite game you play on your phone. For instance, an algorithm you might code in a Yahtzee game is rolling the dice. Or an algorithm you might code in a Space Invaders game is flying a spaceship across the sky every so often.

The algorithms you create connect with each other to build your entire program. As coders, we have three fancy terms to describe how our algorithms connect: sequence, selection, and repetition. Here's what each means:

- **Sequence:** The order in which a process is conducted. Every computer program must be organized so that steps are executed in a logical order. For example, when making pancakes, I must run my algorithm for making batter before running my algorithm for cooking the batter!

- **Selection:** Choosing a path based on certain conditions. For example, when choosing a movie to attend this weekend, you might decide between an action movie or a comedy. The decision you make then directs you to new sequences — and, consequently, other selections — that relate to your choice. Selection is often coded using conditional statements structured this way: if [condition occurs] then [consequence occurs]. These conditional commands let you create as many paths as needed to respond to the conditions of the program.

- **Repetition:** The process of repeating something. When you repeat code, you make it loop over and over again. A *loop* is a structure that tells the computer to run the same commands multiple times, without the need to rewrite those same commands. You already know how loops work: In a song, the drumbeat is looped to provide a continuous rhythm pattern from the first note of the song to the last.

Throughout the book, you'll see references to sequence, selection, and repetition. Check back here to refresh your memory of how each is used when coding a program.

Planning a Program

As you plan and develop your programs, you'll need to have some organized way of writing them down. You can use several methods to represent a program before you translate it into code for use on a computer.

Some people like to draw a picture or a series of pictures (called a *storyboard*) to show how an app, a game, or a website will look onscreen. This type of work is often performed by *graphic designers,* the people who make the images and the animations for computer programs. You will be doing your own graphic design work for the programs you code in this book, so think about doing a little drawing before you touch the keyboard to code.

Other people like to build a flowchart or write pseudocode when planning their programs. A *flowchart* is like a little map with special boxes and arrows that describe the main parts of the program. Table 1-1 shows some of the most important flowchart symbols and what each symbol represents.

Table 1-1   Symbols Used In Flowcharts

Symbol	Name	What It Means
↓ ⟶	Arrow	Shows the program sequence
⬭	Terminal	Starts or ends the program
▭	Process	Performs a task
◇	Decision	Makes a decision, such as yes or no
▱	Input/output	Accepts input or produces output
⬡	Preparation symbol	Sets up a loop counter

In this book, a couple of programs are planned by using a flow-chart. Figure 1-4 is a simple example of a flowchart for a program in which a user searches for, and plays, a song. The great thing about planning a program with a flowchart is that it helps you think about the overall operation of the program. You can think visually and leave writing code for later!

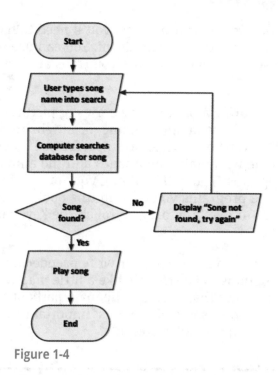

Figure 1-4

Another strategy for planning a program is to jot down your overall ideas in a simplified form of computer code, called *pseudocode*, which means *fake code.* It's not code that the computer can run, but it is written similarly. When writing pseudo-code, you don't have to worry about punctuation such as semicolons or curly brackets, so it keeps your mind on the over-all operation of the program — not the fine details.

For example, if you code part of a *Simpsons* game in which Homer is eating donuts, you might write some pseudocode that looks like this:

```
create variable donuts = 0

if Homer eats donuts
    then add one to donuts

if donuts > 10
    then print "Stop eating donuts!"
    else print "Have another donut!"
```

Whether you choose to draw pictures, flowchart your program, or write pseudocode, it's a good idea to put your plan on paper in some organized form *before* you start coding.

Prepping Yourself to Code

Although coding is about creating new ideas and bringing them to life through computer programs, remember that it's also about your mindset as a coder. Just as you prepare yourself to run a race or compete in a spelling bee, you can do certain things to get ready to code. Here are a few:

✏ **Follow the examples.** The algorithms you learn by coding example programs apply to millions of other programs. For example, learning to make a score increase in one game builds your skill in coding that same process in any game you make. Good coders scour the web and reuse code snippets they find online. Learn by example!

✏ **Think top-down.** Start at the top and work your way down when you're developing a computer program. Don't drill down to the nitty-gritty details of a program when you're first brainstorming a new app. Start by mapping out the overall plan. Then get more specific by drawing pictures or storyboarding your designs. Then create a flowchart. Then write pseudocode. Finally, code the app piece-by-piece.

✔ **Practice patience and resilience.** No matter what you're making — a computer program, a musical performance, or a gourmet meal — patience is required to learn a new skill, and resilience is required to bounce back from challenges to master that skill. You'll need a good dose of both these traits.

✔ **Cultivate your creativity.** Coding is not the cold, calculating discipline many people think it is. From crafting new solutions to a problem to inventing new video games, creativity is a big part of the coding process. Explore as many creative ventures as you can to inspire your programming. Lift your head up from the computer screen, look at the world around you, and listen to the sounds of life. Moving away from your code for a while enables you to come back to it with a fresh new perspective!

✔ **Know that debugging is half the process.** Debugging code means tracing and retracing your steps — sometimes by tracing through each line step-by-step, sometimes by isolating and testing smaller sections of code, and sometimes by testing sample data to examine the output — to find and fix problems. You will spend a lot of time debugging your code to get it fully operational. Managing your frustration during the debugging process is vital to being a successful coder. Keep calm and carry on!

Coding Cool Stuff

Coders make the apps you buy in the app store, but what else do they make? The list of cool things you can create with code is long! For the computer, you can build online games, personal and small business websites, and virtual tours of your photo galleries. For everyday gadgets, you can build backpack alarms, handheld games, health monitors, weather sensors, pet trackers, and remote fish feeders.

If you're into textiles and sewing, you can code programs that control LED lights sewn into fabric so you can craft crazy Halloween and spirit day costumes that literally light up any room you enter! If you're all about security and secret agent activities, you can go cyber, learning Internet basics and encryption techniques to keep online transmissions secure, and information private.

If you have a flair for the theatrical, you can write code to control robots to dance onstage while flying synchronized drones overhead in a stage production. If you love home electronics, you can code devices for use in your smart home, from camera monitors to mood music automated by time of day.

If you want to get wild, you can design, wire, and code an entire yard full of holiday lights, festive music, projection images, and moving figures for the annually televised Great Christmas Light Fight!

And what about those apps in the app store? You can make all sorts of games, from puzzles to wordplay to arcade games. You can build helper tools that assist people with their daily lives. If you're a good Samaritan, you can code apps to connect people in need with available resources, especially in times of crisis. The programs you can code are limited only by your imagination and your skill set.

As a young coder, you can build simple versions of many of these amazing toys and tools today. By doing so, you'll not only have fun and feel the satisfaction of making a real, usable product but also build the foundation for your future.

Working with Programming Languages and IDEs

As a coder, you will work with lots of programming languages. Just like a traveler must know different languages while going from one country to another, you must know a variety of coding languages for different types of projects you'll create. For example, different languages are used for coding a mobile app, a website, a Nintendo Switch game, and a self-driving car. The projects in this book are written in two coding languages that are great for new coders: Scratch and JavaScript.

Scratch is a teaching language made of blocks that you snap together to create programs. You program in Scratch using a website *IDE*, or *integrated development environment*, which is an all-in-one place to build and run your code. The programs you make in Scratch will run on computers and tablets.

JavaScript is a professional language that is text-based, meaning you type commands to create your programs. But don't panic! In this book, you use online IDEs that let you choose whether you want to program JavaScript using text mode or block mode. When you code in the App Lab IDE, you make programs that run on computers and mobile phones. When you code in the MakeCode IDE, you code programs that power an electronics board called a micro:bit. Your programs run on a simulator on the computer screen and — if you want — also on a real micro:bit.

This chapter helps you set up and understand the basic layouts of Scratch, App Lab, and MakeCode. You also learn a little bit about working with images and sounds, so that you can build fun and engaging *UIs,* or *user interfaces,* for your projects.

Basic IDE Setup and Navigation

Scratch, App Lab, and MakeCode are all free, but you need to set up accounts in Scratch and App Lab before you can start coding. MakeCode doesn't require an account.

Setting up your account in Scratch

It's quick and easy to set up an account in Scratch. Just follow these steps:

1. In any web browser, navigate to `https://scratch.mit.edu`.

2. On the Scratch home page, select Join Scratch.

3. In the Scratch dialog box, type a Scratch username and a password, as shown in Figure 2-1. Then click the Next button.

4. Type your birthdate, gender, and country. Then click Next.

5. Type the email of your parent or guardian. Then click Next.

   A screen appears letting you know that you are signed up to use Scratch and that a confirmation email has been sent to your parent or guardian.

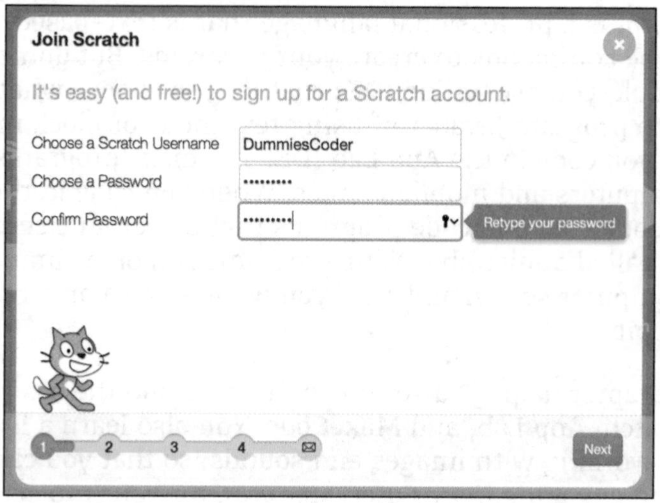

Figure 2-1

6. Your parent or guardian must open the email and confirm that you're permitted to share your work publicly on Scratch.

If the adult doesn't confirm, you can still work in Scratch — but you won't be able to share your programs.

7. Click OK on the final screen to complete the sign-up.

After your Scratch account is set up, you can log in to your account at any time by clicking the Sign In button in the upper-right of the Scratch home page and typing your username and password.

Getting around in Scratch

After you set up your Scratch account, you are taken to the Scratch home page. Here are some of the things you'll see, and some of the actions you can perform.

The Scratch IDE

Select Create on the Scratch home page to open the Scratch IDE. In the Scratch IDE, you see a new, blank project, as shown in Figure 2-2. This is also the same screen you see whenever you choose File⇨New when working in Scratch.

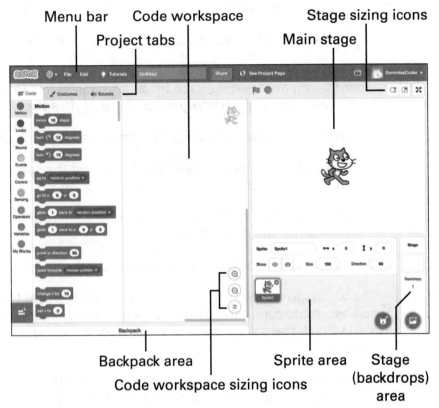

Figure 2-2

The *menu bar* at the top of the Scratch IDE features just a few choices. These are the most important:

- **File⇨New:** Create a new project.

- **Edit:** Allows you turn Turbo mode on or off. When on, this mode executes the program at the fastest possible speed.

- **Project name field:** Name your project.

- **Share button:** Share your project (see Chapter 19).

    ✓ **See Project Page button:** Go to the project page for your current project, where you can give users directions on how to use your program. On the project page, click the See Inside button to get back to the Scratch IDE shown in Figure 2-2.

    ✓ **My Stuff folder icon:** Open projects you've created.

The *tabs* on the left side of the Scratch IDE change depending on whether you are creating code for a *sprite* (an object in Scratch) or for the *stage* (the backdrop where your sprites live):

    ✓ **Code tab:** Access command categories and their blocks.

    ✓ **Costumes tab**: Access sprite costumes and the sprite editor for these images.

    ✓ **Backdrops tab:** Access backdrops for the stage and the backdrop editor for these images.

    ✓ **Sounds tab:** Access sounds and the sound editor.

The *workspace* is the place where you drag command blocks into and assemble command blocks together to make larger *code blocks*. Click the sizing icons to zoom in or zoom out as you build code.

TIP

The Backpack area at the bottom of the Scratch IDE is a place where you can save, store, and reuse project items, sharing them among projects. Just drag a code block, sprite, costume, or sound into the Backpack and it will be available in all projects! Drag any item out of the Backpack for use in any project. Delete an item in the Backpack by right-clicking (Windows) or Ctrl-clicking (Mac) the item.

The *main stage* is the large window that shows you what your user sees. It consists of the sprites and the backdrop. Click a stage sizing icon to resize your view of the stage. Just above the stage are the *green flag* and the *stop* icons; use these to start and stop, respectively, most projects you create.

The *sprite area* displays the sprites (objects) in your project. Each time you start a new project, the Scratch Cat sprite is placed in your project by *default* (something the computer does automatically). Information about this sprite is located just below the stage. The name of the default Scratch Cat sprite is Sprite1. You can find out additional information about Sprite1 in the Sprite area, including position (the *x* and *y* values), *size*, *direction*, and *show* (whether the sprite is showing or hiding, indicated by the eyeball icons).

 If you have more than one sprite in your project, each sprite will appear in the sprite area. The *active*, or selected, sprite has a blue outline around its icon. Clicking a sprite icon to make it the active sprite allows you to write code for that sprite. To add a new sprite, click the *choose a sprite* icon (shown in the margin). To delete a sprite, click the X in the corner of the sprite icon.

The small *stage*, or *backdrops area*, is located in the lower-right corner of the Scratch IDE. Here, an icon shows the current backdrop. Clicking this icon makes the stage active, which means you can write code for the stage, change its background, and add sounds to it.

WARNING

Only one sprite or the stage can be active at a time! Pay attention to which of these is currently selected. If you're writing code, you're writing it for the currently selected object.

Code tab

Figure 2-2 shows the Code tab of the Scratch IDE. You use this tab for both sprites and the stage. It is organized by command categories, as follows:

- **Motion:** Commands to tell sprites (objects) how and where to move. (The stage does not have motion commands.)

- **Looks:** Commands to change the costumes of sprites and backgrounds.

- **Sound:** Commands to play music and sound effects.

- **Events:** Commands to start and end code execution.

- **Control:** Commands to select code or repeat code for execution. (See Chapter 1 for help on code sequence, selection, and repetition.)

✏ **Sensing:** Commands to sense color, sound, position, or user input.

✏ **Operators:** Commands for math and logic operations.

✏ **Variables:** Commands to create and change variables.

✏ **My Blocks:** New commands you define for your project.

To write code for a sprite or for the stage, select a command category and then drag and drop one block into the workspace. Add the next command by dragging a new command below and then snapping it (bringing it close to) the previous command to build a code block. To *execute*, or run, the code block, click the block. The code block will "light up" with a bright yellow outline, and the commands in that block will execute.

You can remove a command block in Scratch by clicking it and dragging it back into the command categories.

TIP

You're using Scratch 3.0, the version released in 2019. It has some cool new features, including text-to-speech and language translation. Click the Add Extension icon below the code categories to check out these features. Also, in this new version, you can create and run code on both computers and tablets!

TIP

Scratch automatically saves your projects, but you can choose to save at any time by choosing File ⇨ Save Now from the menu bar.

Setting up your account in App Lab

Follow these steps to set up an account in App Lab:

1. In any web browser, navigate to https://code.org.

2. On the Code.org home page, click the Sign in button.

3. On the Sign In page, shown in Figure 2-3, click the Create an Account button.

4. Complete the form on the page that appears, and then click the Sign Up button.

A kid can sign up as a student, or a parent can sign up as a teacher. Due to the difficulty level (the inclusion of text-based code), App Lab is designated as a 13+ area of Code.org.

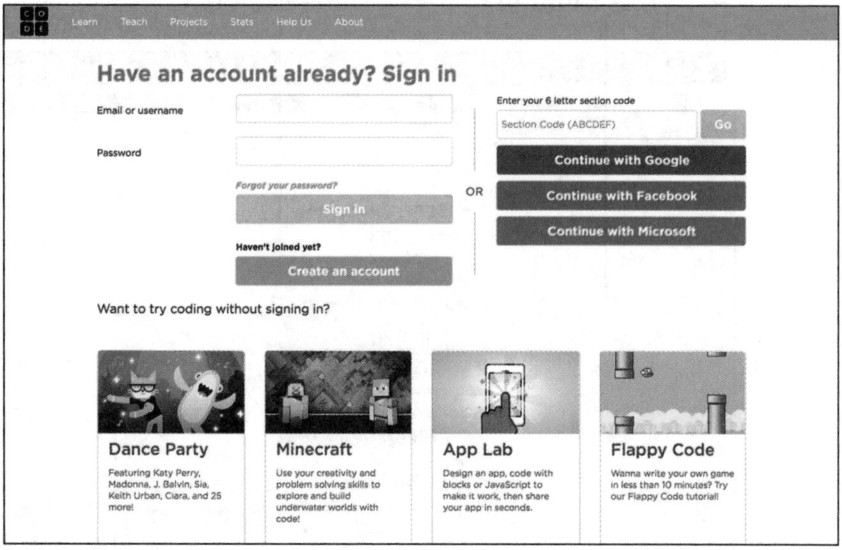

Figure 2-3

5. On the My Dashboard screen, scroll down and click the App Lab icon.

After your Code.org account is set up, you can log in to your account by clicking the Sign In button in the upper right of the Code.org home page and then typing your username and password.

Getting around in App Lab

After you set up your Code.org account, you can sign in at any time and then access App Lab from My Dashboard. Here are some things you can see and do in App Lab.

The App Lab IDE

App Lab opens with a new, blank project, as shown in Figure 2-4. This is also the same screen you see whenever you click the Create New button in App Lab.

Menu bar

Code tab

Design tab

Simulator

Show text or blocks

Version history

Code toolbox

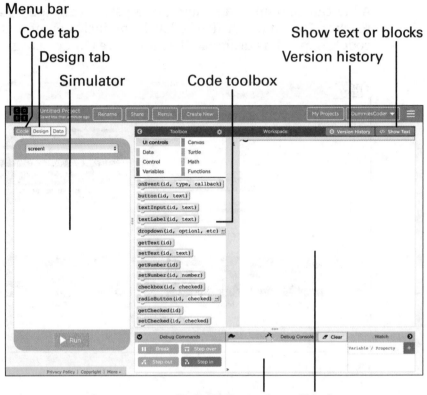

Debug Console   Workspace

Figure 2-4

The *menu bar* at the top of the App Lab IDE features just a few choices. These are the most important:

✔ **Rename button:** Name your project.

✔ **Share button:** Share your project (see Chapter 19).

✔ **Remix button:** Copy and modify the current project.

✔ **Create New button:** Create a new project.

✔ **My Projects button:** Open projects you've created.

The left side of the App Lab IDE has three *buttons.* You'll use two:

- **Code View button:** Access the command categories and their blocks.

- **Design View button:** Lay out the UI of the app shown in the simulator.

The *workspace* is the place where you drag command blocks into, and assemble command blocks together to build your *program.* You can click the *Show Text* button to code in text-based mode. When working in text-based mode, you can click the *Show Blocks* button to code in blocks mode.

TIP

When working, you may want to access a previous version of your code, especially if you make changes that result in some major bugs. (See Chapter 3 for help on debugging.) Click the *Version History* button to "rewind the clock" to an earlier version of your program.

The *simulator* is the window on the left that shows you what your user sees. Here, you can see and interact with your program as it executes. The simulator is always in *portrait orientation* (vertical). The *screen selector,* the drop-down menu at the top of the simulator, allows you to select a screen to work on while you design your app. Click the *Run* button to run your program.

The *Debug Console* is the window at the bottom that gives you clues about mistakes in your program as your code executes. (See Chapter 3 for additional help on debugging code.)

Code View button and the toolbox

When you click the Code View button, the App Lab view shown in Figure 2-4 appears. This view includes the toolbox of coding commands you can use to build your program, organized by of command category:

- **UI Controls:** Commands to control the user interface.

- **Data:** Commands for accessing online data, as well as other advanced features. (The projects in this book do not use the advanced commands.)

✔ **Control:** Commands to select code or repeat code for execution. (See Chapter 1 for help on code sequence, selection, and repetition.)

✔ **Variables:** Commands to create and change variables.

✔ **Canvas:** Commands to control the background of the app.

✔ **Turtle:** Special commands for drawing tools.

✔ **Math:** Commands for math and logic operations.

✔ **Functions:** New commands that you define for your project.

To write code, select a command category and then drag and drop one block into the workspace. Add the next command by dragging a new command below and then snapping it (bringing it close to) the previous command to build your program. To *execute*, or run, the program, click the Run button.

TIP

You can delete a command block in App Lab by clicking it and dragging it back into the toolbox. Or in text mode, select the commands you want to get rid of and then press the Delete key on your keyboard.

When working in App Lab, you're using real JavaScript in a special IDE designed for learning. This book uses only commands that are universal to JavaScript. It avoids the timedLoop commands, which are built into App Lab but not usually seen in other IDEs.

TIP

App Lab automatically saves your projects as you work.

Design View button and the design toolbox

When you click the Design view button, you see the App Lab view shown in Figure 2-5. This view includes the toolbox of design elements you can use to build your program.

To add a design element to the app, you drag it from the toolbox to the simulator screen. Details about how to use each of these components are provided in each project.

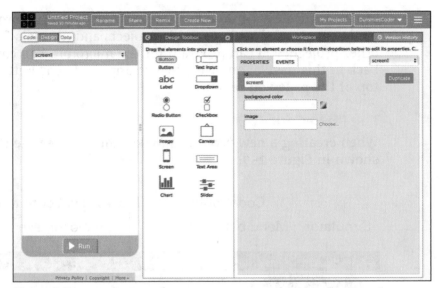

Figure 2-5

Getting around in MakeCode

MakeCode doesn't require you to create an account. Access the MakeCode site, shown in Figure 2-6, at `https://makecode.microbit.org`.

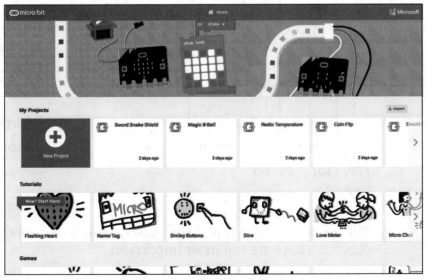

Figure 2-6

This is your page for creating a new project, opening projects you've made, and seeing sample projects and tutorials for lots of other projects you can program for the micro:bit. You can get back to this page at any time by clicking the Home button at the top of the page you're on.

The MakeCode IDE

When creating a new project in MakeCode, you see the IDE shown in Figure 2-7.

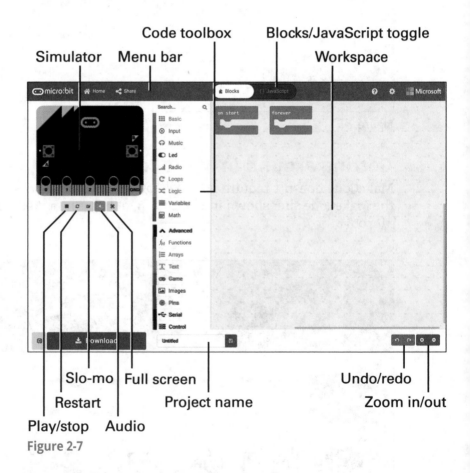

Figure 2-7

The *menu bar* at the top of the MakeCode IDE features just a few choices. These are the most important:

- ✔ **Home button:** Return to the MakeCode home page.

- ✔ **Share button.** Share your project (see Chapter 19).

- ✔ **Blocks/JavaScript toggle:** Choose which mode to code in.

The micro:bit *simulator* is the window on the left that shows you what your user sees. It behaves the way an actual micro:bit will behave, except it's digital (not a real, physical electronics board). Here, you can see and interact with your program as it executes, and get everything working before you transfer your program to the micro:bit. Click the *play* icon (arrowhead) below the simulator to run your program. When your program is running, you can click the *stop* icon to stop program execution. Clicking the *restart* icon, resets the program to the start. You can also click the *slo-mo* icon (snail) to slow the rate of program execution (this is helpful when debugging). You can also click the *audio* icon to mute or unmute sound. Clicking the *full screen* icon makes your micro:bit simulator appear in a large format, on its own screen.

The *workspace* is the place where you drag command blocks into, and assemble command blocks together to build your *program.* You can click the *JavaScript* button to code in text-based mode. When working in text-based mode, you can click the *Blocks* button to code in blocks mode. Click the *zoom in* or *zoom out* icon in the bottom-right corner to adjust your view. If needed, you can click the *undo* or *redo* icon in the bottom-right corner to edit your code

The *debug console* is a window that appears below the simulator if you have an error in your code. This console gives you clues about mistakes in your program and where to look to fix them. (See Chapter 3 for additional help on debugging code.)

The code toolbox

MakeCode provides coding commands for you to build your micro:bit programs. Note that the Advanced option is selected in Figure 2-7, which adds more command categories to your toolbox. Here are the categories:

- ✔ **Basic:** Commands to show images or text by using the LEDs, as well as the on start and forever commands.

- **Input:** Commands to read user input such as clicking a button, shaking the micro:bit, or reading a signal from one of the pins.

- **Music:** Commands to play music. Although audio will play in the simulator, the micro:bit does not have a built-in speaker so you need to hook up headphones or a speaker to make the micro:bit produce sound.

- **Led:** Commands for making the LEDs light up individually.

- **Radio:** Commands for having micro:bits communicate with each other via radio frequency.

- **Loops:** Commands for performing repeats.

- **Logic:** Commands for conditionals, comparisons, and Booleans.

- **Variables:** Commands to create and change variables.

- **Math:** Commands for math operations, including random numbers.

In the Advanced commands, there are many categories. Here are just the categories you'll work with in this book:

- **Functions:** New commands that you define for your project.

- **Arrays:** Commands to create and change array variables.

- **Pins:** Commands for reading and writing an electrical signal to the pins (electrical connections) at the bottom edge of the micro:bit.

To write code, select a command category and then drag and drop one block into the workspace. Add the next command by dragging a new command below and then snapping it (bringing it close to) the previous command to build your program. To *execute*, or run, the program on the simulator, click the *Run* button.

To *save* your program, type the name of your program in the Untitled field at the bottom of the MakeCode IDE and click the Save button.

Delete a command block in MakeCode by clicking it and dragging it back into the Code toolbox. Or in text mode, select the commands you want to get rid of and then click the Delete key on your keyboard.

TIP

Adding Hardware

You can create every project in this book without making additional purchases. If you do want to build the MakeCode projects with a real micro:bit, you'll need to buy one (they're cheap!) along with some optional, inexpensive hardware. Here's some information about the micro:bit and the optional hardware.

The micro:bit Board

A micro:bit is a tiny, programmable computer that's about half the size of a credit card. See Figure 2-8.

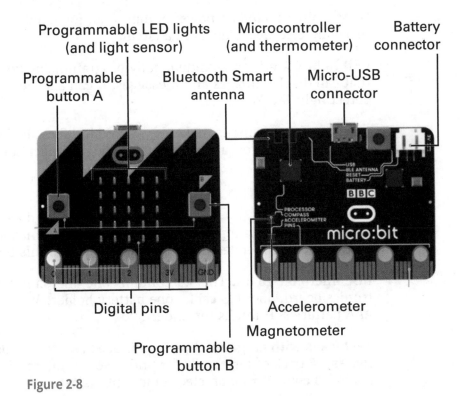

Figure 2-8

A micro:bit contains the following components:

- **Microcontroller:** A tiny computer with a little bit of memory. The temperature of the silicon in this unit also serves as the temperature sensor for the micro:bit.

- **Bluetooth Smart antenna:** Connects the micro:bit to other Bluetooth devices.

- **Micro-USB connector:** Connects the micro:bit to your computer, providing power and a way to transfer your program onto the board.

- **Battery connector:** Connects a battery pack to power the micro:bit away from the computer.

- **Sensors:** An accelerometer, a magnetometer (acting as a compass and metal detector), a thermometer, a light level sensor, and A and B programmable buttons.

- **Digital pins:** Including power and ground, for sending and receiving electrical signals in a circuit.

- **LED lights:** A grid of 25 individually programmable lights that can display images and messages. It can also be used to detect light levels.

The variety of components make the micro:bit a flexible little board that you can program for a wide range of applications.

Buying the board and components

Getting the hardware you need – a micro:bit board and a couple of accessories – is as simple as placing an order on Amazon. Here are the recommended items for the projects in this book:

- **BBC micro:bit go kit.** This kit contains one micro:bit electronics board, one USB cable, one battery holder, and two AAA batteries. It retails for under $20.

- **Test leads with alligator clips:** You'll need two test leads (wires). A pack of ten retails for under $6, or you can just borrow a couple from an electronics enthusiast.

✔ **Earbuds:** You'll need a pair of standard (3.5mm) earbuds. You probably already have a set of these somewhere in your home!

Running a program on the micro:bit board

To transfer and run a program on the micro:bit board, follow these steps:

1. Connect the micro:bit board to the micro USB end of the cable and connect your computer to the USB end of the cable, as shown in Figure 2-9.

   When connected, an icon representing the micro:bit device appears on your desktop.

Figure 2-9

2. In the MakeCode IDE, name the program and click the Save button.

3. In the MakeCode IDE, click the Download button.

   This downloads a .hex file to your computer (usually to your Downloads folder). See Figure 2-10.

4. Transfer the .hex file to the micro:bit by dragging the .hex file from your computer to the icon for the micro:bit device (shown in the Devices area in Figure 2-10).

During the transfer, the orange micro:bit indicator button (on the back of the device) blinks quickly. When the blinking stops, the transfer is complete.

Figure 2-10

5. Power the board.

The micro:bit needs power to operate. You can power the board by leaving it connected to your computer via the USB cable. Or, to make the device portable, attach the battery pack to the micro:bit (and disconnect it from your computer, detaching the USB cable from both devices).

TECHNICAL STUFF The micro:bit stores only the most recent program transferred to it. If you change your program in the IDE, you *must* repeat Steps 2–4 to update the program stored in memory on the micro:bit.

Getting Fancier with User Interfaces

Coders work closely with user interface designers to build engaging and easy-to-understand ways for people to interact with apps, websites, and gadgets. When you're first starting out, you work as both the coder and the UI designer.

As you design user interfaces, you'll want to use a wide variety of images to create the appearance of the UI. Some images will become background images and others will be sprites, buttons, or smaller objects that appear onscreen. Although this isn't coding per se, designing your UI is an important part of creating apps and gadgets that people enjoy and understand how to use. Here's a bit of guidance to help you get fancier with your design work.

Finding images

Using Google image search, search for images to use in your projects. Go to www.Google.com and type any search term that describes the image you want. Then click or tap Images to see all the images. Click or tap the Tools button and choose Usage Rights⇨Labeled for Reuse to narrow the images to only those you can legally use. In Figure 2-11, I searched for *sound effects background* to find images to use in my Foley Sound App in Chapter 5.

Figure 2-11

You can also narrow the images by size. Large images are good for backgrounds, and small or thumbnail images work better for objects placed in front of the background, such as costumes on sprites. Also, by searching only for .png images, you can find images that have transparent backgrounds. This is ideal for images that go in front of the background.

On a computer, save an image you want by right-clicking (Windows) or Ctrl-clicking (Mac) the image. On a tablet, click the Options button that appears with the image. When the pop-up menu appears, choose Save Image As and name the image. Use a short name that makes sense to you.

Editing images

Saved images you want to upload to Scratch or App Lab can be edited. You might want to crop a background, change the image from landscape to portrait orientation, or remove a white background around an object. To edit an image in App Lab, you must use an outside editing program, such as Paint (Windows) or Preview (macOS).

For example, using Preview on a Mac, you can perform the sequence of simple edits shown in Figure 2-12. To open the editing tools in Preview, click the Markup button in the menu bar. Here, I wanted to save an image of a green gob of wasabe for my Sushi Matchup toy. (See Chapter 18 for this project.) I first used the Rectangular Selection tool and the Crop button to crop the wasabe from the other image. Then I used the Instant Alpha tool to "magic wand" across the white background, selecting it. Lastly, I clicked the delete key on my keyboard. Preview asked me if I wanted to convert the image to a .png, and I did. I saved the wasabe image as shown in the last image in the figure.

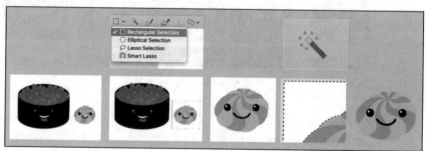

Shutterstock image 418466866 of sushi characters by Rimma Z

Figure 2-12

Finding and recording sounds

Scratch, App Lab, and many other introductory programming languages provide a sound library with sounds you can use in your projects. But what if you want to use a sound from the web or record your own sound? You can!

One of the best resources for a giant collection of free sound effects — without ads or distracting registration pages — is www.SoundBible.com. With a simple search, you can find thousands of great sound effects and background music in .mp3 and .wav formats. Another cool source of sounds is the Video Game Music Archive (www.vgmusic.com), which houses thousands of video game sounds, including those from old platforms. (I found the opening music of Dig Dug for the Atari 2600!) Most of the sounds and music on this site are in .midi format.

Scratch accepts sound files in .mp3 and .wav formats, and App Lab uses only the .mp3 format. If you create or find a sound file in a different format (such as the .midi format), download the file, save it, and convert it before using it in these programming environments. Programs such as GarageBand make it easy to open .midi files and convert them to the .mp3 format.

Uploading sounds

To upload a sound in Scratch, switch to the Sounds tab. Click and hold down on the Choose a Sound icon in the bottom left of the Scratch IDE, and then choose Upload Sound from the pop-up menu that appears. To upload a sound in App Lab, drag a playSound command to the workspace. In the command, click the arrow tab and select Choose. In the Choose Sounds dialog box that appears, select the Make New Sounds category, click the Upload File button, and select the file you want to upload.

Recording sounds

You can also produce your own sounds, whether they're vocals, sound effects, or noises from any location (such as city streets or a public pool). Both Scratch and App Lab allow you to record your own sounds and then use them in any app you create.

To record a sound in Scratch, switch to the Sounds tab and then hover your cursor over the Choose a Sound icon in the bottom-left corner and choose Record from the menu that appears. To upload a sound in App Lab, drag a playSound command to the workspace. In the command, click the arrow tab and select Choose. In the Choose Sounds dialog box that appears, select the Make New Sounds category, click the Record Audio button, and record your sound.

When Things Go Wrong

Programming is a picky enterprise. A program will often contain errors, and you have to fix them before the program will run just right. Whether you're just starting out in coding or you've been programming for a while, you — like everyone else — will make mistakes when writing code. As a coder, you'll spend a lot of time fixing the mistakes, or *bugs*, in your programs. (They're called *bugs* because one of the "mistakes" in the early days of computing was an actual bug in the computer's electronic circuitry!)

9/9

0800 antan started
1000 " stopped - antan ✓
     13° vc (032) MP - MC
        (033) PRO 2   2.130476415
           conect   2.130676415
     Relays 6-2 in 033 failed special speed test
     in relay   " 10.000 test .
              Relays changed
1100 Started Cosine Tape (Sine check)
1525 Started Mult + Adder Test.

1545   Relay #70 Panel F
                 (moth) in relay.

       First actual case of bug being found.
1630 antangent started.
1700 closed down .

Fixing mistakes in your code is called *debugging* — literally, getting the bugs out of your code. Think of your program like an essay you write in English class or a lab report you write in science class. In each written document, you must get the form and content right for the document to make sense and tell its story successfully.

When you write and run your code, you must also get the form and content correct; if you don't, the code will encounter errors. When the bug is due to the code's form, you get a *syntax error*. When the bug is the result of the code's behavior, you get a *logic error*.

Testing your program means running it to see if it operates the way you want it to. In this chapter, you discover some ways that syntax and logic errors pop up when you test your programs. You also learn some strategies for debugging your code in Scratch and JavaScript (using both App Lab and MakeCode). Remember, half of coding is writing the code — and the other half is debugging it!

Syntax Errors

The form, or *syntax*, of what you code consists of the structure, the commands, the grammar, and the punctuation of your program. Here's what each of those pieces means:

- The *structure* of your program is its overall layout. For example, an essay is often structured using five paragraphs: an introductory paragraph, three content paragraphs, and a closing paragraph. In a Scratch program, code is structured to go with the object that executes it. For example, a butterfly sprite has code that makes it fly, and a monkey sprite has code that makes it bounce around. In a JavaScript program, code is structured to feature global variables at the top, then the main program, and then function definitions.

- The *commands* in your program are like the vocabulary in an essay. Commands, like vocabulary, have specific meaning and must be spelled correctly. You can write new commands (and use any spelling you want), but you must define what these new vocabulary words mean in your program.

- The *grammar* of your program is similar to the grammar you use when writing sentences in any language. In English, you say "I'm not hungry," not "I ain't hungry" and not "Hungry not I'm." In the same way, when coding in Scratch, the proper grammar is repeat 10 play sound boom, not repeat 10 boom sounds. Grammar requires that you use certain words together and that you order those words in a specific way.

- The *punctuation* of your program looks a lot like the punctuation in an essay. You must put the periods, commas, and semicolons in the correct places for your code to work. The punctuation of your code also includes some of the symbols you use when writing math equations, such as greater than and less than signs, plus and minus signs, equals signs, parentheses, brackets, and curly braces.

When coding with blocks, it's almost impossible to make syntax errors. Block-based coding requires almost no typing, and the blocks fit together in specific ways. (In fact, the point of coding with blocks is that it helps beginners avoid syntax errors.) When coding in text-based mode, you type everything into the program. You can easily misspell commands and forget to end a line of code with a semicolon. Any error in syntax will be reported to you, either as you type or when you try to run your code. You have to fix errors to execute your program correctly.

TECHNICAL STUFF

Many programming languages, such as Java, require you to compile your program before you can run it. *Compiling* is like checking your code for obvious errors. If you have syntax errors, they are reported to you when you try to compile. Bugs must be fixed to get a successful compilation, after which you can then run your program.

Logic Errors

The *logic* of your program is the behavior that results when you run your code. You can easily get the syntax of a program correct but make mistakes in the logic of the code. For example, if the game score goes down each time a hero defeats an enemy, you may have coded a score variable to decrease, not increase. The code runs because the syntax is correct, but the program doesn't do what you want it to do.

Whether coding with blocks or coding in a text-based mode, you can easily make logic errors. You probably won't notice logic errors until you run your code. At that point, you need to figure out what is going wrong, and then find the part of your code that controls the behavior that is not working correctly. Sometimes tracking down a logic error is easy, but other times it's challenging!

Debugging Scratch Programs

Scratch helps prevent you from making syntax errors because you don't type the commands. Instead, you drag command blocks into the Code workspace. You don't have to worry about misspelling a command or forgetting to add a semicolon because Scratch prevents you from making these types of errors. Instead of typing a premade element such as a variable name, for example, you select it from a drop-down list, as shown in Figure 3-1.

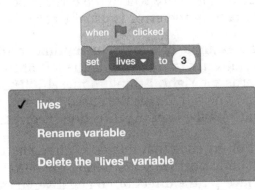

Figure 3-1

When coding in Scratch, you're likely to make mistakes in the logic of your program. These mistakes show up when you run your program, so they are also called *runtime errors.* To fix this type of error, you try to pinpoint the place where something is going wrong in the execution of your program. Then you change the code to correct your error (or errors).

Here are some ways to locate and fix runtime errors in Scratch:

- **Focus on one sprite at a time.** If a sprite is working properly, move on to the next sprite and check its operation. (In many projects, you also write code for the stage, and you can use this method to check the stage as well.)

- **When you identify a sprite with a runtime error, run the program several times to see how the sprite is behaving.** Try to figure out exactly what the sprite is doing wrong and when that behavior occurs.

- **Look carefully at the code for the sprite with the runtime error.** Step through the code one command at a time. Separate some of the code (remove it temporarily by dragging it to the side, away from the event command). Then add sections of your code back in, one or two commands at a time, and test the operation of the sprite after each addition. You should be able to identify where the error is occurring. At this point, correcting the error is usually easy.

Figure 3-2 shows an example of a logic, or runtime, error in Scratch. I want my butterfly to fly towards the left of the screen, but it is flying towards the right. I think to myself, "Hmmm, my butterfly is flying, and he's flying at the speed I want. But he's going the wrong way. Maybe I set my direction incorrectly."

So I look at the part of my code that relates to direction. I see that I have set the direction to positive 90, pointing the butterfly to the right. I should have set the direction to negative 90 (by typing −90), pointing the butterfly to the left.

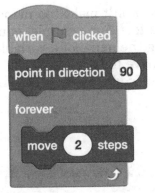

Figure 3-2

Debugging App Lab Programs

As you program in JavaScript using App Lab, you will likely produce some errors in your code. Mistakes in the syntax of your code must be fixed before you can run the program.

In App Lab, syntax errors are displayed as yellow diamonds or red squares. The error symbol appears on the line where you have a bug. If you hover your cursor over the symbol, App Lab provides a clue about the error. Here's a general description of what each error symbol means:

- **Yellow diamond:** Your code has a possible syntax error, but the app might still run. The syntax error might be due to misspelling something or any number of other problems.

REMEMBER

The onEvent() command always display a yellow diamond when you don't delete the default function call name, event. However, this is one error that does not prevent your app from executing, so you don't need to fix it. But if you find that yellow diamond irritating, you can usually just remove event from between the parentheses and the warning will vanish.

- **Red square:** A syntax error is preventing the app from running. For example, you might be using a variable or a function that you haven't declared. You must fix syntax errors before attempting to run your app.

If you program in block mode, you won't make too many syntax errors, but it is possible to make a few. For example, you might make a syntax error when spelling the name of a variable or function — or anything else you have to type in a block. Figure 3-3 shows a snippet of block code that App Lab has flagged with three errors.

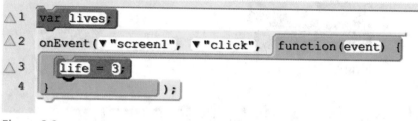

Figure 3-3

If you hover your cursor over the yellow triangle on line 1, App Lab displays the message shown in Figure 3-4. This message tells you that you defined a variable, lives, and then didn't use it in your code.

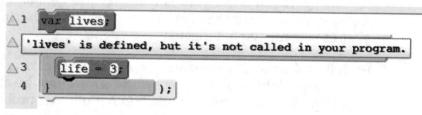

Figure 3-4

If you hover your cursor over the yellow triangle on line 2, the message shown in Figure 3-5 appears. This message tells you that the default function name, event, is not called in your code. As mentioned, in App Lab it's okay to have yellow triangles on all onEvent commands. If you want to correct the error, just delete event.

If you hover your cursor over the yellow triangle in line 3, the message shown in Figure 3-6 appears. This message lets you know that the variable for which you're attempting to set the value, life, doesn't exist. (You never declared it because you meant to set the value of lives not life.)

```
△1   var lives;
△2   onEvent(▼"screen1", ▼"click",  function(event) {
△    'event' is defined, but it's not called in your program.
 4   }                        );
```

Figure 3-5

```
△1   var lives;
△2   onEvent(▼"screen1", ▼"click",  function(event) {
△3      life = 3;
 4
     'life' hasn't been declared yet.
```

Figure 3-6

To debug this code snippet, delete event from line 2 and change life to lives in line 3, as shown in Figure 3-7. Note that changing life to lives also gets rid of the error in line 1.

```
 1   var lives;
 2   onEvent(▼"screen1", ▼"click",  function() {
 3      lives = 3;
 4   }                        );
```

Figure 3-7

Other syntax errors are not flagged as you code but show up at runtime. Figure 3-8 shows a code snippet built in text-based mode. As you can see, App Lab does not display any yellow triangles or red squares.

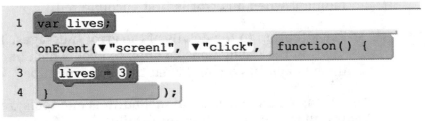

```
1▾ onEvent("catButton", "click", function() {
2     setText("petLabel", "You picked cat!");
3 });
```

Figure 3-8

When you run the JavaScript code, however, a warning message appears at the bottom of the App Lab IDE, in the Debug Console. As shown in Figure 3-9, the warning tells where the error is located and what the error might be. Here, I forgot to name a button in my app. The name `catButton` doesn't exist because I forgot to change the default name from `button1`.

⊘	⚙ Debug Commands	🔊	Debug Console	✂ **Clear**		Show Watch ❮
‖ Break	⊼ Step over		WARNING: Line: 1: onEvent() id parameter refers to an id ("catButton") which does not exist.			
⎇ Step out	⊼ Step in		>			

Figure 3-9

The Debug Console offers several additional tools for helping you debug your app. Besides catching syntax errors that you do not catch while coding, the console can help you track down logic errors that show up at runtime. Here are two key ways you can use the Debug Console to find and fix your errors:

✏ **Use the slider to adjust the speed of execution of your program.** You can change the speed between turtle (slow) and rabbit (fast). Controlling the speed allows you to catch the moment when an error is first encountered.

✏ **Pay attention to the details of the error messages.** The messages in the Debug Console often tell you which line number the bug appears on, and what the error might be.

The Debug Console has additional buttons and tools; read App Lab's online documentation for details.

 Click the Reset button in the App Lab simulator to stop code execution and reset the app.

TIP

Lastly, you can also use the `console.log` command to report tracking information to you in the Debug Console as the program runs. Figure 3-10 shows a code snippet that asks the user to type his or her name. The code should store the name, but because the code doesn't print the name, you can't tell whether the name was stored as you intended. By adding a `console.log` command, you can look behind the scenes by making the name print in the Debug Console. As you can see in the figure, the program read and stored the name.

Figure 3-10

Debugging MakeCode Programs

The block mode of MakeCode is like Scratch in that it keeps you from making syntax errors. Because you use premade blocks, as shown in Figure 3-11, you can't type misspellings or forget to include punctuation.

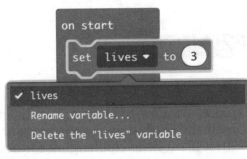

Figure 3-11

However, if you use the JavaScript text-based mode of MakeCode, you type your code, so it is possible to make syntax errors. For example, Figure 3-12 shows you what happens if you try to use a `life` variable when you should be using `lives`. MakeCode underlines the problem code with a red squiggly line and displays the error message, `Cannot find name 'life'`.

```
1  let lives = 0
2  life = 0
   Cannot find name 'life'.
```

Figure 3-12

When coding in MakeCode, errors can also show up at runtime. If you run a MakeCode program in the micro:bit simulator and get an error, an Explorer window appears just below the micro:bit simulator. The window displays the number of errors in the program, as shown in Figure 3-13.

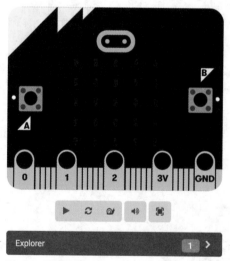

Figure 3-13

You can click the Explorer window to expand it and view additional information about the execution of your program and the errors. But be aware that it's a little challenging for new coders to read and understand the Explorer window!

Your best bet for fixing runtime errors in MakeCode is to run the program several times, tracing the code execution step-by-step. Try to isolate the exact moment when an error takes place, and then go to that part of the code and examine it. Update the code to correct your error (or errors).

TIP

You can press the Slo-Mo button in the simulator to slow the speed at which the program runs, making it easier to trace the action.

Commenting Out Code when Debugging

One final way you can debug code is to comment out sections of code. *Commenting out code* allows you to temporarily remove commands from your program so that you can isolate where things are going wrong. You comment out code by using special symbols in front of one or more lines of code when working in text-based mode. For the projects in this book, commenting out code is a debugging technique you can use with text-based JavaScript in App Lab and MakeCode.

Suppose you wrote the program shown in Figure 3-14, where something is wrong with carrotVotes. When a user clicks carrotImage, the number of votes for the carrot increases only on the first click.

```
1  var carrotVotes = 0;
2  var cookieVotes = 0;
3  onEvent("carrotImage", "click", function() {
4      carrotVotes = 1;
5  });
6  onEvent("cookieImage", "click", function() {
7      cookieVotes = cookieVotes + 1;
8  });
```

Figure 3-14

So you, as the app developer, decide to comment out any code that has to do with the carrot. For a single line of code, as in line 1, you use two forward slash symbols (//) in front of the code. For a larger block of code, as in lines 3 to 5, you use a single forward slash and an asterisk (/*) at the beginning of the block, and an asterisk and a single forward slash (*/) at the end of the block. The code now looks like Figure 3-15.

```
1   // var carrotVotes = 0;
2   var cookieVotes = 0;
3 ▾ /*onEvent("carrotImage", "click", function() {
4       carrotVotes = 1;
5   }); */
6 ▾ onEvent("cookieImage", "click", function() {
7       cookieVotes = cookieVotes + 1;
8   });
```

Figure 3-15

After commenting out the code, you run the program and everything else works correctly. You've confirmed that the errors are in the code that you temporarily removed. You change line 4 to read carrotVotes = carrotVotes + 1. Then you remove the backslashes and asterisks, and run the code again. This time, the program works as you intended.

Debugging your code is a normal part of programming. You won't write code perfectly the first time — no one does. Patience and practice are vital to the debugging process.

The computer only understands the commands you give it, so it's up to you to work carefully and pay attention to every line of code you write. Although debugging your code can be time-consuming (and frustrating), it's just part of the job of being a coder!

Part 2
Sounds, Color, Random Surprises

Animal Sound Effects

```
onEvent(▼"Cat", ▼"click", function() {
    playSound(▼"sound://category_animals/cat.mp3", ▼false); ↵
}                    );
onEvent(▼"Bee", ▼"click", function() {
    playSound(▼"sound://category_animals/bee_buzz.mp3", ▼false); ↵
}                    );
onEvent(▼"Bear", ▼"click", function() {
    playSound(▼"sound://category_animals/bear.mp3", ▼false); ↵
}                    );
onEvent(▼"Cow", ▼"click", function() {
    playSound(▼"sound://category_animals/cow.mp3", ▼false); ↵
}                    );
```

Built on Code Studio ▴

Hailey Nemeth

In this part you'll . . .

■ Code event-driven programs that play sounds

■ Use random numbers to produce a lucky
numbers gadget

■ Build an app for users to create colorful
modern art

Orchestra

Do you like jamming to your tunes? If so, you'll love the project in this chapter! Coding projects that feature music are a fun way to bring together technology and the arts. And because your computer includes a soundboard and speakers, you can run your program and blast out your audio creations to the world.

The orchestra toy in this chapter introduces you to your first big idea in coding: event-driven programming. *Event-driven programming* is just a fancy way of saying that when an event occurs — such as a user clicking a computer mouse or tapping a button on a mobile device — the program responds by doing something.

In the Orchestra project, you use Scratch to create a virtual orchestra on the computer. You write code so that when the user clicks an instrument, the computer plays a sound. Now you're coding!

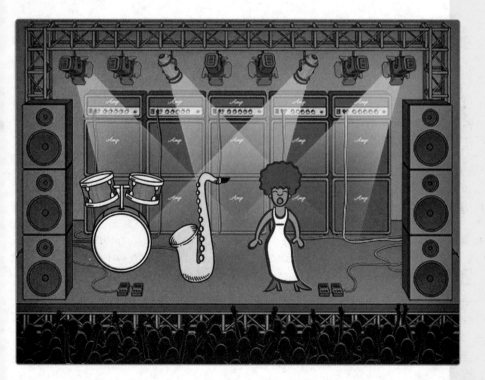

Brainstorm

From rap groups to rock bands to string ensembles, a musical genre exists for everyone! In this project, you work in Scratch to create your own version of an orchestra for use on the computer. Your orchestra can feature any sprites included in the Scratch sprite library and any sounds included in the Scratch sound library.

Brainstorm the design of your program by thinking about what musical objects you want to appear onscreen, such as instruments, percussion, and singers. The *end users* — the people who will be playing with your toys — will play the sound-producing objects you assemble to make their own music. They get to act like DJs, playing different sounds in any combination. You never know exactly how your end users will play with what you give them — that's what makes the Orchestra program so much fun!

Now get coding by following these simple steps.

Event-driven programming

In an *event-driven program,* changing events affect how the program runs. An event can be completed by the user, such as a button click. An event can be triggered by a sensor, such as a thermometer reading a high or low temperature, or an accelerometer sensing movement. Lastly, an event can be triggered when it gets information from another part of the program.

Event-driven programming is different from early ways of programming. Early programming languages were mostly procedural: A program just started at the beginning and ran until the end.

Most of your coding in this book will be event-driven programming. That's why programs like the Orchestra program show you how to write code connecting the action of the user to the action of the program!

Start a New Project

Begin creating your Orchestra program by starting a new project:

1. Open Scratch at `https://scratch.mit.edu`. If prompted, enable Flash to run Scratch. Log in to the account you've created to use Scratch (see Chapter 2).

2. On the Scratch home page, select Create.

   Or if you're already working in Scratch, choose File ⇨ New Project from the menu bar. A new project opens, as shown in Figure 4-1.

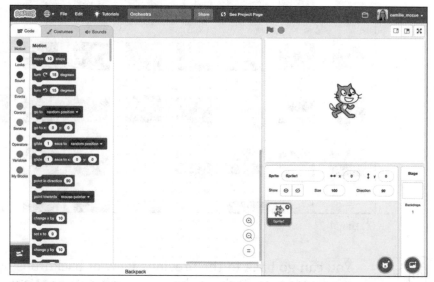

Figure 4-1

3. Name your program by typing a name in the Project Name field at the top of the Scratch interface.

4. Cut (delete) Scratch Cat from the project by clicking or tapping the X in the Scratch Cat icon.

   You can find the icon in the Sprite area in the lower-right corner of the Scratch interface.

Add a Backdrop

The *backdrop* is the background color or image that fills the screen of your toy. Add a backdrop as follows:

 1. At the Stage, click the Choose a Backdrop icon.

   The backdrop library appears on the Choose a Backdrop screen, as shown in Figure 4-2. The library is organized by theme and consists of categories such as Music and Sports.

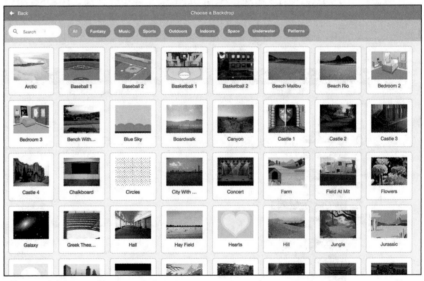

Figure 4-2

REMEMBER

You can go back to the previous view of backdrops by clicking or tapping Back, in the upper-left corner of any category in the backdrop library.

2. Click or tap the Music button to narrow your backdrop choices to a music theme.

   The library now displays only music backdrops.

TIP

The backdrop library offers a search box where you can type the name of a backdrop theme you want, such as *City*, and then click or tap the magnifying lens to search for that theme. If such a backdrop exists, it will appear.

3. From the list of music backdrops, click or tap the backdrop you want.

    Your backdrop appears on the Stage. In Figure 4-3, I chose the Concert backdrop for my program.

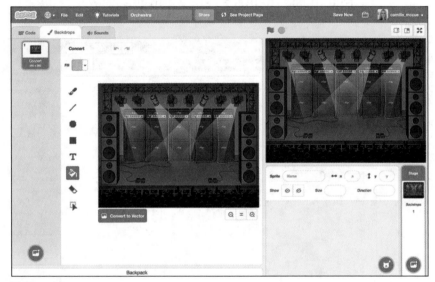

Figure 4-3

Add Instrument Sprites

All programming languages have ways to create objects. *Objects* are usually the physical things that move around the computer screen — cars, birds, paintballs, and so on. Programming languages have different name for objects, and Scratch calls them sprites. A *sprite* is an object that "lives" in a backdrop, like the backdrop you just chose.

You can add an instrument sprite to your toy by following these steps:

1. In the Sprite area of the Scratch interface, click the Choose a Sprite icon.

   The sprite library appears on the Choose a Sprite screen. The library is organized by theme and consists of categories, such as Animals and Food.

2. Click or tap the Music button to narrow your sprite choices to a music theme, as shown in Figure 4-4.

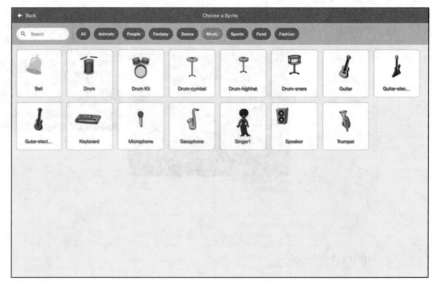

Figure 4-4

The library now displays only music sprites.

REMEMBER

You can go back to the previous view of the sprites by clicking or tapping Back, in the upper-left corner of the Choose a Sprite screen.

3. In the list of music sprites, click or tap the sprite you want.

   Your sprite appears on the Stage.

4. Repeat Steps 1–3 to add more instruments to your toy.

Each new sprite appears on the Stage. An icon for each sprite also appears in the Sprite area of the Scratch interface.

REMEMBER

You can make sprite changes at any time. If you add a sprite and then decide you don't want it, cut it by clicking or tapping the X in its icon, located in the Sprite area of the Scratch interface. You can resize your sprite by selecting it in the Sprite area and then typing a new number in the Size field above the sprite.

TIP

Objects have so many different names! In GameSalad, another programming language you may have heard of, an object is called an *actor.* In MicroWorlds EX, an object is a *turtle.* In some coding languages such as object-oriented programming languages (OOPs), objects can be physical or *informational* — abstract things that possess data and behave in certain ways in a program.

Add a Singer Sprite and Modify Its Costume

Bands and orchestras need vocals. Let's add a singer to your toy!

To add a singer, do the following:

1. In the Sprite area of the Scratch interface, select the Choose a Sprite icon.

2. In the pop-up menu, select Choose a Sprite to open the Scratch library of sprites.

3. In the search box, type singer to locate the singer sprite.

The Singer1 sprite appears.

4. Click or tap the Singer1 sprite to select her.

Your sprite appears on the Stage. But her dress doesn't contrast well with the dark backdrop, so let's recolor the dress.

5. While Singer 1 is still selected, click or tap the Costumes tab in the upper-left corner of the Scratch interface.

   The Costume editor of the Scratch interface opens.

6. Still working on the Costumes tab, click or tap the Fill Color swatch, then the tiny triangle to open up the color palette, and then a new color for the singer's dress. Click or tap outside the palette to accept your selection.

7. Still working in the Costumes tab, click or tap the paint bucket icon and then the dress to recolor it with the fill color.

   As shown in Figure 4-5, the new color of the singer's dress now appears in the Costume editor and on the Stage.

TIP

You can get fancy recoloring and decorating the singer's dress! Play with the Paint tool options to see the different ways you can add colors and special fills to the dress, or use the paintbrush to draw decorations to make the costume amazing!

Your user interface is now complete! It consists of a stage with a backdrop, two instrument sprites, and a singer sprite. Now you can code your program.

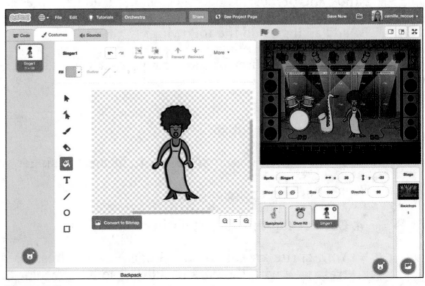

Figure 4-5

Code Each Instrument to Play a Sound

Next, you need to code each instrument to play a sound when an event occurs in your program. You can choose which event you want each instrument to respond to, and what sound you want each instrument to play.

Simply follow these steps:

1. Click or tap an instrument sprite.

   I chose the saxophone sprite.

Events

2. On the Code tab of the Scratch interface, select the Events icon.

   The event commands appear. Here are the most common events:

   • when green flag clicked

   • when x key pressed, where x can be the spacebar (space), an arrow key (up, down, left, or right), or an alphanumeric character (such as a or b or 1 or 2)

   • when this sprite clicked

   The when backdrop switches event is useful when creating games that use more than one scene or level. Events involving broadcast are useful when you want your sprites to communicate with each other. (See Chapter 18 for a project featuring broadcasting.)

3. Drag an event command to the Code workspace.

   I dragged the when this sprite clicked command.

Sound

4. Still working in the Code tab of the Scratch interface, select the Sound icon.

5. Drag the start sound command to the Code workspace and attach it to the event command you added previously.

   The start sound command initially displays the C sax sound.

6. Click or tap the tab on the start sound command tile to see additional sound options, and select the sound you want to use.

   As shown in Figure 4-6, the sound options for the saxophone, such as C sax and D sax, are already built into the saxophone sprite. I chose G sax.

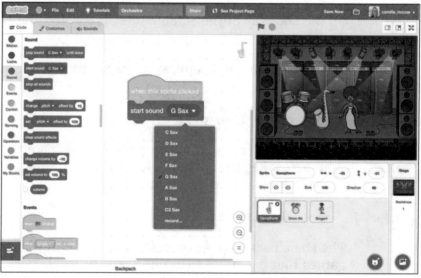

Figure 4-6

7. Click or tap the saxophone sprite (or perform whatever event you selected) on the stage to hear the sound.

8. Repeat Steps 1–7 to add an event and a sound to the other instrument on the stage.

TECHNICAL STUFF

When you select a new sprite, you see only the code for that sprite. You won't see the code you've added to other sprites. Don't let this panic you — you haven't lost any code!

Code the singer to play a sound

The singer sprite is different than the instrument sprites because she doesn't have any built-in singer sounds. She has a built-in sound called pop, but you want her to sing, not pop!

You must add a new sound to your singer sprite, one that sounds like singing. First, you choose an event command to make her start singing. Then you add a sound to the singer so that she has something to sing:

1. Click or tap the icon for the Singer1 sprite.

2. On the Code tab of the Scratch interface, select the Events icon.

   Events

   The event commands appear.

3. Drag an event command to the Code workspace.

   I dragged the when this sprite clicked command.

4. Click or tap the Sounds tab.

   The Sound Editor appears.

5. Click or tap the Choose a Sound button in the lower-left corner of the Scratch interface to open the Scratch library of sounds.

   The sound library appears on the screen.

6. Click or tap the Voice button to narrow your sound choices to a voice theme.

   The library now displays only voice sounds.

7. In the list of voice sounds, click or tap the sound you want.

   Your sound is added to the collection of sounds for the singer. (The Pop sound is also in this collection. You won't need the Pop sound, so click or tap it and then the X to delete it.) Figure 4-7 shows that I've chosen the Singer2 sound.

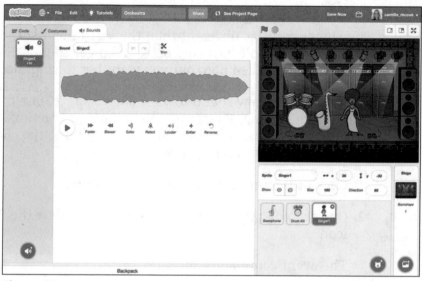

Figure 4-7

When you are working at the Sounds tab, you can select a sound icon (such as Singer2) to edit the attributes of that sound. As shown in Figure 4-7, you can trim the sound, make it play faster or slower, add an echo or a robot effect, make it play louder or softer, or make it play in reverse. You can also rename the sound in the Sound field.

8. Select the Code tab.

Sound

9. In the code area of the Scratch interface, select the Sound category of commands.

10. Drag the start sound command to the Code workspace.

11. Click or tap the small arrow on the start sound command block and select the sound you previously added for the Singer1 sprite.

12. Click or tap the singer sprite to hear her sing (or perform whatever event you selected).

Parallel processing

When you click or tap each of the members of your orchestra, did you notice that the sounds they play overlap, playing at the same time? That's because their code is processing in parallel.

You may have heard the term *parallel* in a math class. *Parallel lines* lie in the same plane and never cross each other. You can have as many lines, running side by side, as you want.

In computer programming, *parallel processing* means that the computer program runs different blocks of code at the same time (in parallel) so you can have more than one thing happening in your program at once. It's like using your left hand to pat your head and using your right hand to rub your tummy; your actions occur simultaneously (at the same time). Right now, I know you're trying to pat your head and rub your tummy, and you're probably finding that it's hard to execute this parallel process! But for computers, parallel processing is easy. And they can run many more than two blocks of code in parallel.

So add as many members to your orchestra program as you want because Scratch will have no problem executing their code in parallel. And instead of having to click or tap each sprite to run its code, you can replace the when this sprite clicked event with when green flag clicked so that you can start all the parallel processing action with a single event!

Save, Test, and Debug Your Program

As you work, Scratch automatically saves your program in the cloud, so you don't have to take any special actions to save your work.

Test your program and fix any bugs to ensure that it works the way you want it to. See the section in Chapter 3 on debugging Scratch programs.

Share Your Program with the World

After your program operates perfectly, it's time to share it! Set the status of your program to Share, then add to your project page a description of your program and directions on how to run it. See Chapter 19 for details on sharing your programs.

Enhance Your Toy

Consider enhancing your Orchestra toy with new features:

- **New instruments:** Add new instruments, including horns and percussion, for the user to play with.

- **New singers:** Add new singers who are singing different songs (including beat boxing!) for your user to try out.

- **Find cool new sounds online:** Tons of music loops, vocals, and sound effects are available to you at sound libraries on the web. See Chapter 2 for additional information.

- **Record your own sound:** Instead of choosing a sound from the Scratch sound library, why not record your own? On the Sounds tab, select and hold down Choose a Sound and then, from the pop-up menu, select Record a Sound. Next, use your computer microphone to record an original sound, like you singing! See Chapter 2 for details on recording your own sound.

- **Use a single event to start the action:** Why bother clicking or tapping each sprite to run its code? Replace the when this sprite clicked event in each sprite with a when green flag clicked command. That way, all the sprites will start running their code blocks with a single event!

Foley Sound Generator

A *Foley artist* **hides** behind the scenes making sound effects to accompany the action in movies and plays. Foley artists used to create sounds with everyday objects — for example, hitting coconuts together to simulate the sound of a clomping horse.

The title *Foley artist* comes from the name Jack Foley — the sound effects pioneer who developed the technique of adding everyday sounds into films during the editing process.

These days, Foley artists use technology and cool digital sound effects to work their magic. You can take advantage of those same tools to build a Foley Sound Generator in App Lab. You can run your finished app on your mobile phone, making it portable and ready to go whenever you need a good sound effect. Then you can use your sound generator for real theater productions or just everyday home pranks!

Building the Foley Sound Generator gives you the opportunity to build event-driven programming and code parallel processing for a mobile app. The fun is in creating your own version of the Foley Sound Generator, featuring alarms, meows, thunder claps, and any other audio you want. Let's get started!

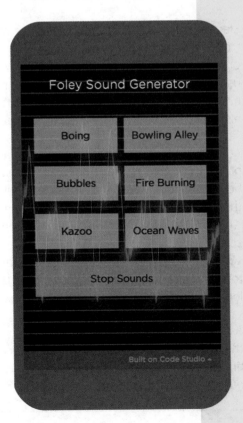

Brainstorm

You can create your Foley Sound Generator so that it plays a weird collection of sounds or only sounds associated with a specific theme. Some of my students have created zoo-themed Foley Sound Generators in the style of the old See-and-Say toys (the cow says, "Moo!"). Others have design the app to play a variety of cool music loops at the same time in different arrangements. Still others have made the app play funny catchphrases from cartoon characters.

Brainstorm some layouts of how you want your Foley Sound Generator app to appear to the end user. The appearance of the user interface should represent the theme of the sounds in the app, such as a jungle scene for zoo animals. Your app should also display a title and clear, readable buttons for your user to click or tap to activate each sound, like those in the first figure in this chapter.

User Interfaces

Electronic devices, large and small, are often operated by humans and controlled by computer programs. Events are coded in a device's event-driven program (see Chapter 4) and triggered when the operator does something, usually by interacting with the device through a *user interface (UI)*. Many times, the UI has a visual layout with buttons, pictures, and menus, but it can also have other elements such as a video camera and microphone.

At home, you operate your digital media tools (television, phone, and computer) through a UI. But think about how people control a car, coffee pot, home climate system, and washing machine. They interact with those devices through a UI, too! Outside home, people use a UI keypad to get cash at an ATM, a UI touchscreen to vote in elections, and a UI handprint and keycard scanner to check in an out of big amusement parks. Even giant electronic systems — such as those used by air traffic controllers, power plant operators, and NFL television broadcast directors — are run by human operators looking at and interacting with specially designed UIs.

As you design your apps, websites, and gadgets, take some time to play with the look of your *user interface* — the "face" your user will see and use every time they run your code. You can always change your user interface later, but it's a good idea to have a layout in mind before you get started.

Start a New Project

Begin creating your Foley Sound Generator App by starting a new project as follows:

1. Open App Lab at `https://code.org/educate/applab`. Log in to the account you created to use App Lab (see Chapter 2).

2. Under the App Lab heading, click the Try it Out button.

   A new project opens as shown in Figure 5-1.

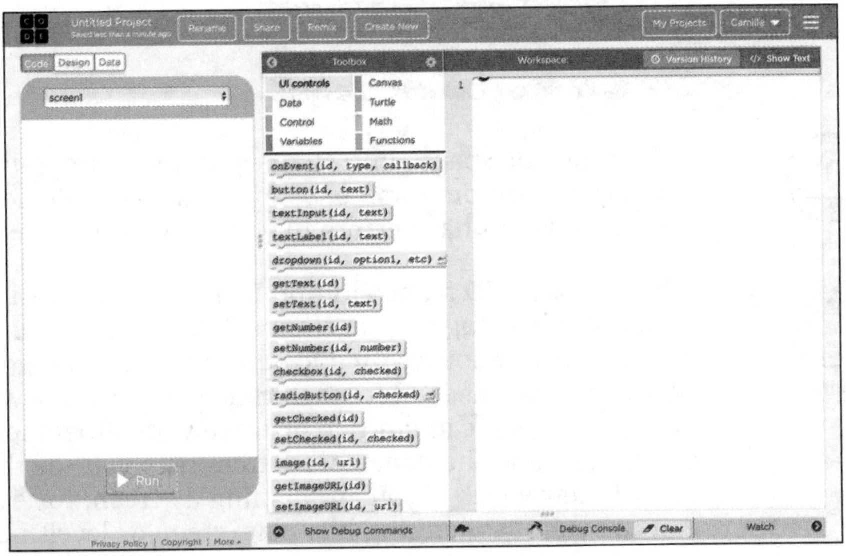

Figure 5-1

3. Name your program by clicking the Rename button and typing a name in the Project Name field at the top.

4. Click the Save button.

Add a Background

Add a background image to your app as follows:

1. Click the Design button to switch to Design mode in App Lab.

   The Design toolbox and workspace are displayed.

2. On the Properties tab of the workspace, rename the ID of screen1 to a more meaningful name such as *playScreen,* as follows:

   id.

   playScreen

WARNING

Do not include spaces in ID names. In most programming languages, including App Lab, spaces are not allowed. If you use them, you'll have errors in your program.

TECHNICAL
STUFF

When creating ID names in App Lab — and in most programming languages — use *camelCase naming.* Like a camel, the name starts low (with a lowercase letter) and goes high (with an uppercase letter) each time you start a new word. In this way, you can put two or three words together, without spaces, and the uppercase letters help you see the start of each new word. If you are naming a screen, for example, you can call it something like playScreen or levelOneScreen.

3. On the Properties tab of the workspace, locate the Image field. Click the Choose link to choose a new background image for this screen.

   The Choose Assets dialog box opens.

4. Click the Upload File button.

5. Navigate to and select the image file that you want upload to your assets. Then click the Choose button.

   The image file is the file you found while brainstorming (for example, in a Google image search) or created previously and then saved.

The image file appears in the Choose Assets dialog box. In Figure 5-2, I uploaded the sound_fx_background.jpg image file.

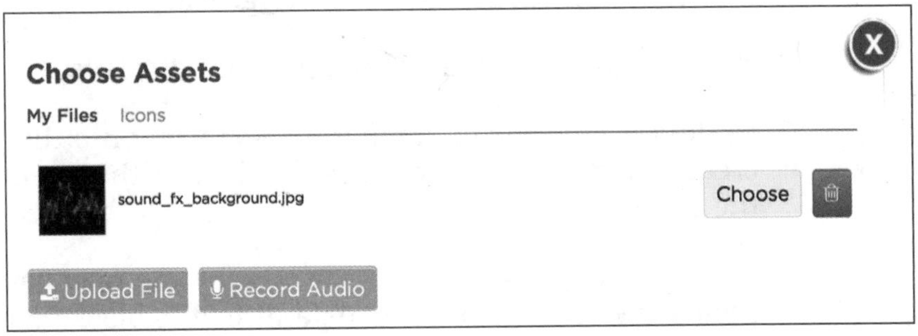

Choose Assets

My Files   Icons

sound_fx_background.jpg   Choose   🗑

⬆ Upload File   🎤 Record Audio

Figure 5-2

6. In the Choose Assets dialog box, click the Choose button next to the image asset you just uploaded.

   The image appears on the background of your app, as shown in Figure 5-3.

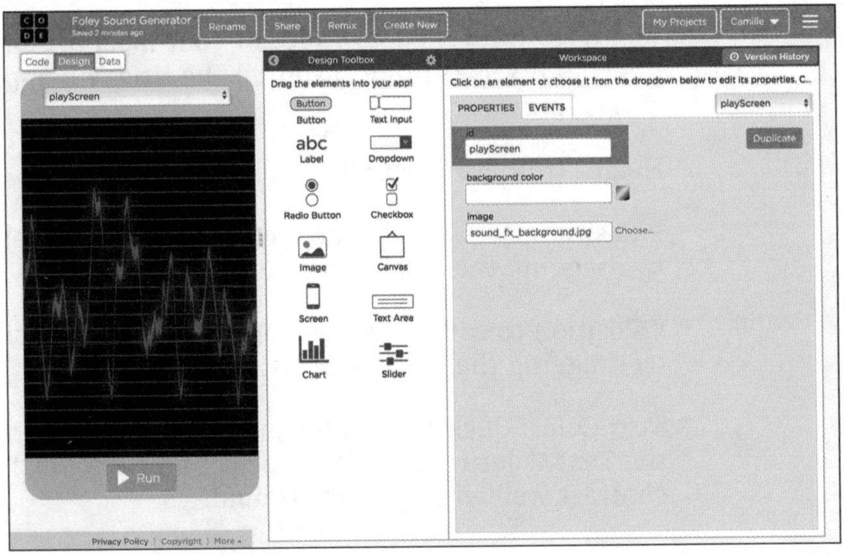

Figure 5-3

Next, you should name your app with a label that helps the user know the purpose of the app. Add a title as follows:

1. Remain working in the Design mode of App Lab. If you're not in Design mode, click the Design button.

   The Design toolbox and workspace are displayed.

abc
Label

2. In the Design toolbox, drag the Label icon onto the screen to create a label in your app. Position it near the top center of the app display.

   With a dark background on the screen, you may have trouble seeing the label because its default text is black. You change the text color in the next step.

3. On the Properties tab of the workspace, change the attributes of the label as follows (and shown in Figure 5-4):

   - ID: Rename the ID to titleLabel.

   - Text: Type the title of your app, such as **Foley Sound Generator**.

   - Width (px): Increase to width of your label to something like 240 pixels (or more) so that the title will appear on a single line.

   - Height (px): No change.

   - x Position (px): No change; you change the x position later by dragging the label into position.

   - y Position (px): No change; you change the y position later by dragging the label into position.

   - Text Color: Click the small square of color to the right of the Text Color field and then select a title color that will contrast well with the background.

   - Background Color: No change.

- Font Size (px): Type a new font size in the field or use the selection arrows to make the title the appropriate size for your app.

- Text Alignment: Click the selection arrows and choose Center.

4. Click the label in your app (see Figure 5-4) and drag the label to position it where you want.

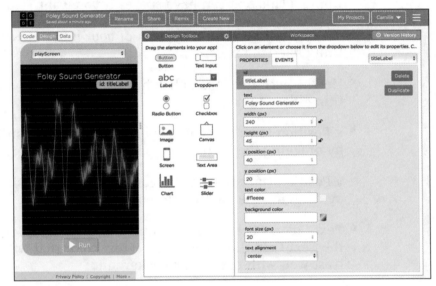

Figure 5-4

Add Sound and Stop Sounds Buttons

Your app will feature buttons that the user can click or tap to play sounds. Follow these instructions to add a button to your app:

1. Remain working in the Design mode of App Lab. If you're not in Design mode, click the Design button.

   The Design toolbox and workspace are displayed.

Button

Button

2. In the Design toolbox, drag the Button icon to the app display to create a button.

3. On the Properties tab of the workspace, change the attributes of the button as shown here and in Figure 5-5:

- ID: Rename the ID to boingButton or something similar to indicate the sound that will be associated with this button.

- Text: Type the text that will appear on the button, such as **Boing**. (This text can have spaces if you want.)

- Width (px): Increase the width of your button to something like 135 pixels.

- Height (px): Increase to height of your button to something like 55 pixels.

- x Position (px): No change; you change the x position later by dragging the button into position.

- y Position (px): No change; you change the y position later by dragging the button into position.

- Text Color: Click the small square of color to the right of the Text Color field and select a text color that will contrast well with the button background.

- Background Color: Click the small square of color to the right of the Background Color field and select a button color that will contrast well with the background color of the app.

- Font Size (px): Type a new font size in the field or click the selection arrows to make the text on your button a good size for your app.

- Text alignment: Click the selection arrows and choose Center.

- Image: No change.

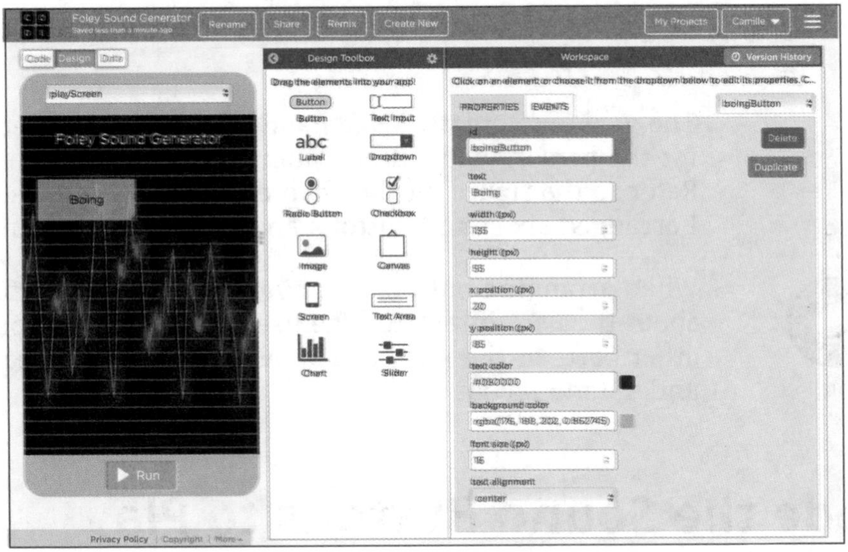

Figure 5-5

4. Click the button in your app display and drag the button where you want.

   When positioning it, remember that you will create several buttons and need room for them all.

5. Create another button by selecting the first button you created and then clicking the aqua-colored Duplicate button in the workspace.

6. Repeat Step 5 until you've created all your buttons.

7. Change the ID and text on each of your duplicate buttons so that each one represents a new sound. Name your last button Stop Sounds.

   If you want to, make the width and the color of the Stop Sounds button different than the other sound buttons so that it stands out. The user will use the Stop Sounds button to stop one or more sounds while they're playing, especially if a sound runs longer than the user wants.

8. Drag each of your new sound buttons to different positions on the app display.

   The goal is to create a clean and readable user interface for the person who will use your Foley Sound Generator. Refer to the figure on the chapter's first page to see how I arranged six sound buttons and a Stop Sounds button.

TIP

When arranging buttons in any project, think carefully about the user interface. The user will expect buttons and other parts of the interface to be organized in an easy-to-understand layout.

Code the Sound Buttons to Play

Next, you need to code each button with commands so that it will play a sound when the user clicks or taps the button. Follow these instructions:

1. Click the Code button to switch to Code mode in App Lab.

   The toolbox of commands and the workspace are displayed.

2. In the toolbox, select UI Controls. Drag the onEvent command into the workspace.

3. In the onEvent command, click the ID tab and select the name of the button you want in the list. I selected boingButton. When the user clicks the Boing button on a computer or taps the Boing button on a smartphone, the code block inside onEvent will execute. Leave the click action as-is, and delete event inside function().

4. Go back to UI Controls. Drag the playSound command into the OnEvent command.

5. In the playSound command, click the ID tab and select the Choose link.

   The App Lab sound library opens, as shown in Figure 5-6.

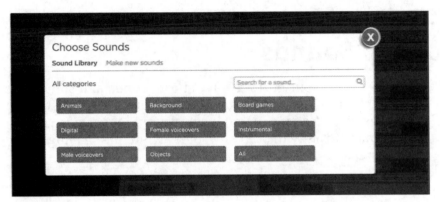

Figure 5-6

6. In the sound library, select a sound category and then a sound in that category. Alternatively, you can search for a sound. Then click the Choose button.

   The sound you select is inserted in the playSound command. I inserted the boing_2.mp3 sound.

7. In the playSound command, leave the false field as-is if you want the sound to play just once. Change this field to true if you want the sound to *loop* (play over and over).

   Your first completed onEvent command should look like this:

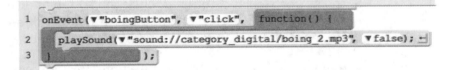

```
1   onEvent(▼"boingButton", ▼"click",   function() {
2       playSound(▼"sound://category_digital/boing_2.mp3", ▼false);
3   }                    );
```

8. Repeat Steps 2–7 to code each of the remaining sound buttons.

   The example shown here features these sounds: Boing, Bowling Alley, Bubbles, Fire Burning, Kazoo, and Ocean Waves.

Code the Stop Sounds Button to Stop Sounds

Some of your buttons have short sounds and some have sounds that last for more than a minute. As a Foley artist, you need to be able to stop a sound when you no longer need it. To create a button that will stop any sound while it's playing, follow these steps:

1. Continue working in the Code mode of App Lab. If you're not in Code mode, click the Code button.

2. In the toolbox, select UI Controls. Drag the onEvent command into the workspace.

3. In the onEvent command, click the ID tab and select stopButton in the list. Leave the click action as-is, and delete event inside function().

   When a user clicks the Stop Sounds button on a computer or taps the stopButton button on a smartphone, the code block inside onEvent will execute.

4. Go back to UI Controls. Drag a stopSound command into the onEvent command.

5. In the stopSound command, click the ID tab and then select the Choose link. Select the name of any long-duration sound (longer than a minute) that you're using in your app.

6. Repeat Steps 4 and 5 to drag all long-duration sounds into onEvent.

   Clicking or tapping the Stop Sounds button triggers onEvent, which causes all the stopSound commands in this code block to execute.

That's it! You've completed all the design and coding for your Foley Sound Generator app. Figure 5-7 shows the complete code in block-based format.

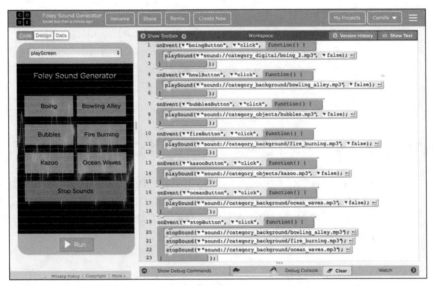

Figure 5-7

Here is the complete code in a text-based format:

```
onEvent("boingButton", "click", function() {
  playSound("sound://category_digital/boing_2.mp3", false);
});
onEvent("bowlButton", "click", function() {
  playSound("sound://category_background/bowling_alley.mp3", false);
});
onEvent("bubblesButton", "click", function() {
  playSound("sound://category_objects/bubbles.mp3", false);
});
onEvent("fireButton", "click", function() {
  playSound("sound://category_background/fire_burning.mp3", false);
});
onEvent("kazooButton", "click", function() {
  playSound("sound://category_objects/kazoo.mp3", false);
});
onEvent("oceanButton", "click", function() {
  playSound("sound://category_background/ocean_waves.mp3", false);
});
```

```
onEvent("stopButton", "click", function() {
  stopSound("sound://category_background/bowling_alley.mp3");
  stopSound("sound://category_background/fire_burning.mp3");
  stopSound("sound://category_background/ocean_waves.mp3");
});
```

Save, Test, and Debug Your App

As you work, App Lab automatically saves your program in the cloud. Test your program and fix any bugs to ensure that it works the way you want it to. For help with testing and debugging, see Chapter 3.

Share Your App with the World

After your app operates as you want it to, you should set the status of your program to Share. You can then share it by sending it to someone's mobile phone via a text message, by publishing it online, and by uploading it to Facebook and Twitter. You can also zip your app and send it as an email attachment, or you can embed it in a web page. See Chapter 19 for details on sharing apps you create in App Lab.

Enhance Your App

Consider enhancing your Foley Sound Generator with these features:

- **New sounds:** Add new sounds, including sounds from the web. In Chapter 2, see the section on recording and finding sounds.

- **Image buttons:** Instead of buttons, upload image files that represent the sounds they play. For example, add an elephant image that, when clicked or tapped, plays the sound of an elephant trumpeting.

Lucky Numbers

Have you ever noticed that the fortunes in fortune cookies often include a list of lucky numbers, usually ranging from 0 to 99? Instead of buying a fortune cookie, you can write a program to make your own lucky numbers, and you can make that program run on a micro:bit to show you the numbers!

To produce your lucky numbers, you'll need to code randomness in your program. *Coding randomness* means creating outcomes that are picked at random so that users experience the program differently each time they run it. In a dice game, each roll of a die produces a number from 1 to 6, at random. In video games, randomness lets you scatter characters onscreen or make a ball bounce off a paddle at different angles. It would be boring if the action in your game never changed: Randomness gives players variation and surprise.

www.flickr.com/photos/rheinitz/8403503137

Randomness is also important when you code a simulation of the real world. Modeling the spread of a flu virus in a population or predicting the motion of traffic on a highway requires using random numbers to predict many different but possible outcomes. In short, coding randomness lets you make your programs more interesting and more realistic.

Brainstorm

Figure 6-1 shows a completed project displaying a lucky number on the micro:bit. To create this cool gadget, you write a short event-driven program and upload it to the micro:bit. (See Chapter 4 for more information on event-driven programming.) The program runs when a user presses button A or button B on the micro:bit.

Figure 6-1

You can make your Lucky Numbers toy show any range of numbers, from any minimum value to any maximum value. For example, if you want your toy to display only one-digit numbers, set the range from 0 to 9. Or you can make your Lucky Numbers toy show lottery numbers for a Powerball game. Powerball numbers range from 1 to 69 for the main numbered balls, and from 1 to 26 for the Powerball. Want to create this toy? You can write code to make the micro:bit display main numbers when you click button A and display Powerball numbers when you click button B.

Start a New Project

Begin creating your Lucky Numbers gadget by starting a new project as follows:

1. Open MakeCode for micro:bit at https://makecode. microbit.org.

2. On the micro:bit home page, click the big New Project button in the middle of the screen.

   A new project opens and displays the workspace.

3. Name your project by typing a name in the Project Name field at the bottom of the micro:bit interface.

4. Click the save icon next to the Project Name field to save your project.

Code Button A

You write your Lucky Numbers code in the workspace. You can work in Blocks mode or JavaScript text mode. The Powerball lottery example (see the "Brainstorm" section) uses code written in Blocks mode. First, code button A to pick lucky numbers in the main lottery range, from 1 to 69, by following these steps:

1. Select the Input category of commands, and drag an on button A pressed command to the workspace.

   When the end user presses button A, it will run the code block (which you create in the next step).

2. Select the Basic category of commands. Drag a show number command to the workspace and drop it inside the on button A pressed command.

   Note that the tile shows a default value of 0. You replace this number in the next step.

3. Select the Math category of commands. Drag a pick random command to the workspace, and insert it in the show number command, replacing the 0.

4. Change the range of pick random to 1 to 69 by typing the new values in the fields.

Your code should look like Figure 6-2.

Figure 6-2

In MakeCode for micro:bit, you see all the code in the work-space, just as you do when working in App Lab. In Scratch, you can see only the code of the sprite or stage you're currently working on.

REMEMBER

Coding Randomness

Programmers rely on randomness to make video games interesting and models of the world more realistic. Randomness is also involved in *cybersecurity* — using mathematical computations to protect your digital information traveling around the Internet. Making a random number for use in a computer program requires an *algorithm,* which is a series of calculations the computer follows the same way every time. You wrote a small algorithm to make the micro:bit produce and display a random number. The computer uses its own algorithm to create the random number that it passes into your program.

Programming languages including Scratch, App Lab, and MakeCode allow you to set the range of the random numbers you want to use in your programs. You just type the minimum number and the maximum number. More advanced programming languages use a command called randomNumber ( ), which sets the minimum value of a random number range to zero. So with these languages, you have to perform some more math to change the starting value and the range of values.

Whatever commands you use for generating random numbers, each number in your random number range will have an equal likelihood of being selected. For example, if you're programming a dice roller, which has a range of 1 to 6, each number on the die face appears 1/6 of time, on average, when the die is rolled many times.

Code Button B

Next, code button B to pick lucky numbers for the Powerball numbers. To do this, you'll duplicate the Button A event and then change a few things:

1. Right-click (Windows) or Ctrl-click (Mac) the on button A pressed event and choose Duplicate from the pop-up menu (shown in Figure 6-3).

The on button A pressed event is duplicated.

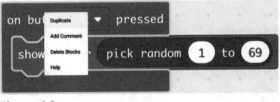

Figure 6-3

2. In the on button pressed command, press the tiny triangle next to the A and change it to B.

   Now, when the end user presses button B, it will run the code block. (You edit the code in the next step.)

3. Change the random number range to display 1 to 26 by typing these new numbers in the Pick Random command.

The completed code for Lucky Numbers is shown in Figure 6-4.

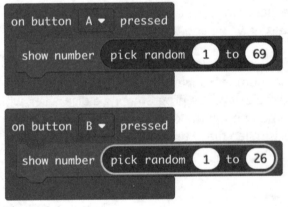

Figure 6-4

Here is the completed code in text-based format:

```
input.onButtonPressed(Button.A, function () {
    basic.showNumber(Math.randomRange(1, 69))
})
input.onButtonPressed(Button.B, function () {
    basic.showNumber(Math.randomRange(1, 25))
})
```

TECHNICAL
STUFF

The MakeCode for the micro:bit IDE gives you several event commands you can use, located in the Input category. Some common events are button presses, motion sensing, and electrical signal sensing. For button presses, you can set an event command to on button A pressed, on button B pressed, or on button A+B pressed (both buttons pressed together). For motion sensing, you can set an event to on shake, on tilt, on free fall, and other types of motion of the micro:bit. For electrical sensing, you can set an event command to on pin pressed, which reads whether an electrical signal is detected through a wire attached to a pin on the board. Data from other parts of the board, such as temperature or compass heading, can also be read and used in commands to cause other events in the program to run.

Save, Test, and Debug Your Program

Press the Save button at the bottom of the screen to save your program. The program is saved in the cloud and also as a micro:bit .hex file in your Downloads folder. The .hex file is a hexadecimal-format program that the micro:bit reads and executes.

You test your program in the on-screen simulator by clicking button A or clicking button B. Each click should show a number in the range you coded. Numbers that don't fit on the screen scroll by, one number at a time. Fix any bugs to ensure that your Lucky Numbers toy works the way you want it to. (See the section in Chapter 3 on debugging micro:bit programs.)

Transfer Your Program to the micro:bit

After your code works the way you want it to, you can transfer it to a micro:bit. See Chapter 2 for guidance in conducting the transfer. Then press button A or button B to see the micro:bit create some Lucky Numbers for you!

After the program is on the micro:bit, you can detach the board from your computer's USB port. If you want to use your toy away from the computer, attach the battery pack to the micro:bit.

Share Your Program with the World

You can share your micro:bit program with others. Set the status of your program to Share, and then copy and paste the link to your project anywhere you want to share it. See Chapter 19 for details on sharing your programs.

Enhance Your Toy

Consider enhancing your Lucky Number toy with new features:

- **Different numbers:** Change the number range of the toy. What's the biggest number you can make the micro:bit display? Can you set the range to make it display only even numbers?

- **New event:** Change the event trigger from on button pressed to a shake or a fall event.

Mondrian Art Toy

Coding color makes programs more interesting and realistic. You may be surprised to know that early video games, such as Pong, were black and white! Now you can mix light from red, green, and blue pixels on the computer screen to make millions of colors.

In this chapter, you add a new level of excitement to a game by coding color. You use skills you gained coding randomness (see Chapter 6) and learn how to use touchscreen sensors to locate position. (You discover even more about position in the next chapter.)

In the Mondrian Art toy, you use App Lab to build an app that lets your end user create art in the style of Piet Mondrian, the Dutch artist known for his abstract paintings of black rectangles filled with the primary colors red, yellow, and blue. You code your program to make rectangles of random sizes with user-selected colors, making every end user's painting a unique work of digital art!

https://commons.wikimedia.org/wiki/File:Piet_Mondriaan_-_03.jpg

Brainstorm

You can create your Mondrian Art drawing toy using lines of any width and color you want. You can set the random range of the rectangles' *dimensions* — the width and length — however you want. And you can offer the end user any fill colors you want, including randomly selected colors or colors with some transparency. Figure 7-1 shows an example of a completed toy featuring a canvas of art digitally painted by an end user.

Figure 7-1

Start a New Project

Begin creating your Mondrian Art toy app by starting a new project:

1. Open App Lab at https://code.org/educate/applab. **Log in** to the account you created to use App Lab (see Chapter 2). Under the App Lab heading, click the Try It Out button.

A new project opens.

2. Name your program by clicking the Rename button and typing a name in the Project Name field at the top of the App Lab interface.

3. Click the Save button.

Add a Background Color

Most Mondrian paintings have a white background, but you can choose to paint your background a different color. To make the colorful rectangles pop, consider changing the background to a light gray.

You can change the background color of your app as follows:

1. Click the Design button to switch to Design mode in App Lab.

   The Design toolbox and workspace are displayed.

2. On the Properties tab of the workspace, rename the ID of screen1 to a more meaningful name such as artScreen, as shown in Figure 7-2.

WARNING

Do not include spaces in ID names. In most programming languages, including App Lab, spaces are not allowed.

PROPERTIES	EVENTS		artScreen ⏶
id			Duplicate
artScreen			
background color			
		◣	
image			
		Choose...	

Figure 7-2

3. Click the small square of color to the right of the Background Color field to open the Color editor for the background.

4. Click the toggle arrows (the up and down arrows) to switch to RGBA color mode.

   Other options shown are HSLA and HEX. HSLA stands for Hue-Saturation-Lightness-Alpha and HEX stands for hexadecimal. Each is a different method of setting color.

5. The default white background color in the Background Color field is rgba(0,0,0,1). Create any background color you want by typing a value from 0 to 255 in each of the R, G, and B fields, and a value of 1 in the A (alpha) field. Or slide the color slider (the first slider) and the alpha slider (the second slider) to create the color and transparency you want.

   To follow along with the example and create a light gray background, type 230 (or thereabouts) in each of the first three fields and 1 in the A field. See Figure 7-3. See the "RGBA Color" sidebar for more information on working with color and transparency.

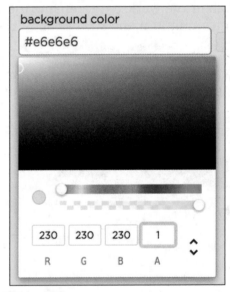

Figure 7-3

RGBA Color

An RGBA color code give values for red, green, blue, and alpha. Red, green, and blue each range from 0 to 255 in value. A value of 0 means no light is displayed in that color, resulting in the darkest color. A value of 255 is the greatest quantity of light in that value, resulting in the brightest color. The alpha parameter is a number from 0 (transparent) and 1 (opaque). If no alpha value is given, it is assumed to be 1. An alpha value of 0.5 would be half transparent and half opaque.

Here are some examples of RGBA values and their associated colors:

(0,0,0,1)	Black
(255,0,0,1)	Red
(0,255,0,1)	Green
(0,0,255,1)	Blue
(255,255,0,1)	Yellow — red light and green light produce yellow light
(0,255,255,1)	Cyan — green light and blue light produce cyan light
(255,0,255,1)	Magenta — red light and blue light produce magenta light
(50,50,50,1)	Dark gray
(150,150,150,1)	Medium gray
(200,200,200,1)	Light gray
(255,255,255,1)	White

Keep in mind that you're mixing colored pixel lights on a computer screen, which produces different results than mixing crayon colors on a piece of paper. For example, mixing red and green light produces yellow light. But mixing red and green crayons produces an icky brown shade.

When coding, you can set a pixel color value by typing a number in the color range, which is 0 to 255. Remember, small numbers means less light and make a darker color on a display. Large number means more light and make a brighter (lighter) color on a display.

Putting together randomness and color, you can write code to make random colors for your apps. Replace any pixel color value with random(0, 255) to create 256 variations for that color. Replacing each pixel color value (each of red, green, and blue) creates 256 color variations for each color channel. That means you can produce 256 * 256 * 256 colors, which is more than 16 million combinations!

Also remember that alpha values less than 1.0 cause your color to have some transparency. When layering colored objects (such as filled rectangles) on top of each other, color blending can be seen in the overlapping regions. This produces some interesting artistic effects.

Add a Title Label

Next, you should name your app with a label that helps the user know the purpose of the app. Add a title as follows:

1. Remain working in the Design mode of App Lab. If you're not in Design mode, click the Design button.

   The Design toolbox and workspace are displayed.

abc
Label

2. In the Design toolbox, drag the Label icon and position it near the top left of the app display.

   The label will be placed in front of the drawing canvas, so that it can be seen.

3. On the Properties tab of the workspace, change the attributes of the label as follows:

   • ID: Rename the ID to titleLabel.

   • Text: Type the title of your app, such as **Mondrian Art.**

   • Width (px): Increase to width of your label to something like 240 pixels (or more), so that the title will appear on a single line.

- Height (px): No change.

- x Position (px): No change; you change the x position later by dragging the label into position.

- y Position (px): No change; you change the y position later by dragging the label into position.

- Text Color: Click the small square of color to the right of the Text Color field and choose a color for your title that will contrast well with the background.

- Background Color: No change.

- Font Size (px): Type a new font size in the field or use the selection arrows to make the title the appropriate size for your app.

- Text Alignment: Click the selection arrows and choose Left.

4. Click and drag the label on your app to position it where you want.

   Refer to Figure 7-1 to see the position of the title label on the app simulator display.

Add Fill and Clear Buttons

Your app will feature buttons that the user can click or tap to select the fill color for each Mondrian rectangle. Follow these instructions to add each of these buttons to your app:

1. Remain working in the Design mode of App Lab. If you're not in Design mode, click the Design button.

   The Design toolbox and workspace are displayed.

Button
Button

2. In the Design toolbox, drag the Button icon to the app display.

3. On the Properties tab of the workspace, change the attributes of the button as shown here:

- ID: Rename the ID to `redButton` (or something similar) to indicate that this button will allow the user to draw a red-filled rectangle (or whatever color you choose).

- Text: Type the text that will appear on the button, such as **Red** (or whatever color you choose).

- Width (px): Increase to width of your button, to something like 55 pixels.

- Height (px): Increase to height of your button, to something like 55 pixels.

- x Position (px): No change; you change the x position later by dragging the button into position.

- y Position (px): No change; you change the y position later by dragging the button into position.

- Text Color: Click the small square of color to the right of the Text Color field and choose a text color that will contrast well with the button background.

- Background Color: Click the small square of color to the right of the Background Color field and choose a button color that will contrast well with the background color of the app. For example a button named Red would logically have a red background color.

- Font size (px): Type a new font size in the field or click the selection arrows to make the text on your button a good size for your app.

- Text alignment: Click the selection arrows and choose Left.

4. Drag the button on your app display to position it where you want. Remember that you will create several buttons and need to leave room for them all.

5. Create another button by selecting the first button you created and then clicking the aqua-colored Duplicate button in the workspace.

6. Repeat Step 5 until you've created all your buttons.

7. Change the ID and text on each of your duplicate buttons so that each one represents a different color. For example, I created a button for Red, Yellow, Blue, and White. I also created a button for Clear, which will be used to clear the screen of a painting.

8. Drag each of your new buttons to the app display, below the drawing canvas.

   The goal is to create a clean and readable user interface for the end user of your Mondrian Art toy. Refer to Figure 7-1.

TIP

To make the use of your app understandable to end users, organize your buttons in easy-to-find locations.

Code a Canvas and Paintbrush

The *canvas* is a rectangle-shaped area on the app screen where end users can paint — like a real artist's canvas! The canvas is see-through, so the background color that you set previously appears. You'll create the canvas and also define the *paintbrush* — the line color and thickness of the rectangles that the user will paint.

Create and code a canvas on the background and then code the paintbrush as follows:

1. Switch to Code mode in App Lab.

   The toolbox of commands and the workspace are displayed.

2. In the toolbox, select Canvas. Drag the `createCanvas` command into the workspace. Click in the `ID` field and type the name "`drawingCanvas`" (include the quotation marks). Set the width (the first number field) to `320`. Set the height (the second number field) to `400`.

   The command looks like this:

   ```
   createCanvas ("drawingCanvas", 320, 400); ←
   ```

3. Drag the `setActiveCanvas` command into the workspace, below the first command. Click in the `ID` field and type the name "`drawingCanvas`" (include the quotation marks).

   The `drawingCanvas` command you previously created is set to the active canvas. The command looks like this:

   ```
   setActiveCanvas (▼ "drawingCanvas");
   ```

WARNING

You can add a canvas also in Design mode. However, it's best to create this element by using code because this is how you would code this JavaScript outside App Lab.

4. Drag a `setStrokeWidth` command into the workspace, below the previous command. Type the number `5` in the empty field.

   The code looks like this:

   ```
   setStrokeWidth (5);
   ```

   When the end user draws a rectangle, its border width will be 5 pixels — very Mondrian in style!

5. Drag a `setStrokeColor` command into the workspace, below the previous command. Type "`black`" in the Color field.

The code looks like this:

```
setStrokeColor(▼ "black");
```

Any rectangle that the end user draws will have a black border.

Code to Draw a Rectangle

Next, you write code so that when the user touches anywhere on the app display, a randomly sized rectangle is painted at that location (read by the touch sensor at event). Follow these steps:

1. Continue working in Code mode.

2. In the toolbox, select UI controls. Drag an onEvent command into the workspace, below the previous command. In the onEvent command, click the ID field and type "drawingCanvas" (include the quotation marks). Leave the other attributes unchanged.

   When the user clicks or taps the drawing canvas, the code block inside this onEvent will execute.

3. In the toolbox, select Canvas. Drag a rect command into the onEvent command. In the rect fields, add the following attributes:

   • x: The first empty field of the rect command is the x-coordinate of the top-left corner of the rectangle. Type event.x in this field. (Note that a purple tile will appear around your typing.)

   • y: The second empty field of the rect command is the y-coordinate of the top-left corner of the rectangle. Type event.y in this field. (A purple tile will appear around your typing.)

- Width (px): The third empty field of the rect command is the width of the rectangle. Type 50 or a similar number in this field.

- Height (px): The fourth empty field of the rect command is the height of the rectangle. In the toolbox, go to the Math commands and drag a random command into this height field. Set the range of the random numbers by typing 20 or a similar number (for the minimum) and 120 or a similar number (for the maximum) in the empty fields.

These new lines of code are shown in Figure 7-4.

```
onEvent ( ▼ "drawingCanvas", ▼ "click", function (event) {
    rect ( event.x , event.y , 50, randomNumber (20, 120) );
}
                            );
```

Figure 7-4

Run your code to test it so far. In the simulator, clicking anywhere on the app display should draw an unfilled rectangle of varying dimensions. Try clicking lots of times to make lots of rectangles!

Code to Fill Rectangles with Color

Now you write some code to allow the user to set the fill color to be used when a rectangle is drawn:

1. Continue working in the Code mode of App Lab.

2. In the toolbox, select UI Controls. Drag the onEvent command into the workspace, below the previous command.

3. In the onEvent command, click the ID tab and choose redButton in the list. Remove event from function(). Leave the other attributes unchanged.

   When the Red button is clicked, the code block inside onEvent will execute.

4. Select Canvas. Drag a setFillColor command into the onEvent command. Type "red" in the field, or click the tab and select an RGB command and then type in values.

   When the user clicks the Red button, the rectangle fill color is set to red. Then, when the user touches the app display at any location, a randomly sized red-filled rectangle will be painted.

5. Repeat Steps 1–4 to code each of the remaining fill color buttons: Yellow, Blue, and White.

Figure 7-5 shows the code for the Red, Yellow, Blue, and White buttons.

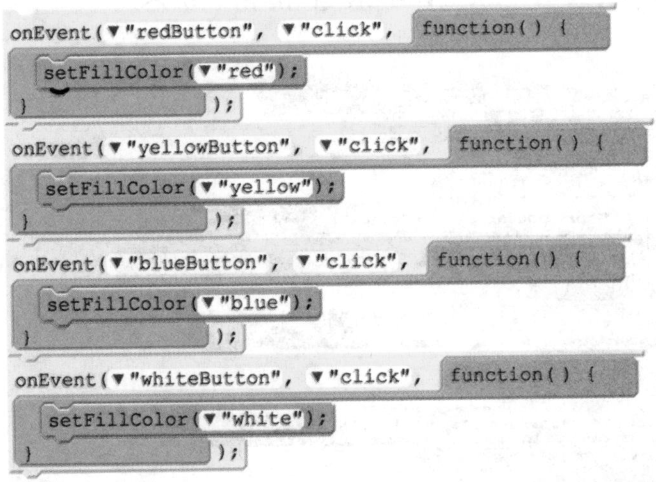

```
onEvent(▼"redButton", ▼"click", function() {
    setFillColor(▼"red");
}                    );
onEvent(▼"yellowButton", ▼"click", function() {
    setFillColor(▼"yellow");
}                    );
onEvent(▼"blueButton", ▼"click", function() {
    setFillColor(▼"blue");
}                    );
onEvent(▼"whiteButton", ▼"click", function() {
    setFillColor(▼"white");
}                    );
```

Figure 7-5

Code a Clear Button to Erase a Painting

After painting several rectangles, the end user may want to clear the painting and start fresh! Code a Clear button as follows:

1. Continue working in the Code mode of App Lab.

2. In the toolbox, select UI Controls. Drag the onEvent command into the workspace, below the previous command.

3. In the onEvent command, click the ID tab and choose clearButton in the list. Remove event from function(). Leave the other attributes unchanged.

When the Clear button is clicked, the code block inside onEvent will execute.

4. Select the Canvas commands. Drag a clearCanvas() command into the onEvent command.

Now, when the end user clicks the Clear button, the painting will be cleared from the display.

That's it! The design and code for the Mondrian Art toy are complete. Refer to Figure 7-1 to see the display of the completed app. Figure 7-6 shows the program in blocks.

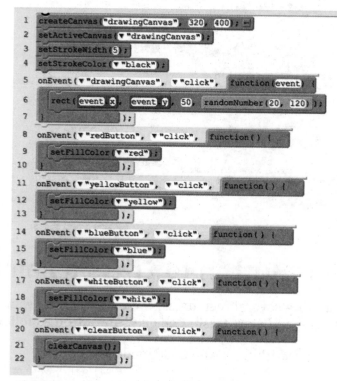

```
1   createCanvas("drawingCanvas", 320, 400); —
2   setActiveCanvas(▼ "drawingCanvas");
3   setStrokeWidth(5);
4   setStrokeColor(▼ "black");
5   onEvent(▼ "drawingCanvas", ▼ "click", function(event) {
6      rect(event x, event y, 50, randomNumber(20, 120));
7   };
8   onEvent(▼ "redButton", ▼ "click", function() {
9      setFillColor(▼ "red");
10  };
11  onEvent(▼ "yellowButton", ▼ "click", function() {
12     setFillColor(▼ "yellow");
13  };
14  onEvent(▼ "blueButton", ▼ "click", function() {
15     setFillColor(▼ "blue");
16  };
17  onEvent(▼ "whiteButton", ▼ "click", function() {
18     setFillColor(▼ "white");
19  };
20  onEvent(▼ "clearButton", ▼ "click", function() {
21     clearCanvas();
22  };
```

Figure 7-6

Here is the complete code in JavaScript:

```
createCanvas("drawingCanvas", 320, 400);
setActiveCanvas("drawingCanvas");
setStrokeWidth(5);
setStrokeColor("black");
onEvent("drawingCanvas", "click", function(event) {
  rect(event.x, event.y, 50, randomNumber(20, 120));
});
onEvent("redButton", "click", function() {
  setFillColor("red");
});
onEvent("yellowButton", "click", function() {
  setFillColor("yellow");
});
onEvent("blueButton", "click", function() {
  setFillColor("blue");
      });
onEvent("whiteButton", "click", function() {
  setFillColor("white");
});
onEvent("clearButton", "click", function() {
  clearCanvas();
});
```

Save, Test, and Debug Your App

As you work, App Lab automatically saves your program in the cloud. Test your program and fix any bugs to ensure that it works the way you want it to. For help with testing and debugging, see Chapter 3.

Share Your App with the World

After your app operates as you want it to, you can set the status of the program to Share. See Chapter 19 for details on sharing apps you create in App Lab.

Enhance Your App

Add some or all of these cool new features to your app:

- **More randomness in rectangle sizes:** As built, only the height of the rectangle is random. Make the width of the rectangle random, too!

- **More color buttons:** Create additional buttons to produce other rectangle fill colors, such as green or purple.

- **Buttons that fill rectangles with half-transparent colors:** Instead of naming a fill color such as red, use an rgb command in the field of setFillColor for each button. The RGB command with four values is actually an RGBA command. Set the fourth value, the alpha (the A value) of each command to 0.5 to make the color half-transparent. For details, see the "RGBA Color" sidebar.

- **A button that fills rectangles with a randomly selected color:** Create a Random button and add this code:

```
onEvent("randomButton", "click", function() {
  setFillColor(rgb(randomNumber(0, 255),randomNumber(0, 255),
  randomNumber(0, 255),1));
});
```

The quantities of each color channel — red, green, and blue — are randomly assigned. Every button click produces a new random color. See the "RGBA Color" sidebar for more on RGBA color.

Part 3
Moving from Here to There, Again and Again

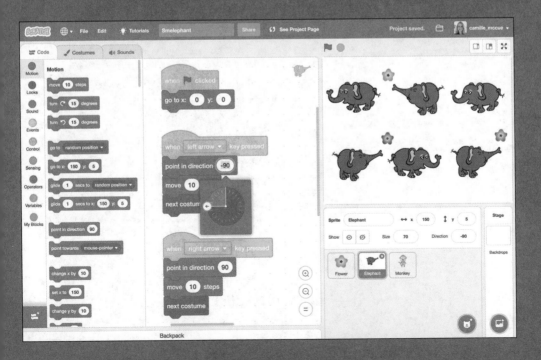

In this part you'll . . .

- Create an algorithm for cloning and scattering objects

- Discover how to animate objects and make them move

- Code key control and detect object collisions

- Construct simple loops and build code blocks (functions)

Emoji Explosion

In this chapter, you code Emoji Explosion, a fun animated scene where emoji objects of many colors bounce around the screen. You learn to set the coordinates and direction of the objects — using randomness to scatter the emojis everywhere! — and then make them move. Simple loops control the action.

To get started, you use Scratch to draw an emoji and then clone it to make a large group of emojis moving and bouncing around the screen. Now that you are writing longer programs, you also create new code blocks (sometimes called *functions*) to organize your code — like a real coder.

Putting together randomness, motion, loops, cloning, and functions in one project is an explosive leap forward. You're really coding now!

Brainstorm

You can draw any emoji you want — a smiling face, a winking face, a face with rolling eyes — countless options are available! Or you can choose any other object to clone and create a population. Star Wars Stormtroopers? Waldo? Cows? Skittles candy pieces? Any object works, just use your imagination. Time to get coding!

TIP

The code you write for this project will be useful for many games and models you may want to code because so many programs require making, scattering, and moving a population of objects.

Start a New Project

Begin creating your Emoji Explosion program by starting a new project as follows:

1. Open Scratch at `https://scratch.mit.edu/`. If prompted, enable Flash to run Scratch. Log in to the account you created to use Scratch (see Chapter 2).

2. On the Scratch home page, select Create. Or if you're already working in Scratch, choose File ⇨ New from the menu bar.

   A new project opens.

3. Name your program by typing a name in the Project Name field at the top of the Scratch interface.

4. Cut Scratch Cat from the project by clicking the X in the Scratch Cat icon in the sprite area in the lower-right corner.

Add a Backdrop

The *backdrop* is the background color or image that fills the screen of your toy. Add a backdrop as follows:

1. At the Stage, hover over the Choose a Backdrop icon.

2. Click Paint from the pop-up menu.

   The backdrop editor opens at the Backdrops tab. The default costume name for this backdrop is `backdrop1`. You can leave this name, or change it. I changed mine to `night`.

3. Click the Convert to Bitmap button.

4. Select a Fill color.

   I selected black, to make the backdrop look like nighttime.

5. Click the Paint bucket and then click the empty backdrop (the checkerboard region) to fill the backdrop with your selected color. Figure 8-1 shows the finished backdrop.

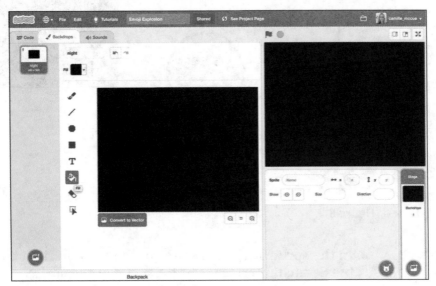

Figure 8-1

Add an Emoji Sprite

Draw an emoji sprite for your animated scene as follows:

1. In the sprite area of the Scratch interface, hover over the Choose a Sprite icon.

2. Click Paint to paint your own sprite costume.

The sprite costume editor opens at the Costumes tab. The default costume name for this sprite is costume1. You can leave this name, or change it. I changed mine to yellow.

3. Use the drawing tools to draw your emoji (see Figure 8-2).

The sprite appears on the stage. Don't worry about its size because you can adjust that later.

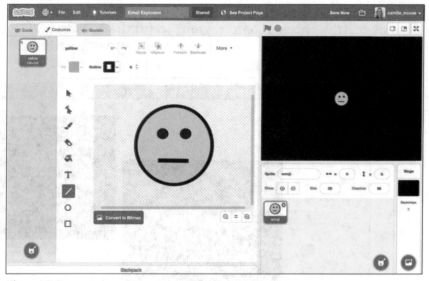

Figure 8-2

4. In the sprite attributes editor in the bottom-right corner of the Scratch interface, edit the name of the sprite.

The default name is Sprite1. I named my sprite emoji.

5. Still in the sprite attributes editor, resize your sprite by typing a new number in the Size field above the sprite.

The default size is 100. I changed the size of my emoji to 20.

Tinker with the drawing tools and the fill colors in the sprite costume editor to see how each can be used to produce different features for your emoji costume.

If you add a sprite and then decide you don't want it, cut it by clicking the X in its icon.

Code the Stage to Play a Sound

Code the stage to play a sound throughout your animated scene. You can choose which sound you want, and set it to play start to finish, over and over, as the animation runs.

1. Click the icon of your backdrop in the stage area.

2. On the Code tab of the Scratch interface, select the Events icon. Drag a when green flag is clicked command to the Code workspace.

3. Select the Control icon. Drag the forever loop command to the Code workspace, and attach it to the previous command.

   The forever command is one of four loop-type control commands. The other three are repeat, repeat until, and wait until. See Table 8-1 for details. (See the "Repeat Loops" sidebar for more information.)

4. Select the Sound icon. Drag the play sound until done command to the Code workspace and attach it inside the forever event command.

5. Click the Sounds tab to open the sound editor for the stage.

6. Click the X in the corner of the Pop sound icon to delete it because you won't be using this sound.

7. Click the Choose a Sound icon in the lower-left corner of the Scratch interface.

   The sound library appears on the Choose a Sound screen.

8. Click the icon for the sound you want to add to the stage.

   I selected Boop Bing Bop, as you can see in Figure 8-3. This is a wacky audio track that sounds like emojis bouncing around!

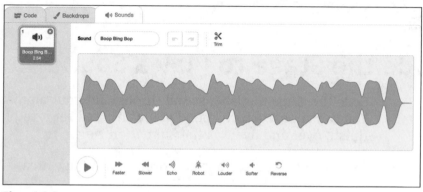

Figure 8-3

9. Return to the Code tab.

10. Click the tab in the `play sound until done` command and select the sound you just added.

Table 8-1   Scratch Control (Loop) Commands

Command	Event
`forever`	The code block runs forever, until the program stops.
`repeat` *number*	The code block runs *number* times.
`repeat until` *condition*	The code block runs until *condition* is met.
`wait until` *condition*	The code block runs after *condition* is met.

Now, when the end user clicks the green flag, the sound you added to the stage will play, looping forever in the background. Figure 8-4 shows the completed code on the stage.

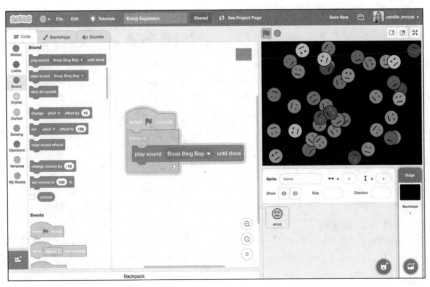

Figure 8-4

REMEMBER

When working on the stage or on a sprite, you see only the code associated with that object. Don't let this panic you — you haven't lost any code!

Code the Green Flag for the Emoji Sprite

The emoji sprite you created should follow a simple program. It should show itself onscreen, clone itself to make more emojis, and then hide.

Write the green flag program for the emoji sprite by following these steps:

1. Select the icon of the emoji sprite in the sprite area.

2. On the Code tab of the Scratch interface, select the Events icon. Drag a when green flag clicked command to the Code workspace.

Cloning and Inheritance

Cloning means making an exact copy of an object. Some people have heard of cloning in the animal world. Back in 1996, at the University of Edinburgh, a sheep named Dolly was born, the first mammal successfully cloned from an adult cell. In programming, cloning allows a coder to quickly create as many copies as needed of an object, such as a sprite.

Cloning takes advantage of a programming idea called *inheritance*. Many programming languages use inheritance so that new objects can be easily created from parent objects. A clone *inherits* the attributes (costume, size, position, and direction) and all code of its parent sprite. Also, after you create clones (also known as *child* objects), you can change them to add or remove attributes or bits of code. In this way, a child object can be *mutated* (changed to do something different) from its parent object.

3. Select the Looks icon. Drag a `show` command to the Code workspace, and attach it to the previous command.

   The emoji sprite must be displayed to be cloned. (This is an issue only if at some point you hide the sprite, which you will do at the end of your main program.)

4. Select the My Blocks icon. Click the Make a Block button to create a new code block.

   The Make a Block dialog box opens.

5. Name this new code block `makeEmojis`, as shown in Figure 8-5, and click OK.

   The new block header is added to your workspace, and the new block command, `makeEmojis` is added to your commands in the My Blocks category.

You haven't defined what the makeEmojis code block does; you do that in the next section. But isn't it neat that you can write your main program without worrying about that detail just yet?

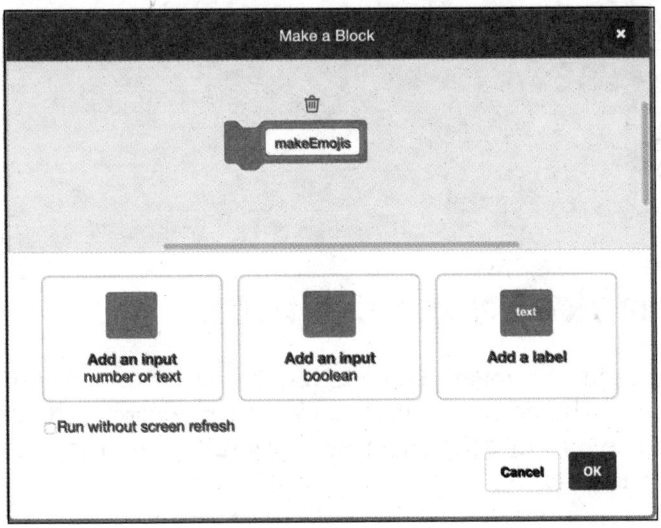

Figure 8-5

6. From the My Blocks category, drag the makeEmojis command to the Code workspace, and attach it to the show command.

7. Drag a hide command to the Code workspace, and attach it to the makeEmojis command.

   After the emoji sprite runs makeEmojis, it hides. You hide it so that you don't have to write commands to make it move — you'll have plenty of emoji clones moving around the screen already.

See Figure 8-6 for the complete green flag code for the emoji sprite.

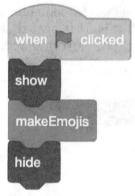

Figure 8-6

Code the makeEmojis Block

You created a makeEmojis code block header and command tile. Now write the code for that block. The makeEmojis code block clones the parent emoji sprite to create many emojis exploding all over the screen.

A *clone* has all of the attributes (costume, size, position, and direction) of its parent sprite and can be made using a clone command in the Control category. You can make lots of clones by putting a clone command in a simple loop. The repeat command (which is also in the Control category) is a simple loop that lets you set the number of times you want it to execute.

Write the code for the makeEmojis code block as follows:

1. Work at the define makeEmojis code block header in the workspace.

2. Select the Control icon. Drag a repeat command to the Code workspace, and attach it to the code block header. Type a number in the repeat command.

   This number is how many times the repeat command will execute. I set mine to 40.

3. Drag a `create clone of` command to the Code workspace, and attach it inside `repeat`. Set the `create clone of` command to `myself`.

4. Select the Looks icon. Drag a `change color effect` to the Code workspace, and attach it to the `create clone` command, inside `repeat`. Type a number in the `change color effect` command.

This number is how much the color of a clone changes each time the `repeat` command executes. I set the change to `10`. A small number makes slight color changes, and a large number makes bigger color changes. The `define makeEmojis` code block is now complete. See Figure 8-7.

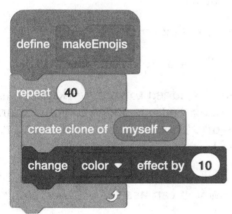

Figure 8-7

Code when I start as a clone for the Emoji Sprite

When the green flag program of the emoji sprite runs, it creates clones. The clones need instructions! Each clone needs to follow one instruction: explode!

Write the when I start as a clone program by following these steps:

1. Select the emoji sprite.

2. Still working in the Code tab of the Scratch interface, select the Control icon.

   Drag a when I start as a clone command to the Code workspace.

   The command you attach to this event will execute each time a new clone is created.

3. Select the My Blocks icon. Click the Make a Block button to create a new code block.

   The Make a Block dialog box opens.

4. Name this new code block explode and click OK.

   The new block header is added to your workspace, and the new block command, explode, is added to your commands in the My Blocks category. The makeEmojis command is there, too! (See Figure 8-8).

   You haven't defined what explode does; you do that in the next section. But now you can use the explode command.

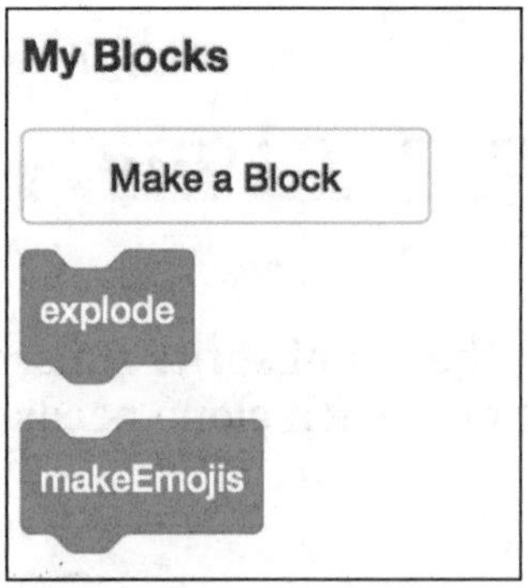

My Blocks

Make a Block

explode

makeEmojis

Figure 8-8

5. From the My Blocks category, drag the explode command to the Code workspace, and attach it to the when I start as a clone command.

See Figure 8-9 for the complete when I start as a clone program for the emoji clones.

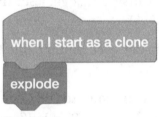

when I start as a clone

explode

Figure 8-9

Code the explode Block for the Emoji Clones

You created an explode code block header and command tile. Now you need to write the code to provide instructions for explode. This code should make each clone scatter to a random position, point in a random direction, and move.

Follow these steps to write the code:

1. Work at the define explode code block header in the workspace.

2. Select the Motion icon. Drag a go to random position command to the Code workspace, and attach it to the code block header.

3. Drag a point in direction command to the Code workspace, and attach it to the previous command.

4. Select the Operators icon. Drag a pick random command to the value field of the point in direction command. Set the range of direction angles from 0 to 360.

5. Select the Control icon. Drag a `forever` command to the Code workspace, and attach it to the previous command.

   The code block you will build inside this command will execute forever until the Stop button is clicked.

6. Select the Motion icon. Drag a `move steps` command to the Code workspace, and attach it inside `forever`. Set the number to steps by typing in number.

   The larger the number, the faster each emoji clone moves. I set mine to a value of `10`.

7. Drag an `if on edge, bounce` command to the Code workspace, and attach it inside the `forever` command.

   This command causes an emoji clone to bounce off the edges of the screen and continue moving.

The `explode` code block is now complete, and should look like Figure 8-10.

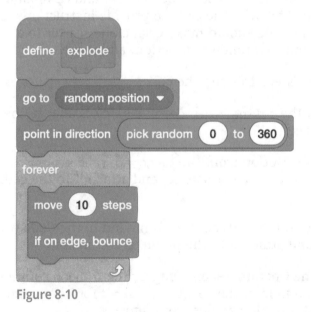

Figure 8-10

Figure 8-11 shows all the code for the emoji sprite. Note that the code for the stage and for the emoji sprite both run when the green flag is clicked. This means they run in parallel (see Chapter 4) — the music on the stage runs forever while the emoji clones move and bounce forever!

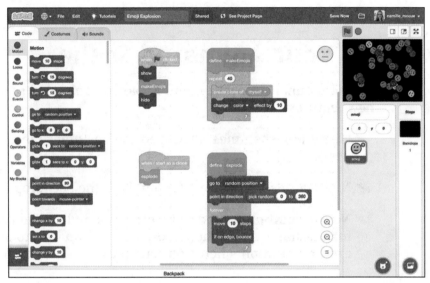

Figure 8-11

Save, Test, and Debug Your Program

Name your project by typing in the Title field at the top of the Scratch interface. As you work, Scratch automatically saves your program in the cloud, so you don't have to take any special actions to save your work.

Test your program and fix any bugs to ensure that it works the way you want it to. (See Chapter 3 for help on debugging Scratch programs.)

Share Your Program with the World

After your program operates perfectly, it's time to share it! Set the status of your program to Share, and then add to your project page a description of your program and directions on how to run it. See Chapter 19 for details on sharing your programs.

Enhance Your Animated Scene

Consider enhancing your Emoji Explosion animated scene with new features:

- **New emoji costumes:** Just open the Costumes tab and draw a new costume.

- **New sounds:** Add different sounds to the backdrop.

- **New backdrop:** Instead of painting a simple, solid backdrop for the stage, select the Choose a Backdrop icon to add an exciting location where your emoji can bounce around!

Setting Position

Coordinates are the mathematical way of naming a position on a graph. In two dimensions, like your screens in Scratch, App Lab, and MakeCode for micro:bit, coordinates are described as a pair of values (x, y). The first number is the x-coordinate (position left to right) and the second number is the y-coordinate (position top to bottom).

In Scratch, the coordinate (0,0) is called the origin and is located at the center of the screen. The x-axis runs left to right across the screen, with x-coordinate values ranging from –240 at the far left to 240 at the far right.

The y-axis runs top to bottom down the screen, with y-coordinate values ranging from 180 at the very top down to –180 at the very bottom. See the figure to locate the x-axis, the y-axis, and the coordinates of the origin and each corner of the screen in Scratch.

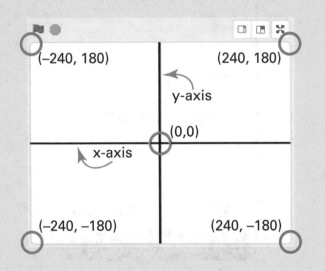

When working in Scratch, you can set the position of a sprite using the go to x: y: command. For example, to set the position of a hero in a game at the center of the screen, you could use the command go to x: 0 y: 0. To place a sprite at a random position, you can use go to random position.

In App Lab, the screen is set up so that the origin — the coordinate (0,0) — is at the top-left corner of the screen. The x-axis runs left to right across the screen, with x-coordinates ranging from 0 at the far left to 320 at the far right. The y-axis runs top to bottom down the screen, with y-coordinates ranging from 0 at the top of the screen to 450 at the bottom. The center of the screen is located at the coordinate (160, 225). The figure shows the x-axis, y-axis, center, and coordinates of each corner of the screen in App Lab.

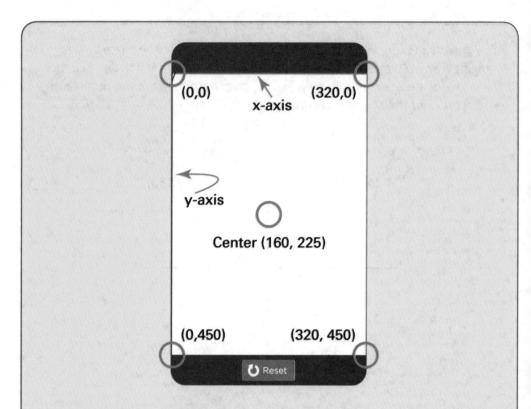

In MakeCode, you can set positions on the micro:bit screen — a very small LED grid with just 25 points. The micro:bit is set up so that the origin — the coordinate (0,0), — is at the top-left corner. The x-axis runs left to right across the screen, with x-coordinates having values from 0 to 4. The y-axis runs top to bottom down the screen, with y-coordinates having values from 0 to 4. Here are the (x, y) coordinates of all the LED positions on the micro:bit:

```
(0,0)(1,0)(2,0)(3,0)(4,0)
(0,1)(1,1)(2,1)(3,1)(4,1)
(0,2)(1,2)(2,2)(3,2)(4,2)
(0,3)(1,3)(2,3)(3,3)(4,3)
(0,4)(1,4)(2,4)(3,4)(4,4)
```

The figure shows the text-based code (JavaScript) in MakeCode for lighting up a diagonal line on the micro:bit. The "line" runs from the top-left corner at (0, 0) to the bottom-right corner at (4, 4).

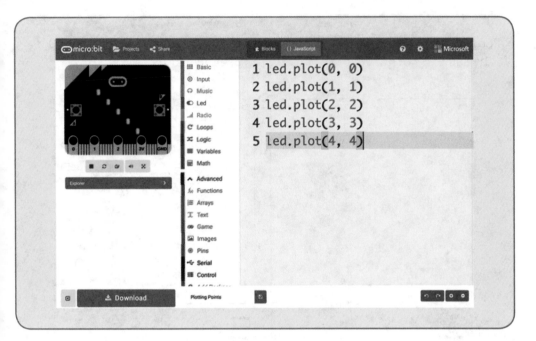

Setting Direction

When working in Scratch, you can make a sprite point in a direction by turn-ing it. Directions are indicated by an angle value (the number of degrees) from 0 to 360. Because a full circle consists of 360 degrees, an angle of 0 degrees is the same as an angle of 360 degrees.

The turn right and turn left commands are *relative turn commands* because they turn the sprite relative to where it currently points. For each of these commands, you must type a number for the angle (the number of degrees) you want the sprite to turn. Turn right 90 is a "hard right," and turn left 90 is a "hard left." A turn of 180 in either direction points the sprite in the opposite direction from where it pointed before the turn.

The point in direction command is an *absolute turn command* because it causes the sprite to point to the selected heading regardless of where it was pointing before the turn. So, point in direction 0 is the direction north, point in direction 90 is east, point in direction 180 is south, and point in direction -90 is west. (Note that point in direction -90 is the same as point in direction 270.) See the figures.

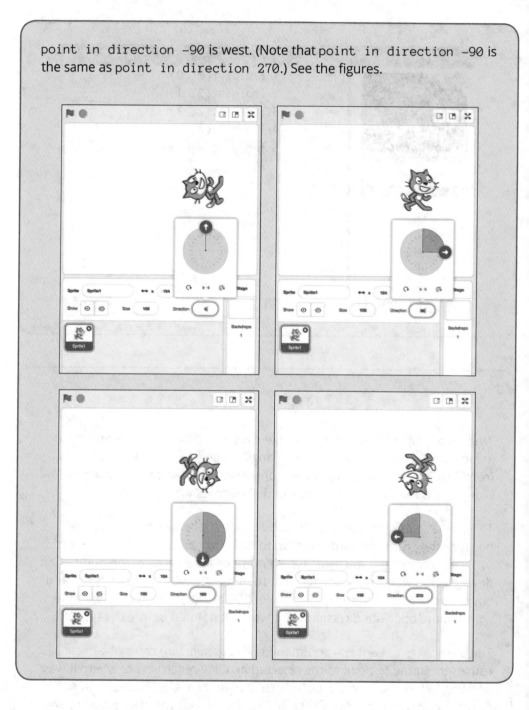

Point towards points the sprite towards something else on the screen. Options consist of mouse pointer or any other sprite on the screen.

Lastly, when setting direction in Scratch, you can decide how you want the sprite to face. The direction indicator has three facing options. The first option (the circle arrow) makes the sprite rotation match its direction. The second option (the mirror image arrows) makes the sprite flip left and right but not up and down. For example, a person sprite would face left or right, but he would not stand on his head! The third option (the circle arrow with the line through it) freezes the look of the sprite: It can still point and move in any direction, but its appearance won't match its heading.

When working in App Lab, MakeCode, and JavaScript in general, be aware that these programs don't make much use of direction commands. (The only exception is the Turtle command category in App Lab.)

Moving

Motion can be coded by making an object change its position from one coordinate to another coordinate, over and over. In Scratch, you can code motion in three ways. The first way is to place a move command (from the Motion category) inside a repeat command (from the Control category). Big moves, such as repeat forever [move 50], make an object go faster than small moves, such as repeat forever [move 10]. You can also set speed by adding a wait command (from the Control category) to each move. For example, repeat forever [move 10 wait 1] makes an object move faster than repeat forever [move 10 wait 2].

The second way to make a sprite move in Scratch is by using the glide command (from the Motion category). Specify the number of seconds for the glide to create smooth motion (great for floating and swimming sprites).

The third way to make an object move in Scratch is by using the change x by and change y by commands. Change x by moves the sprite left or right (when the command is followed by a negative or a positive number, respectively). Change y by moves the sprite up or down (when the command is followed by a positive or a negative number, respectively). The time in which each move runs affects how the user sees the speed of the moving object.

In App Lab, you can create motion by changing the coordinates of an object and specifying how often the move occurs by using the timedLoop(1000, function() { }) command, located in the Control category. The default time of the timed loop is 1000 milliseconds, but you can set the time to any value you want. Another way you can control motion in App Lab is to change the coordinates of an object and add a wait time between each change by using the setTimeout(function() { } 1000) command, also located in the Control category. Again, you set the milliseconds value.

On the micro:bit, motion is accomplished by changing the coordinates of a light on the LED screen and adding a wait time between moves. In MakeCode, several command categories include a wait command, including pause(100) in the Basic category.

Simple Repeat Loops

Sequence, selection, and repetition are the three key processes in any computer program (see Chapter 1). Repetition allows sections of code to execute over and over, or *loop*. Coding loops allows you to make your programs more efficient by identifying the code blocks to be repeated, and then identifying how often they will be repeated — you don't have to keep typing the same code over and over again! In these first chapters, the types of loops you code are fairly simple.

Scratch uses four loop structures: forever, repeat, repeat until, and wait until. Each loop offers a different way to control when code will be repeated and how many times it is repeated. Forever loops run the code block over and over until the program is finished. These loops are great for ongoing processes such as playing background music in a game. Repeat loops specify an exact number of time the loop will run. A repeat loop is useful when you know exactly how many times you want a loop structure to execute, such as cloning 5 players for a basketball team, or counting down a 60-second timer in a game. The repeat until loop executes until a condition is met, and wait until delays execution until a condition is met.

Every programming language, including App Lab and MakeCode, uses loops. App Lab offers timed loops, a while loop (which executes while a condition is met), and a for loop. MakeCode features a forever loop, a while loop, and a for loop. You're probably wondering what a for loop is. The for loop is a more complex loop structure. It's similar to the repeat loop in Scratch but uses a variable to count through the loop. You make use of the for() loop after you work with variables. Numbers variables are covered in Chapter 12 and for loops are covered in Chapter 17.

New Blocks (aka Functions)

Programming languages have built-in commands called *primitives*. Think of primitives as ingredients for making a birthday cake and the computer program as the recipe.

Sometimes, it's easier to understand a computer program or a recipe if we group related instructions. When baking a birthday cake, you make the cake, you make the frosting, and you put them together. The recipe for the birthday cake includes a "frosting" ingredient, but the instructions for making frosting might be on the next page. Instead of explaining all the steps for making frosting in the middle of the cake program, the frosting ingredient represents a smaller program with ingredients and instructions of its own.

By representing this smaller part of the birthday cake with a new name ("frosting") and instructions for making the frosting, the entire recipe-writing process is simplified. In programming languages, the smaller "frosting" program is called a *sub-program*. Scratch calls these sub-programs *blocks,* while App Lab and MakeCode call them *functions.* (Older programming languages called them *procedures.*) You can create as many new blocks (or functions) as you want and then include them in your programs. However, a new block exists only within the program where you made it. Also, the new block executes exactly the same way every time you use it.

You can customize some new blocks (functions). For example, you can include one or more pieces of information, called parameters, with the function. The *parameter* gives extra detail about how to run the function. For example, the frosting recipe function might include a parameter that indicates how many servings the recipe will make — frosting(8) could represent a function that produces frosting for eight servings of cake. (Yum!)

Smelephant

Now that you know how to clone and scatter objects, move around the screen, code loops, and build new blocks, you can create a simple game! Smelephant is a fun collection game that takes place on the savanna and features a bouncy monkey, a field of flowers, and an elephant who loves to roam around, sniffing flowers into his trunk . . . which is why he's called a smelephant!

Your user will move around the screen using a new skill you'll learn to code: key control. This project will also teach you the basics of animating objects and coding object collisions, including hiding and showing objects. Let's get that smelephant moving!

Brainstorm

Your collection game doesn't have to take the form of a smelephant. You can make any hero collect any object you want! My students have made game variations such as a bee collecting pollen, a penguin politician collecting votes, and even Cookie Monster gathering up and munching cookies! The game you create should include a setting, a hero, and objects for the player to collect. The figure on the chapter's first page shows a completed Smelephant game.

Start a New Project

Begin creating your Smelephant program by starting a new project as follows:

1. Open Scratch at https://scratch.mit.edu. If prompted, enable Flash to run Scratch. Log in to the account you created to use Scratch (see Chapter 2).

2. On the Scratch home page, choose Create. Or if you're already working in Scratch, choose File ⇨ New from the menu bar.

   A new project opens.

3. Name your program by typing a name in the Project Name field at the top of the Scratch interface.

4. Cut Scratch Cat from the project by clicking the X in the Scratch Cat icon.

   The icon is in the sprite area in the lower-right corner of the Scratch interface.

Add a Backdrop

The *backdrop* is the background color or image that fills the screen of your toy. Add a backdrop as follows:

1. In the stage area, hover over the Choose a Backdrop icon.

   The Choose a Backdrop library appears.

2. Click the Savanna backdrop from the Choose a Backdrop library.

   The Savanna backdrop appears on the stage, as shown in Figure 9-1.

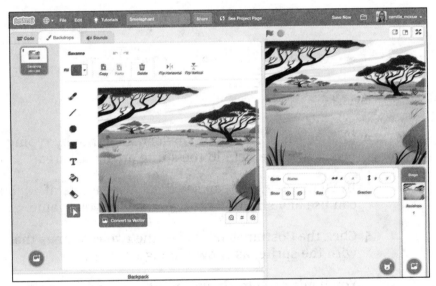

Figure 9-1

REMEMBER

You can delete the default backdrop, backdrop1, by clicking or tapping the Backdrops tab and then clicking or tapping the X in the backdrop1 icon.

Add a Smelephant Sprite

Add an elephant sprite to your game and name it smelephant as follows:

1. In the sprite area of the Scratch interface, click the Choose a Sprite icon.

2. Click the Elephant sprite.

   The Elephant sprite is added to the project. The default sprite name is Elephant.

3. Change the default sprite name by typing smelephant in the Sprite name field in the sprite attributes area, as shown in Figure 9-2.

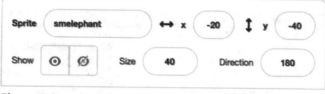

Figure 9-2

4. Change the size of your smelephant sprite by typing a number in the Size field in the sprite attributes area.

   In Figure 9-2, you can see that I used a size of 40, but you can use any size that makes sense for your game.

5. Click the Costumes tab to see the two costumes that come with the sprite, as shown in Figure 9-3.

   You don't need to change anything here, unless you want to tinker with the painting tools to change the color of the smelephant's two costumes. I did!.

TIP

Having more than one costume allows you to create animated motion by switching the costume as the sprite moves. You code this when you code key control for the smelephant in the next sections.

6. Set the rotation style of the smelephant by clicking the Direction field in the sprite attribute area and then selecting the Left/Right rotation option.

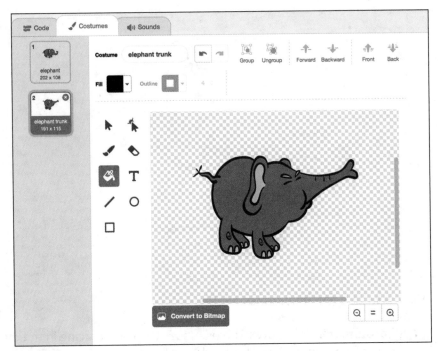

Figure 9-3

This option allows the smelephant to face left when he walks left, and face right when he walks right. When he moves up or down, he remains facing in the direction he was previously facing. For details, see the "Rotation Styles in Scratch" sidebar.

Rotation Style in Scratch

You can set the rotation style of an object in Scratch. If you code an object to rotate, you should also set its rotation style. As shown in the figure, you have three options: all around, left-right, and do not rotate. The rotation style helps the user see which direction the sprite is pointing onscreen.

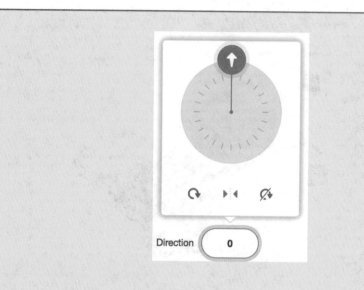

Here is what each option does:

- **All around (circle arrow):** The user sees the object facing in the direction it is heading. This rotation style might be useful for sprite characters that would typically fly or swim.

- **Left/Right (mirror-image arrows):** The user sees the object facing in the direction it is heading when it is moving left or moving right. If the object is moving up or down, the rotation does not change to match the up or down direction. This rotation style is useful for sprite characters that typically walk on the ground, such as people or doggies – or smelephants!

- **Do not rotate (circle arrow with a line):** The sprite does not appear to point in the direction it is heading. Note that a sprite with more than one costume can still change costumes.

Code the Green Flag Code of the Smelephant

Code the smelephant so that when the game starts, he is located in the center of the screen. Follow these steps:

1. Click the icon for the smelephant sprite.

2. Working in the Code tab of the Scratch interface, select the Events icon.

3. Drag the when green flag clicked command to the Code workspace.

4. Select the Motion icon. Drag a go to x: y: command and attach it to the previous command. Set the value in each field to 0, as shown in Figure 9-4.

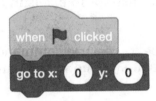

Figure 9-4

When executed, this command sends the smelephant to the center of the screen at coordinates (0, 0).

Code the Smelephant's Up Arrow Key Control

The player moves the smelephant around the savanna and sniffs a flower into his trunk whenever he bumps one. To move the smelephant, the player clicks the arrow keys on the keyboard.

Follow these steps to code the smelephant to move up the screen using the up arrow key:

1. Click the icon for the smelephant sprite.

2. Working at the Code tab of the Scratch interface, select the Events icon. Drag a when space key pressed command to the Code workspace. Change the key selection from space to up arrow.

3. Select the Motion icon. Drag a `point in direction` command to the Code workspace, and attach it to the previous command. Type the number 0 in the field.

   A heading of 0 points the sprite towards the top of the screen. Refer to Chapter 8 for additional information on directional headings.

4. Drag a `move steps` command to the Code workspace, and attach it to the previous command. Type the number 10 in the field.

   This number represents a movement of 10 pixels in the direction set in Step 3.

5. Select the Looks icon. Drag a `next costume` command and attach it to the previous command, as shown in Figure 9-5.

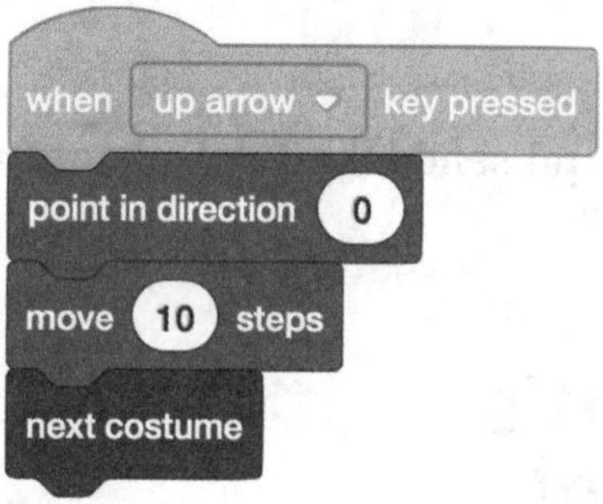

Figure 9-5

This code makes the smelephant sprite wear its next costume. Each time the smelephant moves, in any direction, his costume changes. This simple, animated effect creates the appearance of walking and trumpeting with his trunk! (Refer to the "Animating Shapes" sidebar.)

Now, when a user clicks the up arrow key on a computer keyboard, the smelephant moves up the screen.

Animating Shapes

Animating an object allows you to make it appear to flap its wings or walk while moving. Instead of using a single costume on the object, you add two or more costumes, with each costume showing the object in a different pose. Then, you change the costume each time you move the object.

In Scratch, you animate a shape by using the next costume command in the Looks category. As shown in the first figure, the shark sprite has three costumes, located at the Costumes tab.

The second figure shows sample code for making the shark move with animation. Attaching a next costume command to a move command allows you to animate the sprite when it moves. Including a glide command, a

turn command, and a set rotation style left-right command — all
inside a forever loop — lets you create some fancy shark swimming!

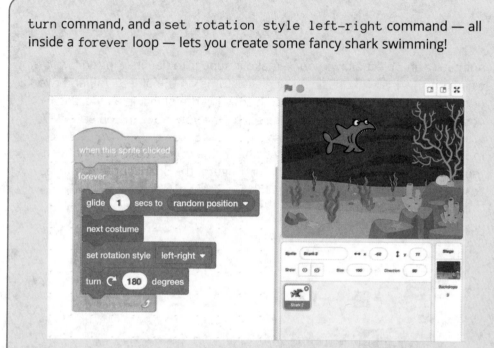

In App Lab, you can create animation by adding an image element to your
app and then changing the image displayed onscreen. Work in Design
mode to add the image element, and upload all the images you want to
display in the animation for that element. Then work in Code mode to add
setImageURL() commands for each new image. Use a timedLoop() to set
the rate at which the image changes. Instead of using different images as
an object moves, a fun alternative is to make an animation in which a single
image grows onscreen. The figure shows how to make the greenie image
element (which is wearing an alien head image) grow, appearing to moving
closer and closer right before your very eyes!

The timedLoop() executes every 100 milliseconds, but you can adjust this to make the growing appear faster or slower. The code uses a variable that changes in value to make greenie grow every time the loop executes. Discover more about variables in Chapter 12.

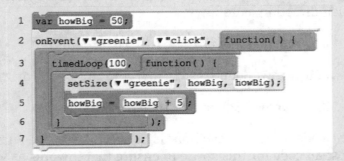

```
1   var howBig = 50;
2   onEvent(▼"greenie", ▼"click", function() {
3       timedLoop(100, function() {
4           setSize(▼"greenie", howBig, howBig);
5           howBig = howBig + 5;
6       });
7   });
```

In MakeCode for micro:bit, you can create very simple animation by switching from one image displayed on the LED grid to another image. Just place a series of showIcon() commands inside a forever() loop and watch the action! Use a pause() command between showIcon() commands to control the speed of execution. The figure a shows a simple heartbeat animation.

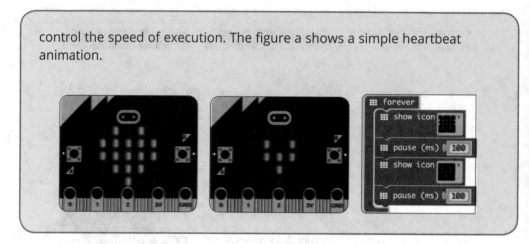

Code Arrow Keys for Moving the Smelephant Down, Left, and Right

Repeat the process in "Code the Smelephant's Up Arrow Key Control" to create key control code moving the smelephant down, left, or right. Set the point in direction command for each direction as follows:

✔ **Down arrow:** Set point in direction to 180.

✔ **Left arrow:** Set point in direction to -90 (or 270).

✔ **Right arrow:** Set point in direction to 90.

The code for the smelephant is now complete! See Figure 9-6. Test all code for this sprite to ensure that it works as you intend.

You can duplicate code by Ctrl-clicking (Mac) or right-clicking (Win) the code block and then selecting Duplicate from the pop-up menu.

TIP

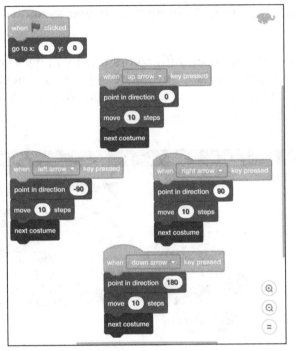

Figure 9-6

Add a Flower Sprite

The user will click the arrow keys to walk the smelephant around the savanna with a goal of smelling the flowers. Create a flower sprite for your game and then clone and scatter the clones as follows:

1. In the sprite area of the Scratch interface, hover over the Choose a Sprite icon.

2. Choose Paint from the pop-up menu to paint your own sprite costume.

   The sprite costume editor opens at the Costumes tab. The default costume name for this sprite is costume1. Leave this name, or change it (I changed it to star).

3. Use the drawing tools to draw your flower as shown in Figure 9-7.

   Tinker with the tools and fill colors until you get the flower costume design you like. The sprite appears on the stage, wearing the costume. Don't worry about the size; you adjust it in Step 5.

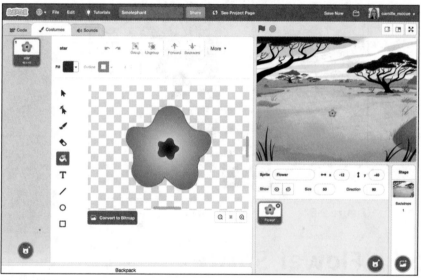

Figure 9-7

4. In the sprite attributes editor in the bottom-right corner of the Scratch interface, rename your sprite.

   The default name is e Sprite1. I named my sprite flower.

5. In the sprite attributes editor, resize your sprite by typing a new number in the Size field above the sprite.

   The default size is 100. I changed the size of my flower to 30.

Code the Green Flag for the Flower Sprite

You will write a green flag program for the flower sprite that positions the parent flower sprite in the savanna. It then calls a block that clones the flower to fill the screen with lots of flowers in different positions.

Write the green flag program for the flower sprite by following these steps:

1. Select the flower sprite by clicking on its icon.

2. On the Code tab of the Scratch interface, select the Events icon. Drag a when green flag clicked command to the Code workspace.

3. Select the Motion icon. Drag a go to x: y: command to the Code workspace, and attach it to the previous command. Type –100 in each field so that the code reads go to x: –100 y: –100.

   This code positions the flower far away from the smelephant so that the two sprites don't collide before the flower sprite is cloned.

4. Select the Looks icon. Drag a show command to the Code workspace, and attach to the previous command.

   The flower sprite must be displayed to be cloned. (This is an issue only if at some point you hide the sprite, which you do at the end of your green flag program.)

5. Select the My Blocks icon. Click the Make a Block button to create a new code block.

   The Make a Block dialog box opens.

6. Name this new code block makeFlowers and click OK.

   The new block header is added to your workspace, and the new command tile, makeFlowers, is added to your commands in the My Blocks category. You define what the makeFlowers code block does in the next section.

7. From the My Blocks category, drag your new makeFlowers command to the Code workspace, and attach it to the show command.

8. From the Looks category, drag a hide command to the Code workspace, and attach it to the makeFlowers command, as shown in Figure 9-8.

After the flower sprite runs makeFlowers, it hides. You hide the sprite so that you don't have to write commands for how it should behave if it is smelled — you'll have plenty of flower clones being smelled.

Figure 9-8

Code the makeFlowers Block

You created a makeFlowers code block header and command tile. Now you need to write the code for that block. The makeFlowers code block clones the parent flower sprite to create lots of flowers and scatter them all over the screen.

Write the code for the makeFlowers code block as follows:

1. Work at the define makeFlowers code block header in the workspace.

2. From the Control commands, drag a repeat command to the Code workspace, and attach it to the code block header. Type a number in the repeat command.

   This number is how many times the repeat command will execute. I set mine to 30.

3. Drag a create clone of command to the Code workspace, and attach it inside repeat. Set the create clone of command to myself.

4. Select the Looks category. Drag a change color effect to the Code workspace, and attach it to the create clone command, inside repeat. Type a number in the change color effect command.

   This number is how much the color of a clone changes each time the repeat command executes. I set the change to 10 to cause the color of the clone to change somewhat from the color of the last clone.

5. Select the Motion icon. Drag a go to x: y: command to the Code workspace, and attach it to the previous command. From the Operators category, drag a pick random command into the first field (the x-coordinate) and another pick random command into the second field (the y-coordinate) of the go to command.

6. In the pick random command, type –240 and 240 as the range of the x position values. These values enable flower clones to be created in any horizontal position on the screen.

7. In the pick random command, type –180 and 40 as the range of the y position values. These values enable flower clones to be created in y positions on the savanna. The y-coordinate values greater than 40 are part of the sky — a flower wouldn't be growing way up there!

   The define makeFlowers code block is now complete. See Figure 9-9.

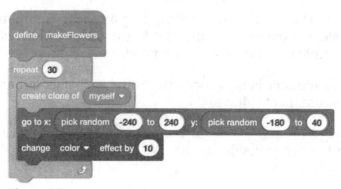

Figure 9-9

When the makeFlowers command is run in the flower's green flag code, it *calls to* the define makeFlowers code block to know what commands to execute.

Code when I start as a clone for the Flower Sprite

When the green flag program of the flower sprite runs, it creates clones. The clones need instructions! Each clone needs to follow one instruction: It needs to know what happens when it gets smelled.

Write the when I start as a clone program by following these steps:

1. Select the flower sprite.

2. Working at the Code tab of the Scratch interface, select the Control icon. Drag a when I start as a clone command to the Code workspace.

   The command you attach to this event will execute each time a new clone is created.

3. Select the My blocks icon. Click the Make a Block button to create a new code block.

The Make a Block dialog box opens.

4. Name this new code block getSmelled and click OK.

The new block header is added to your workspace, and the new block command, getSmelled, is added to your commands in the My Blocks category. The makeFlowers command that you made before is there, too. You define what makeFlowers does in the next section. But now you can use the makeFlowers command.

5. From the My blocks category, drag the getSmelled command to the Code workspace, and attach it to the when I start as a clone command, as shown in Figure 9-10.

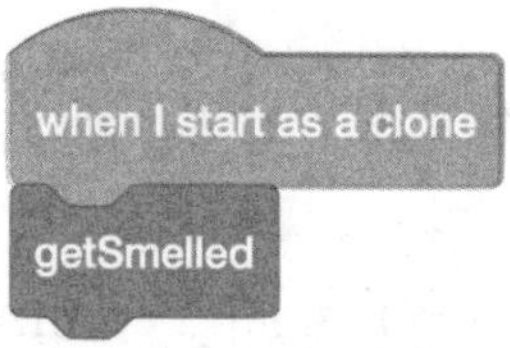

when I start as a clone

getSmelled

Figure 9-10

Code the getSmelled Block for the Flower Clones

You created a getSmelled code block header and command tile. Now you need to write the code to provide instructions for getSmelled. This code should make each clone wait patiently until the smelephant touches it, and then it should hide (because the smelephant sucks the flower clone into his trunk). The code will look like Figure 9-11.

Follow these steps to write the code:

1. Work at the define getSmelled code block header in the workspace.

2. Select the Control icon. Drag a wait until command to the Code workspace, and attach it to the code block header.

Figure 9-11

3. Select the Sensing icon and drag a touching command into the field of wait until. Press the arrow inside touching and select smelephant from the drop-down list.

   The code following the wait until touching smelephant command will not execute until the flower clone is touched by the smelephant.

4. Select the Sound icon. Drag The start sound command to the workspace, and attach it to the previous command. Press the arrow inside start sound and select pop from the drop-down list.

   (The pop sound will accompany any new sprite you paint in Scratch.) When a flower clone is sniffed (touched) by the smelephant sprite, a pop sound will play as though the flower is popping out of the ground.

5. Select the Looks icon. Drag The hide command to the workspace, and attach it to the previous command.

   Now, after the flower clone is smelled, it hides — because the smelephant sucked it up!

Figure 9-12 shows all code for the flower sprite.

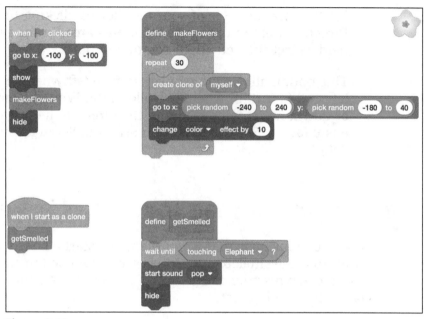

Figure 9-12

Add a Monkey Sprite

A good collection game has something getting in the way of the player reaching the goal of collecting. You'll code a little monkey who constantly moves towards the smelephant. The smelephant must stay away from the monkey. If they collide, it's game over!

Add a monkey sprite to your game and name it monkey as follows:

1. In the sprite area of the Scratch interface, click the Choose a Sprite icon.

2. Click the Monkey sprite. The monkey is added to your sprite collection. Note that its name is Monkey in the Sprite name field in the sprite attributes area.

3. Change the size of your monkey sprite by typing a number in the Size field in the sprite attributes area.

   I used a size of 30, but you can use any size that makes sense for your game.

4. Set the rotation style of your monkey by clicking the Direction field in the sprite attributes area. In the Direction field, select the Left/Right rotation option.

This option allows the monkey to face left when he walks left and face right when he walks right. When he moves up or down, he remains facing in the direction he was previously facing. See the "Rotation Styles in Scratch" sidebar for details.

Code the Green Flag for the Monkey

Code the monkey so that when the game starts, he is located far away from the smelephant. Otherwise, it will be too easy for him to catch his friend! Then add code so that the monkey chases the smelephant.

Follow these steps:

1. Click the monkey sprite.

2. Working on the Code tab of the Scratch interface, select the Events icon. Drag a when green flag clicked command to the Code workspace.

3. Select the Motion icon. Drag the go to x: y: command and attach it to the previous command. Set the value in each field to 100.

When executed, this command sends the monkey to coordinate (100, 100).

4. Select the My Blocks icon. Click the Make a Block button to create a new code block.

The Make a Block dialog box opens.

5. Name this new code block chase and click OK.

The new block header is added to your workspace, and the new command tile, chase, is added to your commands in the

My Blocks category. In the next section, you define what the chase code block does.

6. From the My Blocks category, drag your new chase command to the Code workspace, and attach it to the previous command.

See Figure 9-13 for the complete green flag code for the monkey sprite.

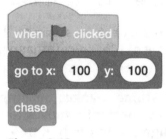

Figure 9-13

Code the chase Block

You created a chase code block header and command tile. Now write the code for that block. The chase code block use a type of loop command (refer to Chapter 8) to make the monkey constantly glide towards the smelephant. If the monkey touches the smelephant, the smelephant is caught and the game is over.

Write the code for the chase code block as follows:

1. Work at the define chase code block header in the workspace.

2. From the Control commands, drag a repeat until command to the Code workspace, and attach it to the code block header.

3. Select the Sensing icon and drag a touching command into the wait until field. Press the arrow inside touching and select smelephant from the drop-down list.

The code that follows the repeat until touching smelephant command will not execute until the monkey touches the smelephant.

4. From the Motion commands, drag a glide to command to the Code workspace, and attach it inside the repeat until. Type a number in the field for the number of seconds. (I typed 2.) Press the arrow inside glide to and select smelephant from the drop-down list.

   The command now shows glide 2 sec to smelephant.

5. Select the Looks category. Drag a next costume to the Code workspace, and attach it to the glide to command, inside the repeat.

   As the monkey moves, his costume changes, making it look like he's walking. The monkey constantly moves towards the smelephant, but slowly enough not to catch him — unless the smelephant gets tired and stops moving. The repeat until code is now complete.

6. Select the Sound icon. Drag a play sound until done command below the repeat until command. Press the arrow inside this command and select chee chee from the drop-down list.

   This sound comes with the monkey sprite when you add him to a project. When the monkey catches his friend, he lets out a '"chee chee" sound of joy!

7. Select the Control icon. Drag the stop all command to the Code workspace, and attach it to the previous command.

   After the monkey yells his "chee chee" sound, the entire game stops.

The define chase code block is now complete and is shown in Figure 9-14.

```
define  chase

repeat until    touching   smelephant ▼   ?
    glide  2  secs to   smelephant ▼
    next costume

play sound   chee chee ▼   until done
stop  all ▼
```

Figure 9-14

When the chase command is run in the monkey's green flag code, it *calls to* the define chase code block to know what commands to execute.

The complete code for the monkey sprite is shown in Figure 9-15.

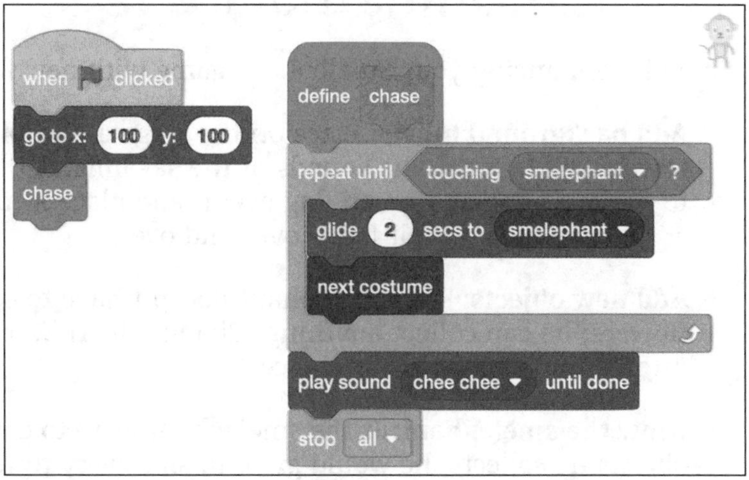

```
when 🏴 clicked
go to x: 100 y: 100
chase

define  chase

repeat until    touching   smelephant ▼   ?
    glide  2  secs to   smelephant ▼
    next costume

play sound   chee chee ▼   until done
stop  all ▼
```

Figure 9-15

Save, Test, and Debug Your Program

Type a name for you program in the Title field at the top of the Scratch interface. As you work, Scratch automatically saves your program in the cloud, so you don't have to take any special actions to save your work.

Test your program and fix any bugs to ensure that it works the way you want it to. (See Chapter 3 for help on debugging Scratch programs.)

Share Your Program with the World

After your program operates perfectly, it's time to share it. Set the status of your program to Share, and then add to your project page a description of your program and directions on how to run it. See Chapter 19 for details on sharing your programs.

Enhance Your Animated Scene

Consider enhancing your Smelephant game with new features:

- **Add background music:** Place on the stage a nice piece of music that features the sounds of the savanna. Set the music to start playing at a green flag event, and place it inside a forever loop so that it loops over and over.

- **Add new objects:** The smelephant doesn't have to collect flowers; he can collect anything! Change the flower to an interesting object of your choice.

- **Grow the smelephant:** If the smelephant were to eat the objects he collects, he would grow in size every time he grabbed a snack! From Make a Block, define a new block (called defineGrow) that grows the smelephant whenever he touches an object he's collecting. Use the change size by command (in the Looks category) and set the value to a small number. Then add your grow command to the smelephant's green flag code. (Note: You'll also need to add a set size to 40% command before the grow command — to return the smelephant to his normal size at the start of each game. The set size command is also in the Looks category.)

✔ **Create nightfall:** At the stage, add a change brightness effect to make it appear that the sun is going down over the savanna. You'll find change brightness in the Looks category. Here is a code snippet you can use:

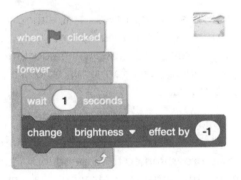

Key Control

Computer keyboard control, or *key control,* is a common method of controlling objects onscreen in a video game. The up, down, left, and right arrow keys are often used to move a character in the game environment. The A, W, S, and D keys are also used frequently for character key control, and the spacebar is sometimes used for shooting or launching in a game.

Because Scratch is well-suited for coding programs to be run on the computer screen, it's easy to write code that includes key control. You can go to the Events category of Scratch and drag a when key pressed command to the Code workspace. This command can serve as an event triggering the movement of a sprite. (See Chapter 4 for details on event-driven programming.) You can set the key press event to respond to the user clicking a letter, a number, the spacebar, or any key on the keyboard.

You can create many different when key pressed commands for a player to move and control a sprite. Coding the left and right arrow keys to respond to clicks allows you to program a paddle ball game, such as Pong. Or code the up and down arrow keys to respond to clicks to create a Flappy Bird game. And coding all four arrow keys to respond to clicks lets you make a Crossy Roads game!

App Lab can also be programmed to respond to key control, although this is not the most ideal use of programming with the environment. App Lab is better suited to touchscreen taps, not keyboard clicks. Online documentation of App Lab commands provides additional information on coding key control should you decide to slay this beast.

MakeCode for micro:bit enables you to code event-driven programs that respond to button (not key) control. The micro:bit has two built-in buttons, Button A and Button B. Each can be programmed to respond individually to a button click. You can also program the buttons to respond to a click of Button A and Button B at the same time. To program a code block to run as a result of a button click event on the micro:bit, use the onButton-Pressed( ) command in the Input category of MakeCode as your event.

Collisions

A collision occurs when two objects are located at the same place onscreen. Being located at the same place means that the objects (sprites) share the same (x, y) coordinates — or that a part of one sprite shares the same coordinates as a part of another sprite.

Checking for collisions is important in programming because this enables you to know when two objects have bumped into each other, crashed, or otherwise overlapped in a game or simulation. For example, if Flappy Bird and a column share a coordinate position, the player has smashed into a column. But collisions aren't always bad! When PacMan collides with a dot, he eats the dot and earns points.

In Scratch, the Sensing category provides a touching command that you can use when checking for collisions. The touching command can be added to any sprite, and the command can be set to check for touching any object in the project. If touching registers a value of true, the sprite and its target object are touching and a collision has taken place. Chapters 12 and 13 show how you can create and use a number variable that changes due to certain conditions. You can use the number variable when writing code that checks for collisions to keep score in a game.

Determining whether a collision has occurred in App Lab requires some calculations because it doesn't have a command to check for two objects touching. A collision between two objects occurs when the distance between the objects becomes smaller than the distance separating the centers of the objects. Measuring the distance between the two objects requires using the distance formula and constantly re-computing the distance as the objects move around. The calculations are beyond the scope of this book, but if you're ambitious, it is possible to code collision detection in App Lab.

Lastly, to detect a collision of two LED lights on the micro:bit, you must check whether two points have converged (come together) at a single (x,y) coordinate on the micro:bit. Because LED lights can't overlap like Scratch sprites or App Lab images, you simply have to check whether the two points on the micro:bit are occupying the same spot.

Show and Hide

Show and hide commands give you control over which objects the user of your program sees onscreen and when the user sees those objects. For example, in the Emoji Explosion scene (see Chapter 8), you hide the emoji sprite you used to create its clones so that you wouldn't have to write additional code to make the parent emoji move around the screen. In the Smelephant game, you hide the flower after the smelephant sniffs the flower out of the ground so that the user sees that the flower has been removed.

Games that feature power-ups or bonus gems make use of show to reveal the objects only at certain times during gameplay. And games such as Space Invaders use hide to remove objects that the player has eliminated from the game field. Additionally, apps that include forms in which the user fills out information require control over which fields the user sees as he or she completes the form — not all fields are visible at all times.

Scratch provides show and hide commands in the Looks category. App Lab provides showElement() and hideElement() commands in the UI Controls category. Use these commands to build and control what's displayed in your user interfaces!

Part 4
Variables, Simple Conditionals, and I/O

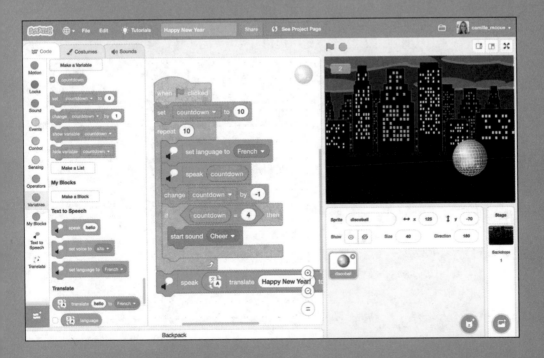

In this part you'll . . .

- [■] Write code to accept user input and produce output

- [■] Work with variables, including strings (text), numbers, and Booleans

- [■] Add text-to-speech and language translation to your apps

- [■] Construct conditionals to make decisions

- [■] Build and code a gadget that reacts to a sensor

Mascot Greeter

Two of the most important skills in coding are learning
how to accept *input* from your user and produce *output* to your
user. These inputs and outputs are often text. In coding, text
that doesn't change is called a *literal*. Text that changes, such
as a user's name, must be stored in a *variable*. A variable is
a container that can store a piece of information that can
be changed as needed. A variable that holds a piece of text is
called a *string variable*. Names, addresses, favorite foods, and
other text that might change depending on the user of the app
are stored in string variables.

In this chapter, you get started with text handling by coding literals and string variables in a simple program that can personalize its greeting. Mascot Greeter is a quick Scratch project in which you code a character to accept string input from a user. You ask the user to input his or her name, and then you store the name. You write additional code to join the user input with other text, and then display — and speak — a greeting.

Brainstorm

Mascot Greeter can feature any character in any setting. And it can say any phrase you want! See Figures 10-1a and 10-1b.

Figure 10-1

Check out the Scratch libraries of backdrops and sprites before deciding on a mascot. And then get coding.

Start a New Project

Begin creating your Mascot Greeter program by starting a new project as follows:

1. Open Scratch at `https://scratch.mit.edu/`. If prompted, enable Flash to run Scratch. Log in to the account you created to use Scratch (see Chapter 2).

2. On the Scratch home page, select Create. Or if you're already working in Scratch, choose File ⇨ New from the menu bar.

   A new project opens.

3. Name your program by typing a name in the Project Name field at the top of the Scratch interface.

4. Cut Scratch Cat from the project by clicking the X in the Scratch Cat icon in the sprite area in the lower-right corner of the Scratch interface.

Inputs and Outputs (I/O)

Input and output are fancy terms you hear all the time in computer science. *Input* means something put into a program, for example, your name in a game app. *Output* means something that comes out of a program, for example, a message announcing that you have achieved the high score! You will often see *input output* written as *I/O*.

Inputs can take a variety of forms, with some inputs being put in by a user, such as typing words into an online form, or looking at your iPhone camera so that its facial recognition system can identify you. Other inputs are put in by sensors that are constantly reading information in the world around you, such as measuring the current temperature by your household thermostat, or determining the compass heading of your car as your drive.

Outputs can also take a many different forms. These include text displayed on a screen, alarms, sensor readings, or automatic activation of devices (such as your smart oven automatically preheating those cookies you plan on baking after school).

Ultimately, the interaction between humans and technology must be coordinated through computer programs. In computer programs, inputs and outputs are the go-betweens that allow you to communicate with your devices and your devices to communicate with you!

Add a Backdrop

The *backdrop* is the background color or image that fills the screen of your toy. Add a backdrop as follows:

1. At the Stage, click the Choose a Backdrop icon.

2. In the Choose a Backdrop window, click any backdrop you want.

I chose the Jurassic backdrop.

REMEMBER

When you start a new project, the stage contains an empty backdrop. The default costume name for this backdrop is backdrop1. After you add a new backdrop, you can delete the empty backdrop by opening the Backdrops tab for the stage and then clicking the X in the icon for backdrop1.

Add a Mascot Sprite

Add a mascot sprite for your toy as follows:

1. In the sprite area of the Scratch interface, click the Choose a Sprite icon.

2. In the Choose a Sprite window, click any sprite you want.

I chose Dinosaur4. (There are so many dinosaur sprites that the Scratch folks at MIT had to number them!)

3. In the sprite attributes editor for Dinosaur4, edit the number in the Size field to change the size of your mascot sprite (if you want to do so). The default size of the sprite is 100.

4. Drag the sprite to somewhere in the middle of the backdrop.

Depending on which sprite you selected, it may have several costumes. Later, you can make use of these costumes by animating your greeter so that he looks like he is moving as he speaks his greeting!

If you add a sprite and then decide you don't want it, cut it by clicking the X in its icon.

REMEMBER

Add Text-to-Speech Commands

Your mascot greeter will not only greet in words but also speak them through Scratch's text-to-speech commands. Add text-to-speech to your Scratch interface as follows:

1. Click or tap the Add Extension icon in the lower-left corner of the Scratch interface.

   The Choose an Extension dialog box opens, including the Text-to-Speech option, as shown in Figure 10-2.

Text to Speech
Make your projects talk.

Figure 10-2

2. Click or tap the Text to Speech box.

   Text-to-speech commands are added to your commands.

Strings and String Operations

Every app displays text to its user, and most apps ask the user to input text as well. Strings allows your computer program to display and accept this text. Some strings are meant to convey information, such as "Welcome to my app!" or "Which weapon do you choose, Cupid's arrow or the Sword of Excalibur?"

If the text never changes, the string is a *literal.* Literal strings are enclosed in quotes — whatever is inside the quotes is shown onscreen. If the text can change, the string is a *variable.* A variable string is like a container which can hold different information at different times. The variable string has a name, such as userName, which never changes. But the values that userName contains can change as needed. For example, during one execution of your program, username could equal "Bart Simpson" but during the next execution, username could equal "Krusty the Clown."

String literals and string variables can be combined, or *concatenated,* to personalize text that appears to the user. To concatenate strings — that is, to connect each literal or variable and produce a new phrase — some programming languages use a join command and others use the plus sign (+).

Scratch, App Lab, and MakeCode for micro:bit all contain special commands for *manipulating* strings. For example, you can use a command to determine the length of a string, select a character at a specific position in the string, or find out whether a shorter string (a substring) exists within a string. You can also compare two strings to see if they match: This is ideal when determining whether a user-entered password matches a previously stored password.

You can combine all of these commands, along with some commands you have learned previously (and a few you'll learn in future chapters), to create some cool programs! One such program is a word reversal program. You may have played with reversing words by spelling them backwards on paper. A well-known tween book, Holes (Louis Sachar), features a main character named Stanley Yelnats, whose last name is the reverse of his first name. Chapter 17 features a project where you can reverse a string and check to see if it is a *palindrome* — a word that is the same spelled forwards and in reverse!

Code the Mascot Sprite to Greet

To personalize the greeting, use the built-in ask command to ask the user to type his or her name. You then store the name in the answer variable. The answer variable is built into Scratch, so you don't have to create it. Finally, you will join the literal (the words that don't change) with the variable (the user's name) and then display the greeting.

Code the mascot sprite to greet as follows:

1. Select the mascot sprite.

2. On the Code tab of the Scratch interface, select the Events icon. Drag a when green flag pressed command to the Code workspace.

   Events

3. Select the Sensing icon. Drag an ask and wait command to the Code workspace, and attach it to the previous command.

   The default question in the ask field is What's your name? You can leave this question, or you can type a new question.

   When the program runs, it presents a blank text field for the user to type her response. After she types her name and clicks or taps the check mark button beside the text entry field (or presses Enter or Return on the keyboard), her text will be stored in the answer variable.

REMEMBER

Scratch doesn't require quotes around a string literal, such as What's your name? However, most other programming languages, including JavaScript, require quotes around a string literal.

4. Select the Looks icon. Drag a say command and attach it to the previous command.

5. Select the Operators icon. Drag a join command to the Code workspace, and place it inside the field of the say command.

6. Type your greeting in the first empty field of the join command.

   I typed Welcome to the Jurassic Period, in the field. Note that this text literal includes a comma and a space after the comma.

7. Select the Sensing icon. Drag an answer command and place it inside the second empty field of the join command.

   This inserts the value of the answer variable — whatever name the user typed — into the greeting.

Text to
Speech

8. Select the Text to Speech icon, drag a set voice to command to the Code workspace, and attach it to the previous command. Select a voice from the menu in the command.

   The choices are alto, tenor, squeak, giant, and kitten. I selected the giant voice (because a dinosaur would have big voice!)

9. In the Text to Speech commands, drag a speak command to the Code workspace, and attach it to the previous command.

10. Create the same greeting as before by Ctrl-clicking or right-clicking the greeting and selecting Duplicate from the pop-up menu. Then place the greeting inside the empty field of the speak command.

The completed code should look like Figure 10-3.

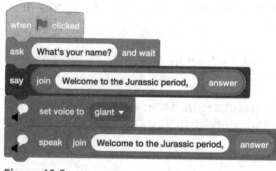

Figure 10-3

Save, Test, and Debug Your Program

Name your project by typing in the Title field at the top of the Scratch interface. As you work, Scratch automatically saves your program in the cloud. Test your program and fix any bugs to ensure that it works the way you want it to. (See Chapter 3 for help on debugging Scratch programs.)

Share Your Program with the World

After your program operates perfectly, it's time to share it! Set the status of your program to Share, and then add to your project page a description of your program and directions on how to run it. See Chapter 19 for details on sharing your programs.

Enhance Your Program

Consider enhancing your Mascot Greeter toy with new features:

- **Change the costume:** Depending on which sprite you selected, if may have several costumes. Select the costume you want to display by clicking it on the Costumes tab.

- **Animate the sprite:** If your sprite has several costumes, drag one or more next costume commands (from the Looks category) into your code so that the sprite changes appearance each time it speaks. Refer to the sidebars in Chapter 9 for help on animating sprites.

- **Add a sound:** From the Sounds tab, add a new sound to your mascot sprite. (Hint: The Grunt sound is what you might expect to hear from a dinosaur!) Then drag a play sound command into your code so that the sound plays before or after the spoken greeting!

- **Add a longer greeting:** By placing a join command inside another join command, you can add another literal following the user's name (which is stored in the answer variable).

CHAPTER 11

Weird Text Message

If you text or send instant messages, at some point you've probably received a weird text message from a friend. Perhaps autocorrect changed one of the sender's words so the meaning of the message was completely altered. I once sent my family a text message saying that I was heading to Zumba (an exercise class), but the message they received was that I was heading to Zimbabwe!

Enter words or phrases:

Food   veggie quesadillas

Place   Mount Rushmore

Celebrity   The Rock

Color   neon orange

Make Weird Text Message

Let's eat at Mount Rushmore tonight. I heard they serve neon orange veggie quesadillas and that The Rock goes there all the time!

In this project, you build a toy in App Lab that uses strings to create a weird text message. The strings are both literals and variables. You create the literals, and your users, when prompted, input text words and phrases stored in variables. The end user can type any text he or she wants to be stored in the string variables. However, the users don't know exactly how their inputs will be used. As you can guess, the values of the string inputs, when assembled with the string literals you create, can result in a rather odd message.

Although the message is not actually texted, when combined with a bit of clever design work, your end user will enjoy the appearance of receiving a weird message on his or her phone. Let the fun begin!

Brainstorm

To get user input for assembling the weird text message, you ask your user to type some words and phrases, as shown in the preceding figure. For example, just imagine if you ask your user for a type of fish, the name of a pop song, and a favorite interjection (a word showing excitement or emotion, such as "wow"). You can *concatenate*, or *join*, those string variable values and some string literals into a really weird text message. Brainstorm as many crazy word categories as you want, and then get coding!

Start a New Project

Begin creating your Weird Text Message app by starting a new project as follows:

1. Open App Lab at https://code.org/educate/applab. Log in to the account you created to use App Lab (see Chapter 2).

2. Under the App Lab heading, click the Try it Out button.

   A new project opens.

3. Name your program by clicking the Rename button and then typing a name in the Project Name field at the top of the App Lab interface.

4. Click the Save button.

Name the Input Screen for the App

Your app will consist of two screens: an input screen where the user types funny words, and an output screen where the weird text message appears. Each screen must be named so that your code knows where to go as it executes.

Name the input screen as follows:

1. Click the Design button to switch to Design mode in App Lab.

   The Design toolbox and workspace are displayed.

2. On the Properties tab of the workspace, rename the ID of screen1 to a more meaningful name, such as inputScreen.

Do not include spaces in ID names. In most programming languages, including App Lab, spaces are not allowed.

WARNING

Add a Background Color to the Input Screen

It is helpful to make the background color of the input screen a different color than the output screen. Different colors allow you to distinguish between the two screens as you work. To change the background color of the input screen, follow these steps:

1. Remain working at the input screen, in the Design mode of App Lab.

2. On the Properties tab of the workspace, locate the Background Color field.

3. Click the small square of color to the right of the Background Color field to open the color editor color for the background.

4. Move the color slider (the first slider) to see the different colors.

5. Click the color swatch (the larger box of color) to choose the color you want.

   The background changes to your selected color.

Add an Instruction Label

Next, you should add a label that helps the user know what to do at the input screen. Add an instruction label as follows:

1. Remain working at the input screen, in the Design mode of App Lab.

2. In the Design toolbox, drag the Label icon and position it near the top left of the app display.

3. On the Properties tab of the workspace, change the attributes of the label as follows:

   - ID: Rename the ID `instructionsLabel`.

   - Text: Type the instructions for your app, such as **Enter words or phrases:**

   - Width (px): Increase the width of your label to something like 240 pixels (or more) so that the title will appear on a single line.

   - Height (px): No changes.

   - x Position (px): No changes; you change the x position later by dragging the label into position.

- y Position (px): No changes; you change the y position later by dragging the label into position.

- Text Color: Leave it black.

- Background Color: No changes.

- Font Size (px): Type a new font size in the field or use the selection arrows to make the title the appropriate size for your app.

- Text Alignment: Click the selection arrows and choose Center.

4. Click and drag the label on your app to position it where you want.

   Refer to the left figure on the chapter's first page to see the position of the instructions label on the app simulator display.

Add Category Labels and Text Input Fields

Next, create category labels so that the user knows what text he or she should enter in the app. Beside each label, place a text input field so that the user has a place to enter a word or phrase. Refer to the left figure on the chapter's first page.

Follow these instructions to add each label and text input to your app:

1. Remain working at the input screen, in the Design mode of App Lab. If you're not in Design mode, click the Design button.

   The Design toolbox and workspace are displayed.

2. Get started by creating the category labels. In the Design toolbox, drag the Label icon to the screen, and position it near left side of the app display.

3. On the Properties tab of the workspace, change the attributes of the label as follows:

- ID: Rename the ID to something representative of the category, such as `foodLabel` or `celebrityLabel`.

- Text: Type the category name, such as **Food** or **Celebrity**.

- Width (px): Set the width of your label to something like 100 pixels so that the category name will appear on a single line.

- Height (px): No changes.

- x Position (px): No changes; you change the x position later by dragging the label into position.

- y Position (px): No changes; you change the y position later by dragging the label into position.

- Text Color: Leave it black.

- Background Color: No changes.

- Font Size (px): Type a new font size in the field or use the selection arrows to make the label text the appropriate size for your app.

- Text Alignment: Click the selection arrows and choose Right.

4. Click and drag the label on your app to position it where you want.

5. Repeat Steps 2 through 4 to create and name three more labels, dragging them into logical positions on the app simulator.

REMEMBER

Don't forget to give each label a unique ID.

Refer to the left figure on the chapter's first page to see the position of the category labels on the app simulator display.

6. Now create the text input fields. In the Design toolbox, drag the Text Input icon and position it beside your first category label.

   I placed my first text input field next to my Food label.

7. On the Properties tab of the workspace, change the attributes of the label as follows:

   - ID: Rename the ID to something representative of the text input field, such as `foodInput` or `celebrityInput`.

   - Text: Leave this blank so that the user sees an empty box.

   - Width (px): Set the width of your label to something like 170 pixels so that the user has room to type his text in the box.

   - Height (px): Set to 40 pixels.

   - x Position (px): No changes; you change the x position later by dragging the label into position.

   - y Position (px): No changes; you change the y position later by dragging the label into position.

   - Text Color: Leave it black.

   - Background Color: No changes.

   - Font Size (px): Type a new font size in the field or use the selection arrows to make the user's text input the appropriate size for your app.

   - Text Alignment: Click the selection arrows and choose Left.

8. Click and drag the text input on your app to position it where you want.

9. Repeat Steps 6 through 8 to create and name three more text input fields, dragging each one into its logical position, next to its companion category label, on the app simulator.

Don't forget to give each text input a unique ID. Refer to the left figure on the chapter's first page to see the position of the text input fields on the app simulator display.

The category labels and text input fields are complete.

Add a Button to Trigger the Action

Now you'll add a button to the input screen. When the user presses the button, he or she triggers the execution of the code, which switches to the next screen, assembles the inputs into a weird text message, and displays the message.

Follow these steps to add the trigger button:

1. Remain working at the input screen, in the Design mode of App Lab. If you're not in Design mode, click the Design button.

   The Design toolbox and workspace are displayed.

2. In the Design toolbox, drag the Button icon to the app display.

3. On the Properties tab of the workspace, change the attributes of the button as shown here:

   - ID: Rename the ID to goButton (or something similar) to indicate that this button will start the action.

   - Text: Type the text that will appear on the button, such as **Make Weird Text Message** (or whatever you want).

   - Width (px): Increase the width of your button to something like 290 pixels.

   - Height (px): Increase the height of your button to something like 45 pixels.

   - x Position (px): No changes; you change the x position later by dragging the button into position.

- y Position (px): No changes; you change the y position later by dragging the button into position.

- Text Color: Click the small square of color to the right of the Text Color field and select a text color that will contrast well with the button background.

- Background Color: Click the small square of color to the right of the Text Color field and select a button color that will contrast well with the background color of the app.

- Font size (px): Type a new font size in the field or click the selection arrows to make the text on your button a good size for your app.

- Text alignment: Click the selection arrows and choose Center.

4. Click and drag the button on your app display to position it below the other elements on the input screen.

See Figure 11-1 for the positioning of the button.

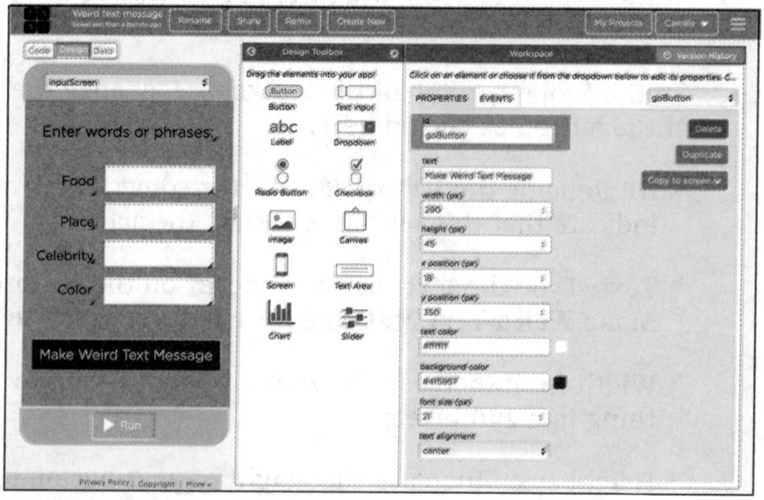

Figure 11-1

Add and Name an Output Screen

The second screen of your app, the output screen, is where the weird text message appears. Create and name the output screen as follows:

1. Continue working in Design mode.

2. Go to the drop-down menu of screens, located at the top of the simulator screen. Click in the menu and choose New Screen, as shown in Figure 11-2.

   A new screen is created in your app. Note that this new screen is called screen2.

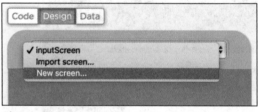

Figure 11-2

3. On the Properties tab of the workspace, rename the ID of screen2 to a more meaningful name, such as outputScreen.

Add a Message Image to the Output Screen

The output screen should have a text message image that mimics the shape and color of what you would see on a typical smartphone. For example, an iOS message usually appears in a blue bubble, and an Android message usually appears in a green bubble.

Find an image of a blank text-message bubble and add it to your output screen as follows:

1. Remain working at the output screen, in the Design mode of App Lab.

2. Perform a quick Google search for *text message bubble* and save the image. Alternatively, you can use Google Slides to draw a text message bubble of the size and color you want.

   Figure 11-3 shows an image I found during my search. Note that whatever image you find or create, you may need to crop the image so that you have a single text message bubble. See Chapter 2 for details on working with images.

Figure 11-3

3. In the Design toolbox, drag the Image icon to the app display to place a new image on the display.

4. On the Properties tab of the workspace, click the Choose link to choose your message image.

   The Choose Assets dialog box opens.

5. Click the Upload File button.

6. Navigate to and select the image file that you want to upload to your assets. Then click the Choose button.

   The image file is the text message bubble you found or created previously and then saved.

   The image file appears in the Choose Assets dialog box.

7. In the Choose Assets dialog box, click the Choose button next to the image asset you just uploaded.

   The image appears in your app's output screen, as shown in the right figure on the chapter's first page. Note that you haven't added the text to the message yet.

8. Click and hold down on the image, then drag it to where you want it positioned on the output screen. Click and drag the sizing tab at the corner of the image to resize it to the dimensions you want.

No other properties need to be adjusted for the text message image.

Add a Message Label to the Output Screen

The text of the weird text message will appear in a label. This label has a transparent background and is layered on top of the text message bubble image you just added to the output screen. Add the label as follows:

1. Remain working at the output screen, in the Design mode of App Lab.

2. In the Design toolbox, drag the Label icon to the app display to create a new label on the display.

3. Drag the label on top of the text message bubble image. Then click and drag the sizing tab at the corner of the label to resize it to the dimensions you want.

The space inside the label should match the size of the bubble image. See Figure 11-4.

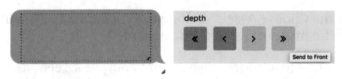

Figure 11-4

4. On the Properties tab of the workspace, change only these attributes:

- ID: Rename the ID to messageLabel.

- Font Size (px): Type a new font size; size 15 works well.

- Depth: If needed, click the Depth button for Send to Front (located below the text alignment attribute) to make the message label appear on top. See Figure 11-4.

You don't have to adjust any other properties for the text message label.

Code the App

Now you need to write code so that the app performs all the steps needed to move from the user's button press to the screen displaying the weird text message. Figure 11-5 is a flowchart that shows the structure of the code. (See Chapter 1 for details on flowcharting a program.)

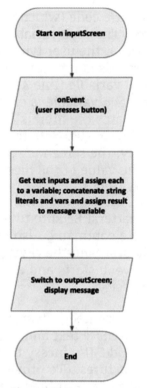

Figure 11-5

To begin coding the app, first switch to Code mode. Then switch to JavaScript mode by clicking the </> Show Text button in the upper-right corner of the screen.

Following the model of the flow chart, construct the code as shown in Figure 11-6.

```
Show Toolbox          Workspace:       Version History    Show Blocks
 1  onEvent("goButton", "click", function() {
 2      var food = getText("foodInput");
 3      var place = getText("placeInput");
 4      var celebrity = getText("celebrityInput");
 5      var color = getText("colorInput");
 6      var message = ("Let's eat at " + place + " tonight." +
 7          " I heard they serve " + color + " " + food +
 8          " and that " + celebrity + " goes there all the time!");
 9      setScreen("outputScreen");
10      setText("messageLabel", message);
11  });
```

Figure 11-6

Here's how the code works: The onEvent code (which begins at line 1) runs when goButton is clicked. The food variable is created and assigned the string text that the user typed in the foodInput text field (line 2). This process is repeated for the place variable (line 3), the celebrity variable (line 4), and the color variable (line 5). Then the message variable is created and assigned the string text that concatenates the literals ("Let's eat at ") and the variable values (lines 6–8). Note that plus (+) signs join the strings together. Finally, the screen is set to display outputScreen (line 9), and the value of the message variable is displayed in messageLabel (line 10).

WARNING

In text-based coding, punctuation matters! Be sure to place a semicolon at the end of each complete command. Also be sure to get the opening and closing curly braces in the right places. They indicate where the code for onEvent starts and ends. Last, be sure to enter the parentheses correctly.

TIP

Are you wondering why this code is presented in text mode instead of block mode? You can concatenate text and write math equations more easily in text mode. It's messy to assemble blocks correctly for these types of structures. (To prove this, switch to Shows Blocks mode and take a look at how the message variable appears!)

TIP

When you create a variable inside a function (in this case, onEvent), it is called a local variable. A *local* variable is known and can be used only inside its function. If a variable value needs to be used in many parts of a program (such as a score or a lives variable), you should make it a *global* variable by creating it outside of your functions.

Save, Test, and Debug Your App

As you work, App Lab automatically saves your program in the cloud.

Test your program and fix any bugs to ensure that it works the way you want it to. Pay particular attention to your punctuation and to the ID names of all your app elements. These are the most likely places where you'll make errors. For help with testing and debugging you App Lab program, refer to Chapter 3.

Share Your App with the World

After your app operates as you want it to, set the status of your program to Share. See Chapter 19 for details on sharing apps you create in App Lab.

Enhance Your App

Add cool new features to your app:

- ✐ **More text inputs:** Add more text input fields to create longer and weirder text messages! Note that you may have to increase the size of the image and label when you display the message on the output screen.

- ✐ **A sound effect when the text arrives:** Add a sound effect such as "ding" or a ringtone that plays when the weird text message is displayed. Then send the app to your phone and run it. Amuse your friends as though you received a real (and very weird) text message!

Dilbert's Jargonator

The Weird Text Message app probably reminds you of a Mad Libs game, in which users supply parts of speech (a proper noun, an adverb, and so on) and accidentally create a crazy story. The app reminds me The Jargonator, a game I owned just before the millennium. The Jargonator was part of Dilbert's Desktop Games, a great collection of silly, 2D games that corporate America played, wasting time before web surfing existed.

https://en.wikipedia.org/wiki/Dilbert%27s_
Desktop_Games#/media/File:Dilbert%27s_
Desktop_Games_cover.gif

Dilbert is a cartoon character created by Scott Adams. He's also a frustrated engineer who works in corporate America, dislikes his boss, and barely tolerates his strange co-workers (who include a cat named Catbert and a rat named, uh, Ratbert). The Jargonator was an especially cool tool for changing text into more corporate-sounding language. Options for transforming your text include "make it sizzle," "punch it up," and "managerialize." Why say, "Our product is selling well," when you can say, "Our multifunctional e-consumable is best-of-breed in the bricks-and-clicks marketplace!" After you know how to work with concatenation, string inputs, and string outputs, you can make your own version of the Jargonator. Try it!

ELIZA, the Turing Test, and AI

The Turing Test is an intelligence test for a computer. It tests whether a person exchanging questions and answers with a computer would be unable to determine whether he or she was talking to a computer or a human. Named for the Englishman Alan Turing, one of the first computer scientists, the Turing test is considered a gold standard for achieving artificial intelligence (AI) in a computer.

ELIZA is a computer program that attempts to pass the Turing Test. It presents itself as a computer therapist that asks and answers questions, interacting with you as you speak or type responses. Written more than fifty years ago by Joseph Weizenbaum, a computer science professor at MIT, it doesn't succeed at passing the Turing Test, but it sure is a lot of fun to play with!

https://www.masswerk.at/eliza/

Put simply, ELIZA *parses*, or separates, words and phrases from user responses, and then inserts them into new questions. If you say, "I'm worried about school," it responds with, "Why are you worried about school?" and so on. Play with the ELIZA machine at www.masswerk.at/eliza/. Then see if you can use your text-handling skills to create your own computer therapist.

Vote Machine

Computer programs often need to keep track of numbers and make decisions based on the values of those numbers. In coding, you can store and use all sorts of numbers. Numbers that don't change, such as the number of days in the month of March, are stored as *constants*. Numbers that can change, such as your bank balance, are stored as *number variables*.

In this chapter, you begin to work with numbers by coding number variables in your programs. You make a vote machine that end users can use to vote for their favorite candidates! Voting is a method for determining relative popularity of anything from foods to athletes to political candidates.

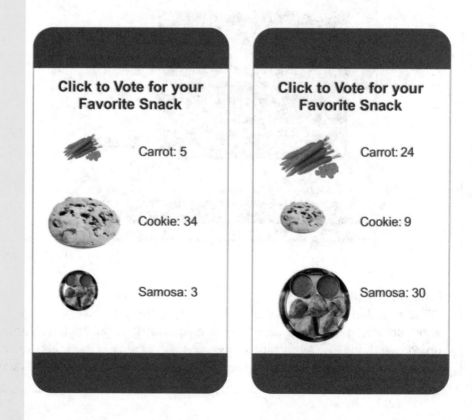

In Snack Vote, you use App Lab to code a voting booth that asks voters to choose their favorite of three snack items. However, you can customize the voting booth to feature any theme and any candidates. In addition to showing the number of votes received, the icon for each candidate changes in size according to its relative popularity — the largest candidate wins!

Brainstorm

Expressing your opinion through voting is something you probably do every day informally among friends, in the classroom, and on SnapChat or Instagram. So ask yourself, what do you want to vote on? Favorite cars? Best pets? Who will win *America's Got Talent* or *American Idol*?

I'm fond of snacks, so the example here is a Snack Vote app featuring three candidate choices: carrot, cookie, and samosa, as shown in the figures on the chapter's first page. After you decide on your theme, search the web for images of your candidates and save the images you find. Make sure you know where you save the images so you can find them later. You could instead digitally draw images using your choice of drawing program.

Start a New Project

Begin creating your Vote Machine app by starting a new project as follows:

1. Open App Lab at https://code.org/educate/applab. Log in to the account you created to use App Lab (see Chapter 2).

2. Under the App Lab heading, click the Try it Out button.

3. Name your program by clicking the Rename button and typing a name in the Project Name field at the top of the App Lab interface.

4. Click the Save button.

Rename the Screen

Switch to Design mode in App Lab. On the Properties tab of the workspace, rename the ID of screen1 to a more meaningful name, such as playScreen.

WARNING

Do not include spaces in ID names. In most programming languages, including App Lab, spaces are not allowed. If you use them, you'll have errors in your program.

Add a Title Label to the App

Next, you should name your app with a label that helps the user know the purpose or use of the app. Add a title as follows:

1. Remain working in the Design mode of App Lab. If you're not in Design mode, click the Design button.

   The Design toolbox and workspace are displayed.

2. In the Design toolbox, drag the Label icon to the screen. Position it near the top center of the app display.

3. On the Properties tab of the workspace, change the attributes of the label as follows:

   - ID: Rename the ID to titleLabel.

   - Text: Type the instructions of your app, such as **Click to Vote for Your Favorite Snack**.

   - Width (px): Increase the width of your label to something like 240 pixels (or more).

   - Height (px): Increase the height of your label to something like 55 pixels (or more). If you have a long title that takes up two lines, you'll need to increase the height to display the second line.

- x Position (px): No changes; you change the x position later by dragging the label into position.

- y Position (px): No changes; you change the y position later by dragging the label into position.

- Text Color: No changes.

- Background Color: No changes.

- Font Size (px): Type a new font size in the field or use the selection arrows to make the title the appropriate size for your app.

- Text Alignment: Click the selection arrows and choose Center.

4. Click the label in your app and drag the label to position it where you want.

Add Images for the Candidates

Add an image that represents each candidate. The image's size will indicate its relative popularity. After many votes are cast, the bigger the image, the more votes it got!

1. Remain working in the Design mode of App Lab.

2. In the Design toolbox, drag the Image icon to the screen to create an image in your app. Position it where the first candidate (carrot) appears in the figures on the chapter's first page.

3. On the Properties tab of the workspace, change the attributes of the image as follows:

- ID: Rename the ID of the image to the name of your first candidate. To follow along with the example, type carrotImage (the first snack candidate).

- Width (px): Set to 60.

- Height (px): Set to 60.

- x Position (px): No changes; you change the x position later by dragging the image into position.

- y Position (px): No changes; you change the y position later by dragging the image into position.

- Image: You upload an image in the next step.

- Fit Image: No changes.

4. On the Properties tab of the workspace, locate the Image field. Click the Choose link to choose an image to be displayed in the image placeholder.

   The Choose Assets dialog box opens.

5. Click the Upload File button. Navigate to and select the image file for the first candidate. Then click the Choose button.

   This image file is the file you found while brainstorming (for example, in a Google image search) or created previously and then saved.

   The image file appears in the Choose Assets dialog box. I uploaded a carrot.png image file.

6. In the Choose Assets dialog box, click the Choose button next to the image asset you just uploaded.

   The image appears in your app.

7. Repeat Steps 2 through 6 to make a total of three candidates for your app. Position the candidates similar to the layout shown in the figures on the chapter's first page.

   My images show three candidates: Carrot, Cookie, and Samosa.

Add Labels for Each Candidate

Your app will feature a label next to the image of each candidate. The label should show the name of the candidate, such as Cookie, along with how many votes the candidate receives. Create your labels as follows:

1. Remain working in the Design mode of App Lab.

2. In the Design toolbox, drag the Label icon to the screen to create a label in your app. Position it beside the image of one of your candidates.

   For example, in the figures on the chapter's first page, the first candidate label, **Carrot**, is positioned next to the image of the carrot candidate.

3. On the Properties tab of the workspace, change the attributes of the label as follows:

   - ID: Rename the ID to a label that indicates your first candidate. To follow along with the example, type `carrotLabel`.

   - Text: Type the placeholder text. This text appears before any votes are cast. The placeholder text in the example app is Carrot.

   - Width (px): Increase the width of your label to something like 145 pixels. This extra width will be used to display the vote count for the candidate.

   - Height (px): Increase the height of your label to something like 20 to 30 pixels.

   - x Position (px): No changes; you change the x position later by dragging the label into position.

   - y Position (px): No changes; you change the y position later by dragging the label into position.

   - Text Color: No changes.

   - Background Color: No changes.

- Font Size (px): Type a new font size in the field or use the selection arrows to make the label the appropriate size for your app.

- Text Alignment: Click the selection arrows and choose Left.

4. Drag the label to position it where you want.

5. Repeat Steps 2 through 4 to create and position your remaining candidate labels.

   The two other candidate labels in the example are Cookie and Samosa.

TIP

When arranging buttons in any project, think carefully about the user interface. The user or player will expect buttons and other parts of the interface to be organized in an easy-to-understand layout.

Code Variables for the First Candidate

Next, you need to create variables for the first candidate. (See the "Working with Number Variables" sidebar.) One variable sets the starting size of the candidate image. A second variable sets the starting number of candidates votes. As voters cast their votes, these variable values increase according to which candidates receive votes. Follow these instructions:

1. Switch to Code mode in App Lab.

   The toolbox of commands and the workspace are displayed. You will be creating two variables.

2. Create your first variable, which is the size of the candidate's image, as follows:

   a. In the toolbox, select Variables. Drag the var x = ; command to the workspace.

   This is a variable declaration that is used to create a variable and set its starting value.

b. Type the name of the variable in the first field.

My first candidate is Carrot, so I typed the name carrotSize in the first field of the command.

c. Type the size of the variable in the second field.

I typed 60 in the second field.

The command looks like this:

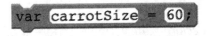

3. Create your second variable, which is the number of the candidate's votes, as follows:

a. Go back to the Variables category. Drag the var x = ; command to the workspace.

b. Type the name of the variable in the first field.

I typed the name carrotVotes.

c. Type the value of the variable in the second field. I typed 0 in the second field.

The command looks like this:

`var carrotVotes = 0;`

Code the First Candidate to Register a Vote

Next, you write code to register a vote for the first candidate. The event that represents voting for the first candidate is when the user clicks the image of the that candidate. The vote is registered by increasing the image size and the vote count for the first candidate.

Working with Number Variables

Number variables are needed in all computer programs. A *number variable* is a container that holds a number that can change. For example, age is a number variable that can have different values for the same person at different stages of life. More specifically, age is an *integer variable*. (An *integer* is a counting number, a negative counting number, or 0.) The bill for a dinner at a restaurant is another type of number variable, specifically a *decimal variable*. (This type of variable is also called a *double*.)

Creating a new variable is called *declaring the variable*. Different programming languages use different rules when declaring a variable, but usually they involve using a command such as var age or double bill. In Scratch or MakeCode, you use the Create a Variable command to declare a variable. In App Lab, you use the var command to declare a variable. After you declare a variable, you usually don't use the var command again with that variable name in the same program. (One exception is declaring a local variable that serves as a counter inside a for loop; you do this in Chapter 17.)

Giving a variable an initial value is called *initializing the variable*. The initial value of an age variable is 0 (when a baby is born). The initial value of a loan might be $25,000. In Scratch, App Lab, and MakeCode, you would initialize these variables with these values using the commands age = 0 and loan = 25000.00 in your code.

Some programming languages, such as App Lab, allow you to declare and initialize a variable in one step, for example, var age = 0. This feature allows you to combine two steps in one, making your code more efficient.

Follow these instructions to code the event for voting for the first candidate:

1. In the toolbox, select UI Controls. Drag the onEvent command to the workspace.

2. In the onEvent command, click the ID tab and select the name of the image for your first candidate.

I selected `carrotImage`. When a user clicks or taps
`carrotImage`, the code block inside `onEvent` will execute.
Delete `event` in the parentheses in `function`. The code
looks like this:

```
onEvent (▼ "carrotImage", ▼ "click", function() {
```

3. Increase the value of the variable for the candidate image's
   size as follows:

   a. Go back to Variables Controls. Drag the `x = ;` command
      into the `onEvent` command.

   b. Write a command to increment the variable for the
      candidate's image size each time the user clicks the first
      candidate.

      You can increment by any number, but a value of 2 or 3
      will increase the image in a visually appealing way.
      I typed `carrotSize` in the first field and `carrotSize + 2` in
      the second field. (Note that App Lab adjusts the formatting
      around `carrotSize + 2`).

      The `onEvent` command now looks like this:

```
onEvent (▼ "carrotImage", ▼ "click", function() {
    carrotSize = carrotSize + 2 ;
```

   The new `carrotSize` equals what `carrotSize` was before,
   plus 2. When the image of the carrot is clicked, `carrotSize`
   will be incremented by 2. (See the "Incrementing Variables"
   sidebar.)

4. Set the image size to the size specified by the variable value
   in Step 3 as follows:

   a. From UI Controls, drag a `setSize` command into `onEvent`
      and attach it to the previous command. At the `ID` field,

press the tab and change the ID to the image ID of the first candidate.

I selected `carrotImage`.

b. In the width field and again in the height field, type the name of the size variable for this candidate.

I typed `carrotSize` in both fields. This command changes the size of `carrotImage`. The value of the size is set by `carrotSize`, which you computed in Step 3.

The entire command now looks like this:

```
onEvent(▼"carrotImage", ▼"click", function() {
    carrotSize = carrotSize + 2;
    setSize(▼"carrotImage", carrotSize, carrotSize);
```

5. Increase the value of the variable for the votes for the first candidate image as follows.

From Variables Controls, drag the `x = ;` command into the `onEvent` command. Write a command to increment the vote count by one each time the user clicks the first candidate.

I typed `carrotVotes` in the first field and `carrotVotes + 1` in the second field. (Note that App Lab adjusts the formatting around `carrotVotes + 1`).

The `onEvent` command now looks like this:

```
onEvent(▼"carrotImage", ▼"click", function() {
    carrotSize = carrotSize + 2;
    setSize(▼"carrotImage", carrotSize, carrotSize);
    carrotVotes = carrotVotes + 1;
```

The new carrotVotes equals what carrotVotes was before, plus 1. The carrotVotes variable is incremented by 1 when the image of the carrot is clicked.

6. Update the label with the vote count for the first candidate when the user casts a vote for that candidate:

   a. From UI Controls, drag a setText command into onEvent and attach it to the previous command. In the ID field, press the tab and change the ID to the label name of the first candidate.

   I selected carrotLabel.

   b. Change the text so that it shows the user a text literal indicating the name of the candidate, joined with the variable value showing the number of votes the candidate has received.

   I typed "Carrot:" + carrotVotes.

   The string literal Carrot: is displayed, followed by the value of the carrotVotes variable you computed in Step 5.

You've now completed all the coding for your first candidate. Figure 12-1 shows the complete code for my Carrot candidate.

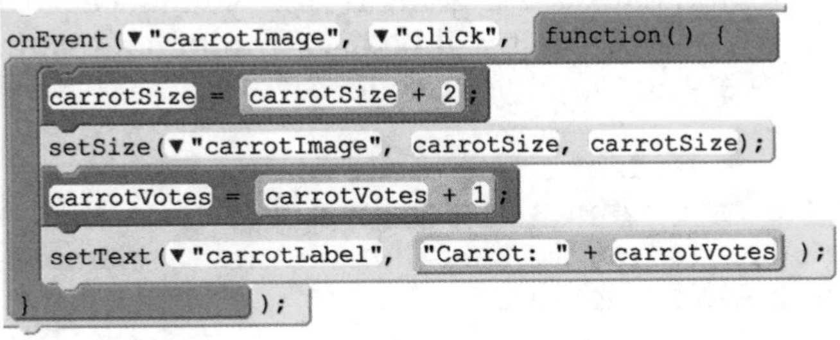

```
onEvent (▼ "carrotImage", ▼ "click", function() {
    carrotSize = carrotSize + 2;
    setSize (▼ "carrotImage", carrotSize, carrotSize);
    carrotVotes = carrotVotes + 1;
    setText (▼ "carrotLabel", "Carrot: " + carrotVotes);
});
```

Figure 12-1

Here is the Carrot code in a text-based format:

```
var carrotSize = 60;
var carrotVotes = 0;
```

```
onEvent("carrotImage", "click", function() {
  carrotSize = carrotSize + 2;
  setSize("carrotImage", carrotSize, carrotSize);
  carrotVotes = carrotVotes + 1;
  setText("carrotLabel", "Carrot: " + carrotVotes );
});
```

Test your code to see how it is working so far! Fix any bugs to make sure that the code for the first candidate works perfectly. Check your variable names and your ID names (in both code and design mode) for accuracy, including letter case. (For help on debugging App Lab code, see Chapter 3.) When the code is bug-free, you can move on to the next section and repeat the process to code your other candidates.

TIP

If you are certain that your code is error-free and it still doesn't work, reload the page. This step often solves the problem!

Code Variables for the Remaining Candidates

Next, you need to create variables for the remaining candidates. Follow the pattern of the instructions in "Code Variables for the First Candidate" to create size and vote variables for each of your other candidates. As a general rule, you place *global variables* — variables that will be used throughout your entire program — at the top of your code.

The variables used for sizing the candidate images and counting their votes are examples of global variables. I created size and vote variables for my Cookie candidate and my Samosa candidate, as shown in Figure 12-2.

Later, in Chapter 17, you learn about *local variables*, which are used for smaller tasks in your events. You use local variables when you need to count something or keep track of information temporarily, but that information is not the main point of the program.

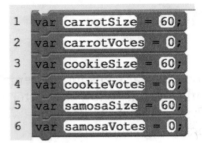

```
1  var carrotSize = 60;
2  var carrotVotes = 0;
3  var cookieSize = 60;
4  var cookieVotes = 0;
5  var samosaSize = 60;
6  var samosaVotes = 0;
```

Figure 12-2

Changing and Incrementing Variable Values

You can change the value of a variable as your program executes. For example, you can change the value of a bank variable, just by assigning a new value to the variable. If bank were part of a Wheel of Fortune app, the value of bank could change based on the action of the game. When a player with $3500 spins the wheel and lands on Bankrupt, the app can take away all his money by using a command such as bank = 0.

Other changes to variables are less drastic than losing all your money and setting the variable to a new value! Often, variables change just a little at a time, such as scoring variables used in games. As a player moves through the game, she scores points that increase her score. For example, when the player blasts an asteroid, she earns 50 points, and her score is 50 points more than what it was before. The command is written as score = score + 50. When increasing a variable by 1, as in tallying votes one at a time, you can also write score++ which means score = score + 1. The process of increasing a number variable, usually a little bit at a time, is called *incrementing the variable.*

A note of caution: New coders sometimes find the format of the incrementing command confusing. The command score = score + 1 is not an algebra equation! Reading the command aloud, you would say, "the score becomes whatever the score was before, plus one more." Or, "the score is now its old value plus one." Practice saying the command to yourself this way whenever you increment a variable in your code.

Code Remaining Candidates to Register Votes

Finally, you need to write code so that votes for the remaining candidates can be counted and shown. Follow the pattern of the instructions in "Code the First Candidate to Register a Vote" to code an onEvent for each remaining candidate.

I created an onEvent that increases the size of my Cookie and the Cookie vote count by 1 when someone clicks the Cookie candidate. I then created another onEvent that increases the size of my Samosa and the Samosa vote count by 1 when someone clicks the Samosa candidate. See Figure 12-3 for the complete code of Vote Machine in block format.

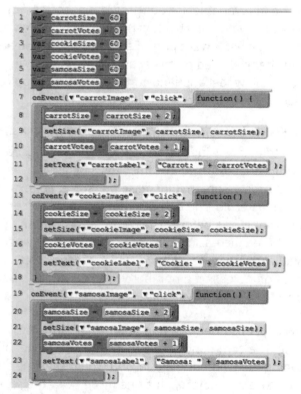

```
1   var carrotSize = 60;
2   var carrotVotes = 0;
3   var cookieSize = 60;
4   var cookieVotes = 0;
5   var samosaSize = 60;
6   var samosaVotes = 0;
7   onEvent (▼"carrotImage", ▼"click", function() {
8       carrotSize = carrotSize + 2;
9       setSize(▼"carrotImage", carrotSize, carrotSize);
10      carrotVotes = carrotVotes + 1;
11      setText(▼"carrotLabel", "Carrot: " + carrotVotes );
12  });
13  onEvent (▼"cookieImage", ▼"click", function() {
14      cookieSize = cookieSize + 2;
15      setSize(▼"cookieImage", cookieSize, cookieSize);
16      cookieVotes = cookieVotes + 1;
17      setText(▼"cookieLabel", "Cookie: " + cookieVotes );
18  });
19  onEvent (▼"samosaImage", ▼"click", function() {
20      samosaSize = samosaSize + 2;
21      setSize(▼"samosaImage", samosaSize, samosaSize);
22      samosaVotes = samosaVotes + 1;
23      setText(▼"samosaLabel", "Samosa: " + samosaVotes );
24  });
```

Figure 12-3

Here is the complete code in a text-based format:

```
var carrotSize = 60;
var carrotVotes = 0;
var cookieSize = 60;
var cookieVotes = 0;
var samosaSize = 60;
var samosaVotes = 0;
onEvent("carrotImage", "click", function() {
  carrotSize = carrotSize + 2;
  setSize("carrotImage", carrotSize, carrotSize);
  carrotVotes = carrotVotes + 1;
  setText("carrotLabel", "Carrot: " + carrotVotes );
});
onEvent("cookieImage", "click", function() {
  cookieSize = cookieSize + 2;
  setSize("cookieImage", cookieSize, cookieSize);
  cookieVotes = cookieVotes + 1;
  setText("cookieLabel", "Cookie: " + cookieVotes );
});
onEvent("samosaImage", "click", function() {
  samosaSize = samosaSize + 2;
  setSize("samosaImage", samosaSize, samosaSize);
  samosaVotes = samosaVotes + 1;
  setText("samosaLabel", "Samosa: " + samosaVotes );
});
```

Save, Test, and Debug Your App

As you work, App Lab automatically saves your program in the cloud. Test your program and fix any bugs to ensure that it works the way you want it to. For help with testing and debugging, see Chapter 3.

REMEMBER

Don't worry about the little yellow triangles that appear on onEvent lines of App Lab code. The warning "Event is defined, but it's not called in your program" occurs at each instance of function(event). You don't have to change this for your app to operate correctly. But if you're bothered by the warnings, just delete the event command inside each function() command (as I did in this project). The warnings will be removed.

Share Your App with the World

After your app operates as you want it to, set the status of your program to Share. See Chapter 19 for details on sharing apps you create in App Lab.

Enhance Your App

Consider enhancing your Vote Machine app with these features:

- **More candidates:** Add as many candidates as you want! For each candidate, create an image, a label, two variables (one for size and one for votes), and an onEvent.

- **Sounds:** Add a sound that plays each time a vote is cast.

- **Total Votes Tally:** Add a new variable, called totalVotes, that counts the total number of votes cast. Declare and initialize the variable to 0 at the start of your program by using the command totalVotes = 0. Be sure to increment totalVotes each time a vote is cast: totalVotes = totalVotes + 1. Also, add a label that displays the total vote tally.

Happy New Year!

Each December 31, people everywhere on Earth count down the final seconds to the start of the new year. Communities stay up late to see the TV broadcast of the glittery ball drop in New York's Times Square as the crowds cheer, "10-9-8-7-6-5-4-3-2-1. Happy New Year!" In this project, you use Scratch to recreate the iconic scene. To code your program, you work with number variables (see Chapter 12) and use a new process called *decrementing* to make a countdown variable get smaller as the seconds tick away. You also use text-to-speech and language translation to hear the countdown — and you can do it in a variety of languages, as if you're watching the scene on television in another country!

https://pixabay.com/en/disco-ball-mirror-ball-glitter-ball-160937/

You also use a new set of commands called conditionals. *Conditionals* allow your code to make decisions based on different variable values. A conditional is sometimes called an *if-then* statement. Conditional decisions can then be used to *branch*, or select different paths, to run through your program. (Refer to Chapter 1 for details on selection.) In Happy New Year! you use a conditional to trigger the cheering of the crowd based on the time remaining on the clock. You can build other conditionals to customize the scene any way you want.

Brainstorm

Your Happy New Year! scene can take place in any city. The project in the figure on the chapter's first page shows a city with a splendid skyline of skyscrapers, be it New York City or Tokyo. You can choose any city to stage your celebration.

Brainstorm some layouts of how you want your celebration to look to the end user. Do you want to feature a city you've visited during a countdown to the new year? Or one you enjoy viewing on television during its New Year's festivities? Perhaps you want to show fireworks, or just a banner that reads *Happy New Year!* The choices are yours.

Start a New Project

Begin creating your Happy New Year! program by starting a new project:

1. Open Scratch at `https://scratch.mit.edu`. If prompted, enable Flash to run Scratch. Log in to the account you created to use Scratch (see Chapter 2).

2. On the Scratch home page, select Create. Or if you're already working in Scratch, choose File⇨New from the menu bar.

3. Name your program by typing a name in the Project Name field at the top of the Scratch interface.

4. Cut (delete) Scratch Cat from the project by clicking or tapping the X in the Scratch Cat icon.

   The icon is in the sprite area in the lower-right corner of the Scratch interface.

Add a Backdrop

The *backdrop* is the background color or image that fills the screen of your toy. Add a backdrop as follows:

1. At the Stage, click the Choose a Backdrop icon.

   The backdrop library appears on the Choose a Backdrop screen.

2. Scroll through the backdrops and click or tap the one you want to use.

   The backdrop appears on the stage. I selected the Night City backdrop.

Add a Glittery Ball

The ball that drops in Times Square on New Year's Eve is large and glittery. Search online to find an image. I searched for *disco ball clip art.* Save the image on your computer, in a location where you can find it later. You may need to edit the image to remove background color. (See Chapter 2 for details on image editing.)

TIP

Try to save thumbnail-sized versions of images for your sprites. Saving sprite images in large sizes forces you to shrink the sprite a lot, which also reduces the quality of the image onscreen. Smaller images result in better looking sprites.

TIP

Name the image something simple and clear. I named mine `discoball`. This name is used when naming the sprite and its costume. You can always change the names of the sprite and the costume later.

Now follow these steps to add your saved image as a sprite:

1. In the sprite area of the Scratch interface, hover over (or tap and hold down) the Choose a Sprite icon and select Upload Sprite.

2. Navigate to and select the image you previously saved for the glittery ball. Click or tap the Choose button.

   On the stage, a sprite appears wearing the glittery ball costume. The name of the sprite is whatever name you used when you saved the image. My sprite, shown in Figure 13-1, is named `discoball`.

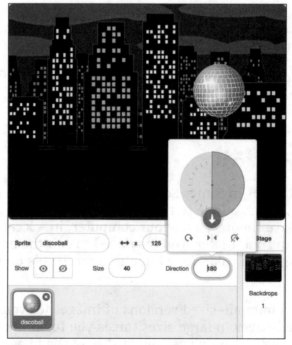

Figure 13-1

3. In the sprite attributes area, type a new size for the ball. The size depends on how large you want the ball to appear in the scene.

   I typed a size of 40.

4. Still in the sprite attributes area, set the direction and orientation of the ball. Set Direction to 180 (pointing down) and Orientation to Do Not Rotate.

   The ball needs to point down so that it drops down the screen. Setting the orientation to Do Not Rotate keeps the ball from looking like it is tipped over on its side when it is rotated to point down.

Code the Ball to Drop

Next, you code the ball to drop down the screen. The fall should take ten seconds because it occurs during the ten-second count-down to the new year. Simply follow these steps:

1. Click or tap the discoball to select it.

2. On the Code tab of the Scratch interface, select the Events icon. Drag the when green flag clicked command to the Code workspace.

3. Select the Motion icon. Drag the go to x: y: command to the Code workspace and attach it to the previous command. Type values in the x and y fields to set the x-coordinate and y-coordinate positions of the ball starting its drop.

   My command reads go to x: 125 y:125.

TIP

I dragged the ball to a spot near the top of the screen. I then looked in the sprite attributes area for my discoball and checked the x-coordinate and y-coordinate of the sprite to locate the position I wanted.

4. Drag a `glide secs to x: y:` command to the Code work-space and attach it to the previous command. Type values in the x and y fields to set the x-coordinate and y-coordinate positions of the ball ending its drop.

I dragged the ball to a spot near the bottom of the screen. I then looked in the sprite attributes area for my discoball and saw that the x position was still 125 but the new y posi-tion was −125. The drop should take 10 seconds. The com-mand reads `glide 10 secs to x: 125 y:−125`.

Now when the green flag is clicked, the ball takes its starting position in the air, falls (glides) down the screen for ten seconds, and stops at its ending position on the ground. Figure 13-2 shows the complete code block for the ball drop.

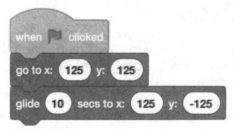

Figure 13-2

Create a Countdown Variable

A countdown clock displays numbers, one at a time, counting down the seconds left until the new year. Create the variable for your countdown clock by following these steps:

1. Click or tap the discoball to select it.

2. On the Code tab of the Scratch interface, select the Variables icon.

3. Click or tap the Make a Variable button.

A New Variable dialog box opens.

4. In the New Variable Name field, type a name for the variable that will count down the number of seconds until the new year.

I named my variable countdown, as shown in Figure 13-3.

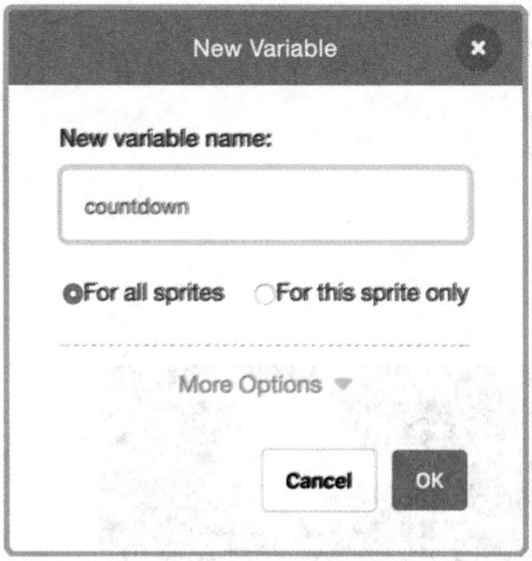

New Variable ✖

New variable name:

countdown

⦿For all sprites ◯For this sprite only

More Options ▼

Cancel OK

Figure 13-3

5. Leave the For All Sprites radio button selected.

6. Click or tap the OK button.

The countdown variable now appears with the variable commands, as shown in Figure 13-4. However, the variable appears also on the stage.

7. To display only the value and not the name of the countdown variable, Ctrl-click (Mac) or right-click (Win) and select Large Readout from the pop-up menu, as shown in Figure 13-5.

Variables

Figure 13-4

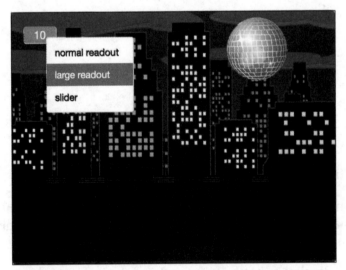

Figure 13-5

Google Language Translation

Scratch uses Google Translate to translate text into different languages for use in your programs. It can translate text into over 100 languages, and for many languages, it can pronounce the translated text in an authentic accent. To translate text, Google uses a process called neural machine translation (NMT). In NMT, the translation process works sort of like a human brain, looking for connections in information to find meaning, as opposed to searching a database of translated words. To make those natural language connections, the translator looks through large numbers of sentences in documents to understand what words are likely to go together in common phrases. It then assembles the phrases into complete, translated sentences.

Google is using this technology in many other ways. World Lens enables you to use your computer's or cell phone's camera to "look at" text and automatically convert it to another language. This program is especially helpful when trying to read signs, menus, and other text when visiting another country. Google is also perfecting real-time audio translation, where you can speak to people in your native language, but they hear your voice in their language. Star Trek's universal communicator has come to life!

Add Text-to-Speech and Translate Commands

Just as a television news anchor says the numbers counting down to the new year, you can make your program speak, too! And because every nation around the world rings in the new year (not necessarily on the same date), your program will need to say "Happy New Year!" in several languages.

Add text-to-speech commands and language translation commands to your Scratch interface as follows:

1. Click or tap the Add an Extension icon in the lower-left corner of the Scratch interface.

   The Choose an Extension dialog box opens.

2. Click or tap the Text to Speech box.

   Text-to-speech commands are added to your commands.

3. Click or tap the Add an Extension icon again.

4. Click or tap the Translate box, shown in Figure 13-6.

   Translate commands are added to your commands.

Translate
Translate text into many languages.

Figure 13-6

Add a Cheer Sound to the Ball Sprite

The crowd always cheers in the last few seconds before midnight, so you should add a Cheer sound to the ball sprite. You'll use the sound later when you write the code for the sprite. Follow these steps:

1. Click or tap the Sounds tab in the upper-left corner of the screen.

   The sound editor appears.

2. Click or tap the Choose Sound icon in the lower-left corner of the sound editor to open the Scratch library of sounds.

   The sound library appears on the screen.

3. Click or tap the Cheer sound.

   The sound is added to the collection of sounds for the disco-ball. (The Pop sound is also in this collection. You won't need the Pop sound, so click or tap its X to delete it.

Code the Countdown Clock

Now it's time to put all the pieces together and code the count-down clock. The clock starts at 10 seconds and ends at 0 sec-onds. Make the countdown variable decrement once each second.

Show the updated value of the countdown clock by following these steps:

1. Click or tap the discoball to select it.

2. On the Code tab of the Scratch interface, select the Events icon. Drag the `when green flag clicked` command to the Code workspace.

   The code block you attach to this event will run when the green flag is clicked on a computer or tapped on a tablet. Note that this code will run in parallel with the code you previously wrote for the ball drop. (See Chapter 4 for infor-mation on parallel execution of code.)

3. Select the Variables icon. Drag the `set countdown` command to the workspace, and attach it to the previous command. Type `10` in the field. The command is now `set countdown to 10`.

4. Select the Control icon. Drag the `repeat 10` command to the workspace, and attach it to the previous command.

   Inside the repeat command, you will code a block that announces the seconds left in the countdown.

5. Select the Text to Speech icon. Drag the `set language to` command inside the `Repeat 10` command.

   This command will set the accent to whatever language you pick. It will also automatically translate the numbers in the countdown to that language. I selected Japanese.

6. From the Text to Speech commands, drag the `speak` command inside the `repeat 10` command, and attach it to the previous command. From the Variables commands, drag the `countdown` variable to the `speak` command to replace the default value of `Hello`.

   The command is now `speak countdown`. Each time the command is executed, it speaks aloud the value of the `countdown` variable, in the language you chose in Step 5. It takes about one second for the computer speaker to say each number; this sets the correct pace for the countdown clock.

7. From the Variables commands, drag the `change countdown by` command inside the `repeat 10` command, and attach it to the previous command. Make the value `–1`.

   The command is now `change countdown by –1`. The countdown variable will decrement (go down) each time it executes. (See the "Decrementing a Variable" sidebar for details.)

Decrementing a Variable

The process of decreasing a number variable is called *decrementing a variable,* and it's a common coding process when working with timers and lives. Timer variables, such as the countdown clock in Happy New Year!, are often used in games. Each round of a game lasts for a certain time period, and the timer counts down until it reaches zero, indicating that the game is over. (One of my favorite Atari 2600 cartridges was a carnival arcade game that lasted for two minutes. The last few seconds of the game featured frantic firing at plastic ducks and giant clown heads before the clock reached zero.)

The command for the timer countdown would be written as timer = timer – 1. When decreasing a variable by 1, as in subtracting seconds of a time, you can also write timer--.

Many games also include a lives variable that decrements as your hero character experiences damage during a game. Decrementing a lives variable would look something like lives = lives –1. You could also write this as lives--.

An if-then conditional is often written with a command that decrements a variable. This is because the program needs to know what action to take when the variable reaches a *threshold* value, such as zero. When a timer variable or lives variable reaches a value of zero, the game is over or the animated scene is finished.

8. From the Control commands, drag an if-then command inside the repeat 10 command, and attach it to the previous command. Create a conditional in which the crowd cheers during the final four seconds of the ball drop:

   a. Create the *condition*: From the Operators commands, drag an equals (=) operator to the hexagon field following the if. Then, from the Variable commands, drag your countdown variable to the first field of the operator, and type the value 4 in the second field. The condition is now if countdown = 4.

b. Create the *consequence*: From the Sound commands, drag a start sound command to the then area of the conditional. Click or tap the tab and select the cheer sound (it's probably the default sound). Now the cheer sound will play during the last four seconds of the countdown.

9. From the Text to Speech commands, drag a speak command and attach it outside the repeat command. From the Translate commands, drag a translate to command to the field of the speak command you just added. In the translate to command, type the phrase you want translated. Click or tap the arrow in the language selector and select the language you want to use.

I created the command translate Happy New Year! to Japanese. The program will speak this phrase in Japanese and using a Japanese accent (which was set in Step 5).

The complete code block for the countdown clock is shown in Figure 13-7.

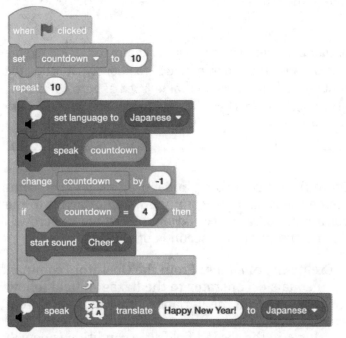

Figure 13-7

TIP

The Translate command list features a huge collection of languages. from Albanian to Zulu! However, the set language command list has fewer accents. So you can make Scratch speak French with a French accent, Russian with a Russian accent, and Japanese with a Japanese accent, but you'll have to live with a less authentic-sounding accent when Scratch speaks phrases translated into Hindi or Welch.

Save, Test, and Debug Your Program

As you work, Scratch automatically saves your program in the cloud, so you don't have to take any special actions to save your work. Test your program and fix any bugs to ensure that it works the way you want it to. (See Chapter 3 for details on debugging Scratch programs.)

Simple Conditionals and Booleans

You work with conditionals every day. *Conditionals* enable you to make decisions when different things happen in your life. For example, you might say, "*If* it is cold outside, *then* I will wear a coat." This is a simple if-then conditional. The *if* part of the decision is called the *condition,* and the *then* part is called the *consequence.*

When the condition is true, the consequence is executed. When the condition is false, the consequence is not executed. Sometimes the condition is true and sometimes it is false; in other words, the condition is a variable. This type of variable is not a string variable and it's not a number variable. A variable that has the value of true or false is called a *Boolean variable* (named for the Irish mathematician and philosopher, George Boole).

Conditionals allow computer program to make decisions. They're the commands that give you control over the paths your program selects as it executes. (See Chapter 1 for information on sequencing, selection, and repetition). When flowcharting a program, you use a diamond to represent an if-then decision. More complex conditional structures give you even greater control over how your program branches. (For more information, see Chapter 14, especially the sidebar on advanced conditionals in that chapter).

Share Your Program with the World

After your program operates perfectly, it's time to share it. Set the status of your program to Share. Then add to your project page a description of your program and directions on how to run it. See Chapter 19 for details on sharing your programs.

Enhance Your Toy

Consider enhancing your Happy New Year! scene with new features:

- **New sprites:** Add new sprites, such as New Year's revelers or fireworks, to the scene.

- **New music:** Add a command to play an additional song when the ball reaches the ground and the countdown reaches zero. The command should follow in sequence after the repeat command. Try "Auld Lang Syne," the traditional song for ringing in the New Year, or a festive party song you like! Search the web and then download your song choice in .mp3 format. Finally, upload the song to the sound editor in Scratch, and add the code to your program to make the song play.

- **New languages:** Say "Happy New Year!" in more languages. Add as many translate commands as you want!

Light Theremin

A *theremin* **is an** odd electronic instrument, patented in
1928 and known for its spacey sounds. A musician plays a
theremin without ever touching it! To make music notes, she
moves one hand into different positions near a metal rod
sticking out of the top of the theremin. To adjust the loudness
of each note, she moves her other hand near a metal loop
sticking out of the side of the theremin.

https://en.wikipedia.org/wiki/Theremin#/media/File:Theramin-Alexandra-Stepanoff-1930.jpg

In this project, you code and play your own version of a theremin using MakeCode for micro:bit. You make music with your theremin by moving your hand or shining a flashlight to control the quantity of light that falls on a light sensor. The light sensor on the micro:bit can read values from 0 (dark) to 255 (bright light). The code reads the input light level (a variable) and then uses advanced conditional statements to decide which sound to play. These more advanced conditionals, called *if-then-else if-else* commands, allow your program to branch to many different decisions based on different variable values.

You can then transfer your code to a micro:bit, attach a few wires and some earbuds and have a real working theremin!

TECHNICAL STUFF

The LED light grid on the front of the micro:bit acts as a light sensor and light level meter for the device. LED lights are *directional*; they light up only when they are connected to an electrical circuit in one direction. When they are connected in the opposite direction, they can perform the opposite process: They take in light energy and produce a tiny bit of electricity. So in this project, the LEDs take in the light shining on them and then produce an electrical signal to tell a device to play a sound!

Brainstorm

The MakeCode interface includes commands for producing all the notes from low C to high B. Even if you don't know anything about music, you can select any notes you want your theremin to play on the micro:bit. If you do know a little about music, you might choose to select notes that form a chord, such as middle C, E, G, and high C, which form the C major chord. Regardless of what musical notes you choose to code, your finished theremin will look something like Figure 14-1. Get coding by following these steps.

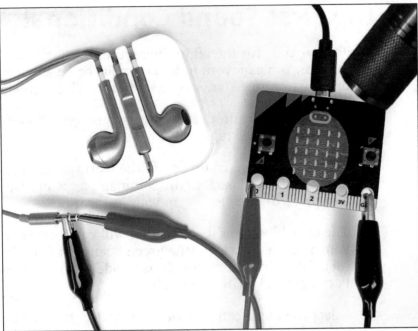

File:Flashlight CleanBackground.png - Wikimedia Commons

Figure 14-1

Start a New Project

Begin creating your theremin gadget by starting a new project as follows:

1. Open MakeCode for micro:bit at `https://makecode.microbit.org`.

2. On the micro:bit home page, click the big New Project button in the middle of the screen.

   A new project opens and displays the workspace.

3. Name your project by typing a name in the Project Name field at the bottom of the micro:bit interface.

4. Click the Save button next to the Project Name field to save your project.

Code the First Sound Conditional

Write your code for the Light Theremin project in the workspace. You can work in Blocks mode or JavaScript text mode. The example shows code written in Blocks mode.

You code the theremin to run its code forever, without a starting event. Follow these steps:

1. Keep the `forever` command in the workspace. Drag the `on start` command back to the command area, or else click it and press the Delete key on your keyboard.

   The code block you'll be creating will run forever as soon as you click the Play icon (the green triangle below the simulator). On a physical micro:bit, the code will run as soon as it is transferred to the micro:bit.

2. Select the Logic category of commands, and drag the `if true then` command to the workspace, placing it inside the `forever` command. The command looks like this:

3. From the Logic category of commands, drag the `0 = 0` command to the workspace. Make the `0 = 0` command the condition of the `if true then` command (that is, replace `true`).

   The *condition* is the `if` part of the `if true then` command. Note that the hexagon shape of the `0 = 0` command fits inside the `if` condition.

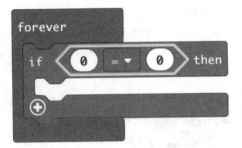

4. Change the 0 = 0 condition to `light level` ≥ `200` as follows. From the Input category of commands, drag the `light`
   `level` variable to the first 0, replacing it. Click the tab where
   the equals sign (=) is located and change the operator to ≥.
   Type 200 in the field following the ≥ operator.

   The command looks like this:

5. Complete the `if-then` conditional by adding a *consequence* as
   follows. From the Music category of commands, drag the
   `play tone Middle C for 1 beat` command inside the `if-`
   `then` conditional command. The command looks like this:

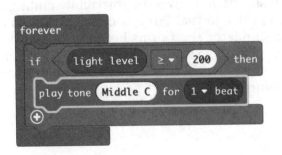

In the play tone Middle C for 1 beat command, click the note name (Middle C). This opens a piano keyboard where you can select a new note, as shown in Figure 14-2. Select High C.

Figure 14-2

Test how your coding is working so far. Click the green Play icon on the simulator. Note the circle-shaped light meter, which measures the quantity of light falling on the micro:bit, in the upper-left corner. The default light level for the simulator is 128.

Using the mouse pointer, click and hold down on the dividing line where the yellow touches the gray inside the circle. Drag the line up and down to manually decrease and increase, respectively, the value of the light sensor variable. (The simulator is not changing the light level; it simply allows you to test how the micro:bit behaves under different lighting conditions.) If you reach a value of 200 or more, the micro:bit simulator plays the high C note.

Note that the simulator shows the micro:bit sending an electrical signal to Pin 0, and that Pin 0 is connected to an external speaker. The simulator shows this because the physical micro:bit board has no built-in speaker, but it can set a voltage at a pin (connection point), which causes a connected speaker to play a sound. See Figure 14-3.

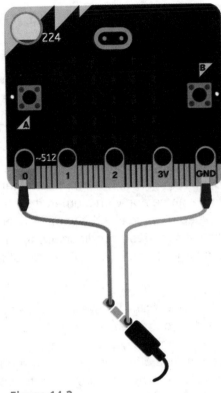

Figure 14-3

Code More Sound Conditionals

Continue writing your Light Theremin code in the workspace. Code more sound conditionals, with each sound conditional responding to a different light level.

Note that you will use a series of if–then–else conditionals to decide which sound to play. See the "Advanced Conditionals" sidebar.

1. At the if then conditional you have already placed in your code, click the small plus sign (+) located in the lower-left corner of the conditional.

   This adds an else command to the conditional. You're not done yet!

Advanced Conditionals

Conditionals can be simple if—then commands (see Chapter 13), or they can be more advanced if—then—else commands. Depending on the Boolean value (true or false) of a condition, a path is selected for the next command to be executed in the program.

The if—then—else command is a common command for making your code select one of two different paths to run. (See Chapter 1 for details on *selection.*) For example, when playing a game app with a timer, *if* there is time left on the clock, *then* you can keep playing, *else* the game is over. By expanding from an if—then to an if—then—else conditional, you can ensure that you create a specific outcome for both possible states of the condition.

Here's another example: "*If* it is cold outside, *then* I will wear a coat, *else* I will wear a swimsuit." This structure provides you more control over the consequences of the decision. When the condition is true, you make one decision, and when the condition is false, you make a different decision. Without the else, you would have exited the conditional without taking any action. For example, you don't know what to wear if it isn't cold outside!

When needed, conditionals can be even more complex, taking the form of if—then—else if—else commands (as in the Light Theremin project). This structure lets you create many alternative outcomes by adding as many else if statements as you need. For example, "*If* it is less than 40 degrees, *then* I will wear a coat; *else if* it is less than 65 degrees, I will wear a light jacket; *else if* it is less than 90 degrees, I will wear shorts and a T-shirt; *else* I will wear a swimsuit." Note that the else at the end of your decision is executed only when all of the if and else if statements are false. The else is a catchall in your conditional because it catches all the cases that are not caught by the previous statements. It is the "outcome of last resort."

Putting together many else if statements in a conditional allows you to create a *conditional sieve:* the different levels of else if statements allow you to bypass a condition that is false and get "caught" by a condition when it is true. Once caught, a statement can't be caught again;

the consequence of the else if that caught the statement is executed and the program exits the conditional sieve. (You may have seen a different type of sieve at a construction site: There, sieves are used to sort rocks of different sizes.) Both the Light Theremin program and the weather clothing example are structured as conditional sieves.

2. At the if then else conditional, click the small plus sign (+) three more times.

   You now have one if-then, three instances of else if, and one else as shown in Figure 14-4.

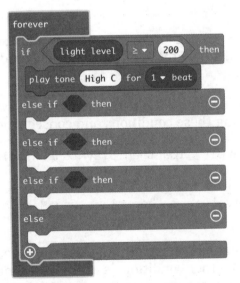

Figure 14-4

TIP

When writing a conditional in MakeCode, you can click the plus sign (+) on a conditional to add new conditions to it, and you can click the minus (–) key to remove conditions you previously added.

3. From the Logic category of commands, drag the 0 = 0 command to the workspace. Place it inside the condition of the first else if-then command.

4. Change the 0 = 0 condition to read `light level ≥ 150`. Follow these steps:

   a. From the Input category of commands, drag the `light level` variable to the first 0, replacing it.

   b. Click the tab where the equals sign (=) is located and change the operator to ≥.

   c. Type 150 in the field following the ≥ operator.

5. Complete the `else if-then` conditional by adding a *consequence* as follows:

   a. From the Music category of commands, drag the `play tone Middle C for 1 beat` command inside the `if true then` conditional command.

   b. In the `play tone Middle C for 1 beat` command, click the note name (`Middle C`). This opens a piano keyboard where you can select a new note. Select `Middle G`.

6. Repeat Steps 3 through 5 for the remaining two `else if-then` conditionals by using these conditions and consequences:

   ```
   else if light level ≥ 100 then play tone Middle E
   for 1 beat
   ```

   ```
   else if light level ≥ 50 then play tone Middle C
   for 1 beat
   ```

7. The `else` conditional has no condition; its consequence executes if none of the other conditionals are `true`. From the Music category of commands, drag the `rest (ms) 1 beat` command inside the consequence of `else`.

   When the light level on the micro:bit is very low, less than a value of 50, none of the other conditionals are `true`. That's when this `else` consequence executes. It "plays" a rest, which is no music sound.

Your completed code should look like Figure 14-5.

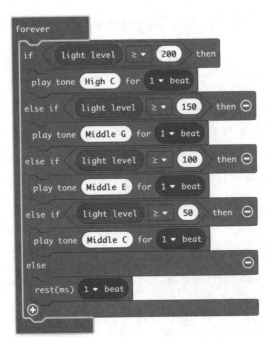

Figure 14-5

Here is the complete code in a text-based (JavaScript) format:

```javascript
basic.forever(function () {
    if (input.lightLevel() >= 200) {
        music.playTone(523, music.beat(BeatFraction.Whole))
    } else if (input.lightLevel() >= 150) {
        music.playTone(392, music.beat(BeatFraction.Whole))
    } else if (input.lightLevel() >= 100) {
        music.playTone(330, music.beat(BeatFraction.Whole))
    } else if (input.lightLevel() >= 50) {
        music.playTone(262, music.beat(BeatFraction.Whole))
    } else {
        music.rest(music.beat(BeatFraction.Whole))
    }
})
```

Save, Test, and Debug Your Program

Click the Save button at the bottom of the screen to save your program. Test your code by clicking the green Play icon on the simulator and then dragging the light level line up and down on the light meter. As you artificially adjust the amount of light falling on the micro:bit, you should hear the different notes (and the rest) you coded.

Fix any bugs to ensure that your Light Theremin toy works the way you want it to. (For details on debugging micro:bit programs, see Chapter 3.)

IoT and Sensors in Circuits

With the world becoming more connected than ever, you've probably been hearing a lot about the Internet of Things, or IoT. Not only are your computer, tablet, and phone able to communicate over the Internet, other devices in your home can too, including your television, security cameras, appliances, and thermostat. Computer programs use sensors on these devices to record a TV program at a certain time, start streaming live video of the person currently ringing your doorbell, turn on the coffee pot before you wake up, and adjust the household temperature when no one is home.

Similarly, wearable electronics have code-controlled sensors that can track your health and wellness by monitoring your sleep patterns, record how many steps you take each day, determine your heart rate, and even measure your blood sugar levels.

Even cities make use of IoT by connecting sensors on infrastructure — such as transportation, power production, and water systems — to the Internet. These sensors respond to computer programs that control how they perform their jobs, including changing the timing of traffic lights, balancing power distribution, and adjusting water levels during droughts and floods.

Sensors in electronic circuits perform the same roles as senses in living creatures: They measure information about the world around them. But sensors don't do much by themselves. Sensors require a computer program to understand and "do something" with the information they measure in the same way that your senses (your eyes, ears, and nose) need your brain to make meaning of the information they take in.

The micro:bit board is a simple electronics board with built-in sensors: pushbuttons, a light sensor, a thermometer, a magnetometer (compass), and an accelerometer. See Chapter 2 for additional information on each of these sensors.

The pins can also measure whether or not a circuit (of which the micro:bit board is a component) is complete — in other words, whether electricity is running through the circuit. In MakeCode for micro:bit, the Input category of commands is used to measure information about the micro:bit sensors. You write the code so that the events and conditionals can respond to sensor readings — just like in the Light Theremin project.

Transfer Your Program to the micro:bit

When your code works the way you want it to, you can transfer it to a physical micro:bit. For details on transferring programs to the micro:bit, see Chapter 2.

Continue powering the micro:bit from your computer or attach the portable battery pack to the micro:bit. Use an alligator clip to connect Pin 0 of the micro:bit to the tip of the headphone jack. Use another alligator clip to connect the Ground pin of the micro:bit to the base of the headphone jack. Refer to Figure 14-1.

Put on your headphones, and then change the quantity of light falling on the LED grid. You should hear different notes playing through the headphones as you change the light level.

Share Your Program with the World

If you want, you can share your micro:bit program with others. Set the status of your program to Share, and then copy and paste the link to your project anywhere you want to share it. See Chapter 19 for details on sharing your programs.

Enhance Your Toy

Consider enhancing your Light Theremin gadget with new features:

- **Additional sound levels:** Add more conditionals to create new sound levels and associated sounds. Can you create an entire scale?

- **Button key shift:** Change the key from C major to a different music key by writing new code. Add an on button a pressed event and create a new conditional sieve that uses a new chord progression such as F major.

- **Speaker hardware:** Instead of connecting your micro:bit to headphones, connect it to a speaker. Inexpensive speakers for electronics projects can be purchased online or at hobby shops. Just connect the alligator clips to the lead wires from the speaker and you'll have a theremin everyone can hear, so you can play for an audience!

Part 5
Lists, Loops, and Logic

In this part you'll . . .

- Code simple lists (arrays)

- Create an easy sort algorithm of the bucket sort type

- Build a simple search algorithm to identify palindromes

- Use logical operators and broadcasting to build a matchup toy

Magic 8-Ball

The classic Magic 8-Ball is a fun retro toy that gives a randomly chosen answer to a question the user asks. Magic 8-Ball can give 20 answers, with some answers positive ("Big Yes!"), some negative (No Way), and some neutral ("Answer is Cloudy"). The user asks a question, jiggles the ball, and an answer appears!

In this project, you create your own Magic 8-Ball using MakeCode for micro:bit. You first code a list of answers using a new type of variable (called a *list variable,* or *an array variable*). Then you code the micro:bit to respond to a shake by scrolling a randomly chosen answer across the screen. If you want, you can transfer your code to a real micro:bit, and if you're really ambitious, you can design and 3D-print a Magic 8-Ball shell for your toy!

https://commons.wikimedia.org/wiki/File:Magic_8_Ball_-_Instrument_Of_Evil%3F_(2426454804).jpg

Brainstorm

Your MakeCode program can scroll predictions as part of any toy you create. You can just play with your program on the computer screen, or you can transfer your code to a micro:bit and build a toy around the electronics board. That toy can be made of any craft materials you have access to, from cardboard and Styrofoam to wood and 3D filament.

Also, your toy can look any way you want — it doesn't need to look like a Magic 8-Ball. You can create any device to display text predictions for your user. What will you design? A crystal ball? A Zoltar genie machine? A fortune cookie? A closeup of Yoda's head? Tea leaves in a cup of hot tea? You can also write the predictions any way you want, but consider using a combination of "yes," "no," and "maybe" predictions. Figure 15-1 shows the 3D design I created in Tinkercad and then 3D-printed!

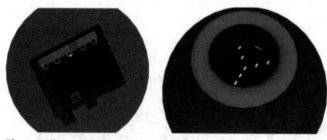

Figure 15-1

Start a New Project

Begin creating your Magic 8-Ball toy by starting a new project as follows:

1. Open MakeCode for micro:bit at https://makecode.microbit.org.

2. On the micro:bit home page, click the big New Project button in the middle of the screen.

A new project opens and displays the workspace.

3. Name your project by typing a name in the Project Name field at the bottom of the micro:bit interface.

4. Click the Save button next to the Project Name field to save your project.

Code on start

You write your Magic 8-Ball code in the workspace. You can work in Blocks mode or JavaScript text mode.

The example uses code written in Blocks mode to create a list variable containing three predictions. The on start event is the starting point for the MakeCode program you will write for the Magic 8-Ball. Follow these steps:

1. Keep the on start command in the workspace. Drag the forever command back to the command area, or else click it and press the Delete key on your keyboard.

2. In the Variables category of commands, click the Make a Variable button. In the dialog box that opens, type predictions (see Figure 15-2) and click OK.

   The predictions variable is now added to your available variables.

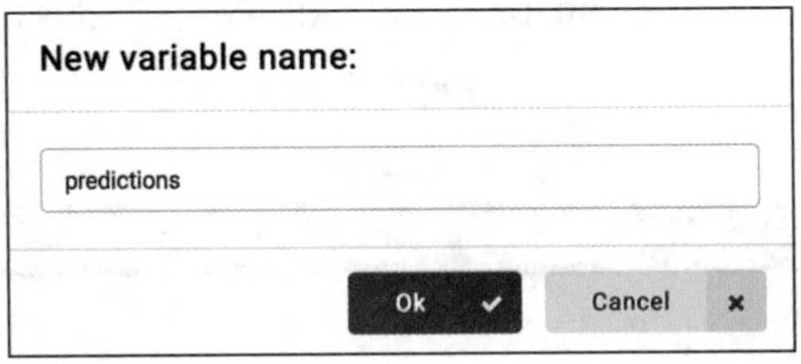

New variable name:

predictions

Ok ✔   Cancel ✗

Figure 15-2

3. Open the Advanced commands, select the Array category of commands, and drag a `set text list to` command to the workspace. Place this command inside the `on start` command. Press the small down arrow at `text list` and select `predictions` from the drop-down menu.

4. Build your list (array) of predictions by typing one prediction into each field of the array.

   You don't need to type the quotes in each prediction — MakeCode adds them automatically to any string you type in a field. (For details on working with strings, see Chapter 10.)

   a. In the first field, replace the a by typing a prediction such as `BIG YES!`.

   b. In the second field, replace the b by typing a prediction such as `NO WAY`.

   c. In the third field, replace the c by typing a prediction such as `ANSWER IS CLOUDY`.

   If you want to add more predictions, add new fields for them by pressing the plus (+) button. Remove unwanted fields from the end of the list (array) by pressing the minus (–) button.

Your complete `on start` code should look like Figure 15-3. When the micro:bit program starts executing, it sets the list variable, `predictions`, to all the string values you typed. In this example, the value of `predictions` at position 0 is `"BIG YES!"` and the value of `predictions` at position 2 is `"ANSWER IS CLOUDY."`

Figure 15-3

TECHNICAL STUFF

In MakeCode — and most programming languages — you start counting list (array) positions at 0. You stop counting list positions at the last item in the list. The last item in the list is at a position that is one less than the number of items in the list. In the example, three items are in the list, but the last item is at position 2.

Simple Lists (Arrays)

A *list* is a variable that represents a group of items stored together in a certain order. *Array* is another word for list. (There are some technical differences between the two, but the explanation of those differences is beyond the scope of this book.) Items in a list (array) are usually called *elements.* Many different types of elements are available, such as numbers, strings, and even other lists.

Programming languages use lists to store related information in some way. For example, a grocery list has items such as broccoli, cheese, and juice boxes. A teacher might have a list of scores earned by students on a test. A school might have a list of classrooms, and for each classroom, and a list of students in that classroom (this is a "list of lists"). For all practical purposes, your list can be as long as you want it to be.

In a block programming language, you name a list in the same way you do any variable, such as groceries, predictions, scores. In a text-based programming language, you might use additional symbols, such as square brackets to show that the variable is a list. Lists usually order their elements starting at the number 0 and counting up to the last element. (But it's important to note that Scratch starts numbering its list elements at 1.) This way, your program can identity the value of an element by its position in the array.

Parallel lists (arrays) are two or more lists that have related information. For example, a teacher might have these arrays:

```
String [] students = ["Alice", "Benito", "Carol", "Dan"];
int [] scores = [87, 93, 94, 80];
```

The value of students[0] is "Alice" and the value of scores[0] is 87. For this classroom of students, the teacher has set student number 0 to Alice, so we know that Alice's score on the test is 87.

Note that although the students[] array has four students, the last student in the list is at position 3. This is because you start counting the positions in the array at 0, not 1. So the value of students[3] is "Dan" and the value of scores[3] is 80. See Chapter 16 to for an additional project on lists.

Code on shake

The user shakes the micro:bit to reveal a prediction. When the user shakes the micro:bit, the accelerometer sensor detects the movement and runs the code associated with the on shake event. (See Chapter 3 and the sidebar on IoT and sensors in Chapter 14 for additional information on micro:bit sensors.) Write this code by following these steps:

1. From the Input category, drag the on shake command to the workspace.

2. In the Basic category of commands, drag the show string command to the workspace and attach it inside the on shake command.

3. Open the Advanced commands, select the Array category of commands, and drag the list get value at command to the workspace.

4. Place the list get value at command in the field of the show string command. Press the small down arrow at list and select predictions from the drop-down menu.

5. From the Math commands, drag the pick random command to the workspace and place it inside the predictions get value at field.

6. Set the range of value for `pick random` by typing numbers in the empty fields. Type 0 in the first field, which is the position value of the first item in your array.

The value of the second field depends on the position of the last item in your array. In my example, I have three predictions, so the range of my `pick random` is 0 to 2 (the three predictions are at position 0, position 1, and position 2 in my array). The second field of your `pick random` has a value of *one less* than the number of items in your array.

Your complete on `shake` code should looks like Figure 15-4.

Figure 15-4

When the user shakes the micro:bit, its accelerometer measures motion and triggers the execution of the code block at the on `shake` event. The on `shake` event causes a randomly selected prediction string to be scrolled across the LEDs of the mico:bit. Figure 15-5 shows the micro:bit simulator scrolling a prediction, letter by letter.

The complete code in JavaScript follows:

```
let predictions: string[] = []
predictions = ["BIG YES!", "NO WAY", "ANSWER IS CLOUDY"]
input.onGesture(Gesture.Shake, function () {
    basic.showString(predictions[Math.randomRange(0, 2)])
})
```

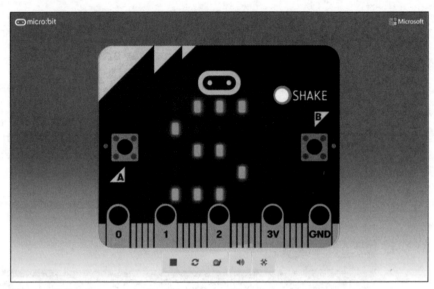

Figure 15-5

TECHNICAL
STUFF

MakeCode might place the line showing the string values in the `predictions` array below the event handler (`input.onGesture()`). However, when writing the text-based code, you should write the code as shown here. The standard way of organizing JavaScript code is to place the variable assignments before the event handlers.

Save, Test, and Debug Your Program

Click the Save button at the bottom of the screen to save your program. The program is saved in the cloud and also as a micro:bit .hex file in your Downloads folder.

You test your program in the on-screen simulator by clicking the Shake button (which simulates shaking the micro:bit). Each click should show a prediction from your `predictions` array. The letters in the prediction scroll by, one letter at a time.

Fix any bugs to ensure that your Magic 8-Ball toy works the way you want it to. (See the section in Chapter 3 on debugging micro:bit programs.)

Transfer Your Program to the micro:bit

After you test and debug your code, you can transfer it to a physical micro:bit. For details on transferring programs to the micro:bit, see Chapter 2. After the program is on the micro:bit, you can detach the board from your computer's USB port. Attach the optional battery pack to use the micro:bit and your Magic 8-Ball toy away from the computer.

Share Your Program with the World

You can share your MakeCode for micro:bit program with others. Set the status of your program to Share, and then copy and paste the link to your project anywhere you want to share it. See Chapter 19 for details on sharing your programs.

Enhance Your Toy

Consider enhancing your Magic 8-Ball toy with new features:

✏ **Add predictions associated with acceleration changes:** Right now, a random prediction of any type is selected from the array in response to on shake. You can measure the direction of motion when the micro:bit is shaken and associate a prediction type with the direction of motion.

For example, you can make positive responses appear when the 8-Ball is shaken along the x-axis, neutral responses for y-axis motion, and negative responses for z-axis motion. That way, you can secretly control the types of responses you get, making it appear that you're truly magical! You'll need to create three arrays to replace your original array, with each array featuring a response type: positive, neutral, or negative. Then you'll need to create some if-then conditionals to display one of those response types according to the direction and measure of the micro:bit's accelerometer values. To learn more about measuring accelerometer values, refer to the micro:bit online documentation at `https://makecode.` `microbit.org/reference/input/acceleration`.

- ✔ **Create a Magic 8-Ball shell to house the micro:bit:** Check out the sidebar on making a cool container for your toy! You can use free design software such as Tinkercad to design the 8-Ball shell. Then you can use a 3D printer (or send your design to a company that does 3D printing) to fabricate your design. I bought some black filament and printed mine on a FlashForge Finder 3D printer. Then I placed my micro:bit and battery pack inside and — voila! — I have my own, custom-made 8-Ball.

TIP

If you choose to print your own 3D designs, a FlashForge Finder single-filament 3D printer runs about $300, and a daVinci Color mini 3D printer costs a whopping $1600. Filament costs approximately $30 per roll (it lasts a long time). If you choose to send out your 3D design for printing, plan on paying around $10 to $30 per pound, depending on the filament materials you request.

eToys

You've probably noticed many devices named i*Something* or e*Something* these days. The *i* stands for *Internet* and the *e* stands for *electronic.* Devices named i*Something,* such as smart watches and mobile phones, use the Internet in some way. Devices named e*Something* include all sorts of toys that use electronic circuitry in them. Everything from remote-controlled cars to the old-school game of Operation can be considered an eToy.

The micro:bit board can serve as electronics component of a toy, turning it into an eToy. Sensors on the micro:bit can make measurements about its environment. Onboard memory allows it to store code that provides instructions to the device. And external batteries provide the power needed to operate it! But the micro:bit itself is just an electronics board, so as an eToys designer, you need to think about the fancy and fun physical parts you'll need to add to make your eToy say, "Play with me!"

For the Magic 8-Ball toy, you can create a real eToy by making plastic shell and adding the coded micro:bit board and battery pack to it. You can use all sorts of materials to make the shell, from Styrofoam to a Nerf ball to Play-Doh. Another option is to design a shell in a 3D design program such as Tinkercad (www.tinkercad.com/) and then print it using a 3D printer.

I created a design at www.tinkercad.com/things/8QdTqoXzVnl-8-ball-with-microbit/edit. I first found a micro:bit created and shared in Tinkercad, and then I designed my 8-ball shell around the micro:bit design. You can use this design, "tinkering" with it to make it your own or creating something new. Keep in mind, though, that many 3D printers print in a single filament color, so even if you make your design with lots of colors, it will print in the one color loaded into the 3D printer. I used a FlashForge Finder, but you can find many other 3D printers. And if you don't have a 3D printer, you can send your saved 3D design (as an .stl or .obj file) to a company that will print it for you for a small fee (search online for *3D printing companies*). After you have your shell in hand, just pop in the micro:bit and battery pack (add a bit of tape to hold these in place) and shake to see a prediction in your eToy!

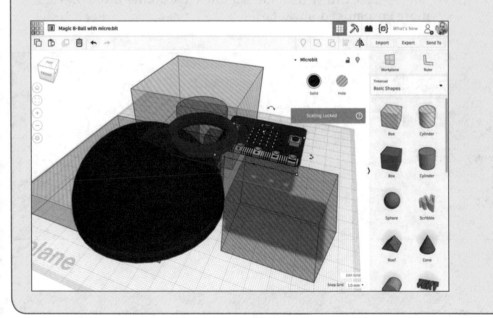

16

Sock Sort

Sorting socks on laundry day is a necessary — but oh so boring! — job. If you don't *sort*, or separate, them by color, your red socks and your white socks will produce a new batch of pink socks when they exit the washing machine. Sorting is an important job in programming, too! You start with a list of items, then you decide how you want to group them: by color, by size, alphabetically, or by some other feature. Next you take each item off your list and add it to one of the new lists, where it's grouped with items that have similar features.

In the Sock Sort project, you work in Scratch to create a pile of mixed-up socks containing red socks and white socks. Then you code a sorting algorithm to separate the socks into two piles. When writing your code, each pile will be a special type of variable called a *list* (or an *array*) — a variable which can contain more than one item. By creating a program that sorts socks, you're learning the general strategy of coding a *bucket sort* — a sort in which you separate list items into two (or more) organized buckets.

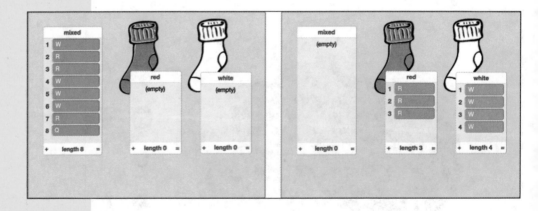

Brainstorm

The figures on the chapter's first page show the Sock Sort app — but your sorting app doesn't have to feature socks. What about sorting dogs (Corgi, Beagle, Chihuahua) by breed (herding, hound, toy)? Or family members by age (kids, teens, adults)? You can create any list of items, and you can write an algorithm to sort that list into category lists you create. You can have as many category lists as you want, but try just two or three to start.

Start a New Project

Begin creating your Sock Sort program by starting a new project:

1. Open Scratch at `https://scratch.mit.edu`. If prompted, enable Flash to run Scratch. Log in to the account you created to use Scratch (see Chapter 2).

2. On the Scratch home page, select Create. Or if you're already working in Scratch, choose File ➪ New from the menu bar.

   A new project opens.

3. Name your program by typing a name in the Project Name field at the top of the Scratch interface.

4. Cut (delete) Scratch Cat from the project by clicking or tapping the X in the Scratch Cat icon.

   You can find the icon in the Sprite area in the lower-right corner of the Scratch interface.

Add a Backdrop

The *backdrop* is the background color or image that fills the screen of your app. Add a backdrop as follows:

1. At the Stage, hover over on the Choose a Backdrop icon. Click Paint from the pop-up menu.

   The backdrop editor opens on the Backdrops tab. The default costume name for this backdrop is backdrop1. You can leave this name or change it.

2. Click the Convert to Bitmap button.

3. Select a Fill color.

   I selected yellow.

4. Click the paint bucket icon and then click the empty backdrop (the checkerboard region) to fill the backdrop with your selected color.

   Figure 16-1 shows the finished backdrop.

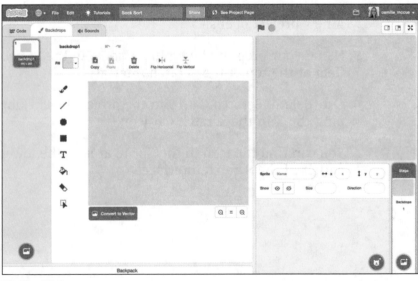

Figure 16-1

Add Red and White Sock Sprites

The Sock Sort app features two sprites, redSock for red socks and whiteSock for white socks. Each sprite is placed beside its associated list. These sprites exist only to give the app user visual cues as to where each list is located. You write code not on the sprites but on the stage.

Search online to find a red sock and a white sock that you like. Save the images on your computer where you can find them later. You may need to edit the images to remove any background color. (See Chapter 2 for details on image editing.)

TIP

Try to save thumbnail-sized versions of images for your sprites. Smaller images result in better-looking sprites.

Then follow these steps to add your saved images as sprites:

1. In the Sprite area of the Scratch interface, hover over the Choose a Sprite icon and choose Upload from the pop-up menu.

2. Navigate to the image you previously saved for the red sock. Select the image and click or tap the Choose button.

   A sprite appears on the stage, wearing the red sock costume. The name of the sprite is whatever name you used when previously saving the image. My sprite is named redSock.

3. If you want to rename the sprite, type a new name in the sprite attributes area.

4. In the sprite attributes area, type a new size for redSock.

   The size depends on how large you want the sock to appear in the scene. As shown in Figure 16-2, I typed a size of 40.

5. Duplicate the red sock sprite by Ctrl-clicking (Mac) or right-clicking (Windows) the sprite icon and selecting Duplicate from the pop-up menu.

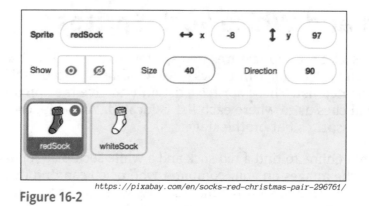

https://pixabay.com/en/socks-red-christmas-pair-296761/

Figure 16-2

6. Go to the Costumes tab for the duplicate sprite and edit its costume to make it a white sock. You can either upload the white sock image you saved or paint the existing costume white.

7. Name the sprite whiteSock in the sprite area.

Add Mixed, Red, and White Lists

In Scratch, a list consists of items, in order, that can be identified by their positions in the list. The first item is at position 1, and you can count how many items are on any list. You can ask the user to add or remove list items. You can also code your program to add or remove list items.

In Sock Sort, you create three lists:

✔ mixed is the main list, where the user types a list of sock colors, R or r (for red), and W or w (for white).

✔ red is the list where red socks are added when they're removed from mixed.

✔ white is the list where white socks are added when they're removed from mixed.

TECHNICAL STUFF

Scratch reads the uppercase and lowercase version of a letter the same way. So the letter A is the same as the letter a. However, most programming languages read uppercase and lowercase as different letters.

REMEMBER

The socks sprites don't serve a function in the coding. They are there only for decoration.

Follow these steps to create the lists on the Stage:

1. Click or tap the Stage icon to select the main stage.

2. On the Code tab of the Scratch interface, select the Variables icon.

3. Click or tap the Make a List button.

   A New List dialog box opens.

4. In the New List Name field, type a name for the list of mixed-up sock colors.

   I named the list mixed, as shown in Figure 16-3.

New List   ✕
New list name:
mixed
This variable will be available to all sprites.
More Options ▼
Cancel   OK

Figure 16-3

5. Click or tap the OK button.

   The mixed list name and the commands associated with the list now appear with the list commands. See Figure 16-4.

6. Repeat Steps 3 through 5 to create a list named red and a list name white.

   The red list name, the white list name, and the commands associated with these lists now appear with the list commands. See Figure 16-4.

Variables

Make a Variable
Make a List
✓ mixed
✓ red
✓ white

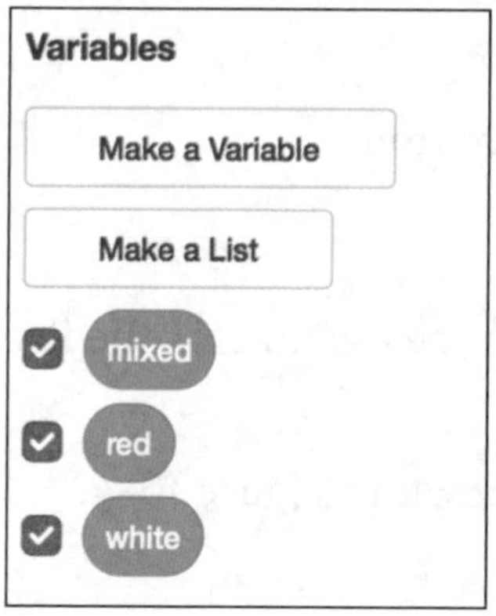

Figure 16-4

7. Click and drag each list to move it where you want it on the Stage.

   Refer to the figures on the chapter's first page to see the placement of the lists.

8. If you want to resize a list, click and drag its corner.

Code the Green Flag (Create List)

You'll write code so that when the user clicks or taps the green flag, the program starts. The program will call a code block that clears all items from all lists; you write this block later.

The program then asks the user for the color of the sock (red or white). The user types R or W (or anything he or she wants) and presses the Enter (Return) key after each entry. R or W (or whatever the user typed) is then added to the `mixed` list. The user keeps adding sock colors.

When the user has finished adding to the list, he or she types Q or q (for quit) and presses the Enter (Return) key. The Q (or q) is added to the list as the final item and the green flag code stops executing. Figure 16-5 shows the flowchart of the green flag code.

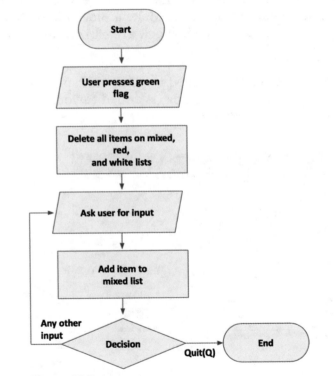

Figure 16-5

Follow these steps to write the green flag code as shown in Figure 16-6:

1. Click the Stage icon to select the main stage.

2. In the Code tab of the Scratch interface, select the Events category. Drag the when green flag clicked command to the Code workspace.

   The code block you will attach to this event will run when the green flag is clicked on a computer or tapped on a tablet.

3. Select the My Blocks icon. Click the Make a Block button to create a new code block. In the Make a Block dialog box that appears, name this new code block clearLists and click OK (see Figure 16-6).

   The new block header is added to your workspace, and the new command tile, clearLists, is added to your commands in the My Blocks category.

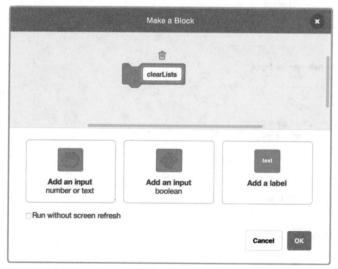

Figure 16-6

4. From the My Blocks category, drag your new clearLists command to the Code workspace, and attach it to the previous command.

When this command runs, it calls the `clearLists` code block (which you build in the next section) to clear all three lists of any items.

5. Select the Control icon and drag the `repeat until` command to the Code workspace. Attach it to the previous command. Continue building this command as follows:

   a. From the Operators category, drag an = command and place it inside the empty field of the `repeat until` command.

   b. From the Sensing category, drag an `answer` command to the Code workspace, and place it inside the first field of the = command.

   c. Type the letter Q in the second field of the = command.

   The `repeat until answer = Q` command now looks like this:

   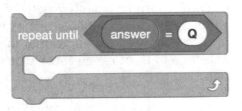

   The commands in this `repeat until` loop will be executed until the user inputs a Q (or q).

6. From the Sensing category, drag an `ask and wait` command to the Code workspace, and attach it inside the `repeat until` loop. In the field, type the input request, such as GIVE ME A SOCK, R OR W.

   This `ask` command is inside the `repeat until` loop and serves the purpose of prompting the user over and over for new input to the `mixed` list.

7. From the Variables category, drag an add to list command inside the repeat until command, attaching it to the ask command. Continue building this command as follows:

a. From the Sensing category, drag out an answer command and place it inside the add to list command.

b. Click the small arrow on the list part of the command and select mixed from the menu (the command might already display this).

The add answer to mixed command now looks like this:

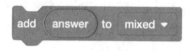

This command adds whatever the user typed as input to the mixed list. Because it is inside the repeat until loop, this add command executes as long as the loop continues. When the user enters a Q (or q), the Q (or q) input is added as the final item in the mixed list. Then the repeat until loop stops executing because answer = Q. (See Chapter 1 for additional information on how a program selects a path of execution.) This completes the repeat until loop.

The entire green flag code block is now complete. See Figure 16-7.

Figure 16-7

The program doesn't prevent the user from typing any other letter — someone could type P for pink, Y for yellow, or anything! But note that the program won't stop running the `repeat until` loop until the user types Q or q.

Code the `clearLists` Block

You created a `clearLists` code block header and command tile. Now it's time to write the code for that block. The `clearLists` code block deletes all the items in the `mixed`, `red`, and `white` lists, so that the user starts fresh with each run of the program.

Write the code for the `clearLists` code block as follows:

1. Work at the `define clearLists` code block header in the workspace.

2. From the Variables commands, drag a `delete all of list` command to the Code workspace, and attach it to the code block header. Click the small arrow on the `list` part of the command and select `mixed` from the menu (the command might already display this).

   The command now reads `delete all of mixed`.

3. Repeat Step 2 two more times, changing the new commands to read `delete all of red` and `delete all of white`, respectively.

The `define clearLists` code block is now complete, as shown in Figure 16-8.

When the `clearLists` command is run in the Stage's green flag code, it *calls to* the `define clearLists` code block to know what commands to execute.

Figure 16-8

Code the Sorting Process

Now you write code so that when the user presses the S (or s) key, the associated program sorts the mixed list into two lists, red and white. This code block is separate from the green flag code block.

Figure 16-9 shows the flowchart of the sorting algorithm. When the user presses S (or s), the code reads Item 1 in the mixed list:

- If the item is R (or r), the item is added to the red list.

- If the item is W (or w), the item is added to the white list.

- If the item is neither R (r) nor W(w), it is not added to any list.

Then Item 1 is deleted from the mixed list. The process is repeated until the mixed list has no more items, at which point the program stops.

The result is an empty mixed list, a red list displaying all the red socks, and a white list displaying all the white socks. Note that if a sock doesn't match R or W (or r or w), it is not added to either list but it is still deleted from mixed. It is ignored, or lost, as often happens with socks!

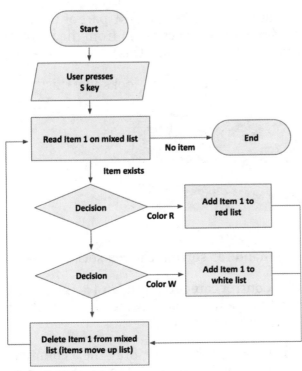

Figure 16-9

Follow these steps to write the s key code:

1. Click the Stage icon to write code for the main stage.

2. Working on the Code tab of the Scratch interface, select the Events category.

3. Drag the when key pressed command to the code workspace. Change the key to s (for sort).

   The code block you will be attaching to this event will run when the S or s key is pressed on a computer or tapped on a tablet.

4. Select the Control icon and drag a repeat command to the code workspace. Attach it to the previous command. Make this command display repeat length of mixed as follows:

   a. From the Variables category, drag the length of list command into the field of the repeat command.

b. Click the small arrow on the `list` part of the `length of list` command and select `mixed` from the menu (the command might already display this).

When complete, this command looks like this:

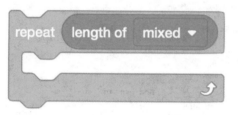

5. Build a command for sorting the red socks.

a. From the Control category, drag an `if-then` conditional command to the workspace. Attach it inside the `repeat length of mixed` command.

b. From the Operators category, drag the `=` command and place it inside the condition of the `if-then` command.

c. From the Variables category, drag the `item 1 of list` command to the Code workspace, and place it inside the first field of the `=` command. Press the small arrow on the list part of the command and select `mixed` from the menu (the command might already display this). In the second field of the `=` command, type the letter R.

d. From the Variables category, drag an `add thing to list` command inside the `if-then` command.

This serves as the consequence of the conditional command.

e. Drag an `item 1 of mixed` command to the Code workspace, and place it inside the first field of the `add thing to list` command (replacing `thing`). Set the end of the command by pressing the small arrow and selecting `red` from the menu.

When complete, this command looks like this:

6. Repeat Step 5 to build an additional `if-then` command for sorting the white socks. Attach this conditional to the previous `if-then` command, inside the `repeat` loop.

   Your new command should be `if item 1 of mixed = W then add item 1 of mixed to white`.

7. From the Variables category, drag an `delete 1 of list` command inside the `repeat` loop, following the previous `if-then` command. Click the small arrow on the `list` part of the command and select `mixed` from the menu (the command might already display this).

The S code block is now complete. Figure 16-10 shows the finished block.

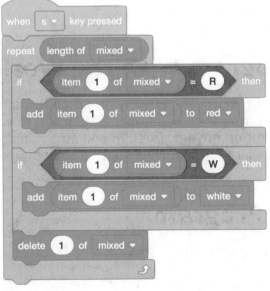

Figure 16-10

TECHNICAL STUFF

The program doesn't account for lost socks. A sock that isn't red or white is removed from the `mixed` list but it isn't sorted (added to some other list). When writing programs, try all the ways your users will likely interact with your program and then make sure that your program will still run. Better yet, create a way of getting around the problems. For example, you could create a third list — an "everything else" list — and use an `if-then-else` conditional to catch items that don't end up in the `red` or `white` list. Or write code to prevent users from typing an illegal sock color in the first place! (See the "Enhance Your Program" section for details.)

Save, Test, and Debug Your Program

As you work, Scratch automatically saves your program in the cloud, so you don't have to take any special actions to save your work.

Test your program and fix any bugs to ensure that it works the way you want it to. Type a variety of sock colors to create your `mixed` list, and then sort the list to see it produce your `red` and `white` lists. (Also see the information in Chapter 3 on debugging Scratch programs.)

Share Your Program with the World

After your program operates perfectly, it's time to share it! Set the status of your program to Share, and then add to your project page a description of your program and directions on how to run it. See Chapter 19 for details on sharing your programs.

Enhance Your Program

Consider enhancing your Sock Sort with new features:

✏ **New list:** Add a new sprite and a new list to catch the other socks that don't get sorted into the `red` and `white` buckets.

You will need to change your if-then code structure to an if-elseif-else structure, with the else catching all the items that aren't sent to the red or white list.

↙ **User warning:** To prevent other items from being added to your mixed list, you can block users from adding anything other than R, W, or Q. Just add an if-then-else conditional to your green flag code: if the user answer is R or W or Q, then the input is allowed, else the user receives a warning message and the answer is not added to the mixed list. (See Chapter 18 for more information on working with logical operators such as the or operator.)

Sorting Algorithms

Sorting is one of the most common processes that computer programs perform. Items can be sorted in a variety of ways depending on the type of item. Socks, M&M candies, and Hot Wheels cars can be grouped according to category (for example, color), so these objects are often sorted using a *bucket sort* — the type of sort in this project. Bucket sorts can be used also to separate numbers. Using modular math, you can separate even numbers from odd numbers. Or using a cutoff, such as a minimum height value for riding a roller coaster, visitors at an amusement park are separated into two buckets: those who are tall enough to go on a ride and those who are not tall enough.

Numbers of all types can also be sorted by order, such as from small to large or from large to small. Student scores on a test can be sorted by order to look at the distribution of student performance on the test. Salaries in a company can be sorted to look at the range of paychecks from the lowest paid worker to the highest paid worker. Weights of passengers who will be flying in a small airplane can also be sorted by order so that the pilot can easily arrange the passengers to balance the total weight on the left and right sides of the plane.

Words can be sorted alphabetically by comparing the first letter of each word, then the second letter of each word, and so on, arranging the words in order from A to Z. A new word can be added to the alphabetized list by comparing the new word to those already in the list and then moving it to its correct location.

You can use many different programming techniques for sorting a list. In one type of sort called a *selection sort*, the code runs through all the items in a list, then pulls out a selected item (such as the smallest number) and puts it in a new list. The process repeats over and over until a new, sorted list is produced.

In another type of sort called a *bubble sort,* two items are compared. If the items are in order, they are left alone. If they are not in order, the items are switched. Imagine telling a roomful of students to stand against a wall, and then ordering them by height by looking at each pair and switching the order if needed. The process repeats over and over, in place, until the original list is sorted.

You have already worked with the bucket sort: You remove items one at a time from a master list and add each item to a specialized list (or else throw out the item). You repeat the process over and over until the master list is empty.

Different sort algorithms require different amounts of time to complete, depending on the lists items and how organized they were before the sort. The time requirement matters to computer programmers who need to sort billions of items in a short period of time!

After the items are sorted, programmers often want to search the sorted list for a certain item. You learn more about searching in Chapter 17.

One of my favorite sorting games, *Sock Works,* features a character named Pajama Sam, who sorts his socks in a giant factory. My kids loved helping Sam control the direction and speed of conveyor belts and the positioning of gates to move differently colored socks into their matching color buckets!

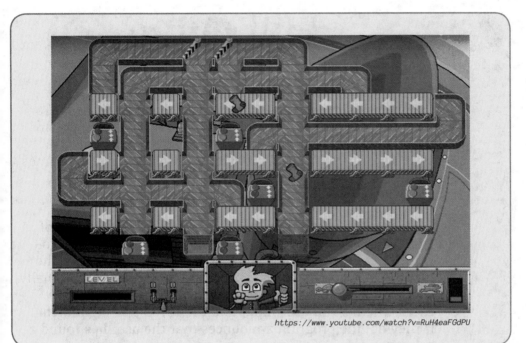

https://www.youtube.com/watch?v=RuH4eaFGdPU

Evil Olive

In this project, you build a fun program in App Lab that helps users find palindromes. A *palindrome* is a word or a number that is the same forward and backward. The word *racecar* and the number 12321 are palindromes. Once you start looking, you'll find many other interesting palindromes, including the superhero TACO CAT and her arch nemesis, EVIL OLIVE (without the spaces, of course!).

To code your palindrome-checker, you'll use a new type of loop, called a *for loop.* Your program will consist of an algorithm that reads a string input by a user, and then uses the for loop to move letter-by-letter, reversing the string. Finally, you'll code a Boolean operator (see Chapters 13 and 14) to check whether the user input and the reverse string match. If they do, the program announces that the user has found a palindrome!

https://pixabay.com/en/bokeh-pink-background-1958563/

Brainstorm

You can create any type of interface for your palindrome-checking app. I called mine Evil Olive because *EVILOLIVE* is a cool palindrome and it allowed me to create an angry-looking (yet funny) character who evaluates user input. You can design your character and interface any way you want. As shown in the left figure on the chapter's first page, the end user is given an empty field in which to type a word or a number — any string to be checked. (See Chapter 10 for an introduction to strings.) The center image shows the output when the user tries a word that is not a palindrome. The right image shows the output when the user tries a word that is a palindrome.

Start a New Project

Begin creating your Evil Olive app by starting a new project as follows:

1. Open App Lab at https://code.org/educate/applab. Log in to the account you created to use App Lab (see Chapter 2).

2. Under the App Lab heading, click the Try it Out button.

3. Name your program by clicking the Rename button and then typing a name in the Project Name field at the top of the App Lab interface.

4. Click the Save button.

Add a Background Image to the Screen

Your app will consist of one screen, named screen1 by default. Spice up the color of screen1 by adding a background image to it. Search online to find an image. I searched for pink background.

Save the image on your computer, in a location where you can find it later. When you save the image, you might want to change its name to something easy to understand. Also, you might need to edit the image, such as rotating it from landscape to portrait orientation. (See Chapter 2 for details on image editing.)

Now follow these steps to add your saved background image to screen1:

1. Switch to the Design mode of App Lab.

2. On the Properties tab of the workspace, locate the Image field. Click the Choose link to choose an image to be displayed on the background of the display.

   The Choose Assets dialog box opens.

3. Click the Upload File button. Navigate to and select the background image file you found and saved previously. Then click the Choose button.

   The image file appears in the Choose Assets dialog box. I uploaded the pink_background.jpg image file.

4. In the Choose Assets dialog box, click the Choose button next to the image asset you just uploaded.

   The background changes to the image. Refer to the figures on the chapter's first page to see the background on the app simulator display.

Add an Instruction Label

The display of screen1 should provide simple instructions so that the user knows how to use the app. Add an instruction label as follows:

1. Continue working in the Design mode of App Lab.

2. In the Design toolbox, drag the Label icon and position it near the top left of the app display.

3. On the Properties tab of the workspace, change the attributes of the label as follows:

   - ID: Rename the ID instructionsLabel.

   - Text: Type the instructions for your app, such as: **Type a word or number, and then click Evil Olive to find out if it is a palindrome**.

   - Width (px): Increase the width of your label to something like 260 pixels (or more).

   - Height (px): Increase the height of your label to something like 70 pixels (or more).

   - x Position (px): No changes; you change the x position later by dragging the label into position.

   - y Position (px): No changes; you change the y position later by dragging the label into position.

   - Text Color: Leave it black.

   - Background Color: No changes.

   - Font Size (px): Type a new font size in the field or use the selection arrows to make the title the appropriate size for your app. I used a font size of 18.

   - Text Alignment: Click the selection arrows and choose Left.

4. Click and drag the label on your app to position it where you want.

   Refer to the figures on the chapter's first page to see the position of the instructions label on the app simulator display.

Add a Text Input Field

Next, create a text input field so that the user has a place to enter a word or number. Refer to the figures on the chapter's first page. Follow these instructions:

1. Remain working in Design mode. In the Design toolbox, drag the Text Input icon and position it below your instructions label.

2. On the Properties tab of the workspace, change the attributes of the text input as follows:

   - ID: Rename the ID to something representative of the text input field, such as input.

   - Placeholder: Leave blank.

   - Width (px): Set the width of your label to something like 260 pixels so that the user has room to type his or her word or number in the box.

   - Height (px): Set to 70 pixels.

   - x Position (px): No changes; you change the x position later by dragging the label into position.

   - y Position (px): No changes; you change the y position later by dragging the label into position.

   - Text Color: Leave it black.

   - Background Color: No changes.

   - Font Size (px): Type a new font size in the field or use the selection arrows to make the text input the appropriate size for your app. I made mine 20.

   - Text Alignment: Click the selection arrows and choose Center.

3. Click and drag the text input field on your app to position it where you want.

The text input field is complete.

Create and Add Evil Olive to the Screen

Now you'll add Evil Olive — or any other character you want — to the input screen. Search online to find an image you want, or draw one digitally. I searched for `evil olive`, but I didn't find anything I liked. So I used the simple shapes and colors in Google Slides to draw my own Evil Olive. I then removed the background and saved the image as a .png to use in my app. (See Chapter 2 for help on editing images.)

However you get your image, save it in a location where you can find it later — and make sure the name is something easy to understand.

Follow these instructions to add your character to the display:

1. Remain working in the Design mode of App Lab.

2. In the Design toolbox, drag the Image icon to the screen to create an image in your app. Position it where the character appears in the figures on the chapter's first page.

3. On the Properties tab of the workspace, change the attributes of the image as follows:

   • ID: Rename the ID of the image to the name of your character. To follow along with the example, type `evilOlive`.

   • Width (px): Set the width to any size that make sense in your app.

   • Height (px): Set the height to any size that make sense in your app.

   • x Position (px): No changes; you change the x position later by dragging the label into position.

- y Position (px): No changes; you change the y position later by dragging the label into position.

- Image: You upload an image in the next step.

- Fit Image: No changes.

4. On the Properties tab of the workspace, locate the Image field. Click the Choose link to choose an image to be displayed in the image placeholder.

   The Choose Assets dialog box opens.

5. Click the Upload File button. Navigate to and select the image file for the first candidate. Then click the Choose button.

   This image file is the file you found while brainstorming (for example, in a Google image search) or created previously and then saved. The image file appears in the Choose Assets dialog box. I uploaded the olive.png image file.

6. In the Choose Assets dialog box, click the Choose button next to the image asset you just uploaded.

   The image appears in your app.

TIP

Sometimes an image placeholder seems to vanish when working in Design mode of App Lab, especially before you've added an image to it. If this happens, just switch to Code mode, and then switch back to Design mode again — the image placeholder should reappear.

Add a Message Label to the Screen

When the user clicks or taps the image of Evil Olive, he or she triggers the execution of the code, which results in the display of the *"Palindrome!"* or *"Not a palindrome"* message.

Add the label as follows:

1. Remain working in the Design mode of App Lab. In the Design toolbox, drag the Label icon to the app display to create a new label on the display.

2. Click and drag the sizing tab at the corner of the label to resize it to the dimensions you want.

   Size the label so that it fits in the space next to your character, as if your character is stating its decision about whether the user input is a palindrome or not. See the figures on the chapter's first page.

3. On the Properties tab of the workspace, change only the following attributes:

   • ID: Rename the ID to messageLabel.

   • Font Size (px): Type a new font size; size 18 works well.

   You don't have to adjust any other properties for the message label.

Code the App

Now you need to write code so that the app performs all the steps to accept user input and checks if the input is a palindrome. Figure 17-1 is a flowchart that shows the structure of the code. (See Chapter 1 for details on flowcharting a program.)

To begin coding the app, first switch to Code mode. Then switch to JavaScript mode by clicking the </> Show Text button in the upper-right corner of the screen.

WARNING

Don't type the line numbers; these appear automatically and are not part of the program. The line numbers just keep track of where you are in the program, which is helpful when debugging.

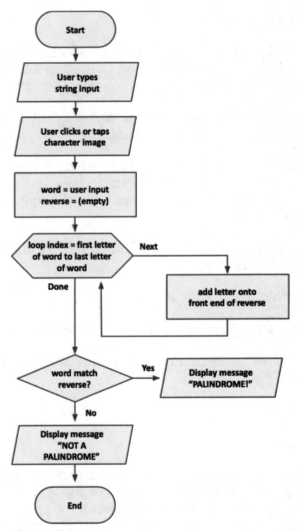

Figure 17-1

Following the model of the flow chart, construct the code as follows.

```
1  onEvent("evil0live", "click", function() {
2    var word = getText("input");
3    var reverse = "";
4    for (var i = 0; i < word.length; i++) {
5      reverse = word.charAt(i) + reverse;
6    }
```

```
 7    if (word == reverse) {
 8        setText("messageLabel", "Palindrome!");
 9    } else {
10        setText("messageLabel", "Not a palindrome");
11    }
12 });
```

Here's how the code works: Lines 1–3 set up the onEvent function and the two variables. (See Chapter 4 for help on event-driven programming.) The onEvent code runs when the evilOlive image is clicked or tapped. The word variable is created and assigned the string text that the user typed in the input text field. Also, the reverse variable is created and assigned an empty value (shown by the double quotation marks).

Lines 4–6 are the for-loop. The loop variable, i, starts at 0 (the position of the first letter in word) and ends before reaching word.length (it ends at the last letter of word), incrementing by i++ (one letter at a time). Each time the loop runs, the value of reverse is updated: It joins the current letter with the current value of reverse. This process reverses the letters in word to make reverse.

For example, suppose the user types *CAT*, which means word = CAT. Figure 17-2 shows the reversing process step-by-step, from just before entering the loop through loop execution.

Before loop		
word = CAT	reverse =	
Loop execution		
i = 0 word.charAt(0) = C	reverse = C +	= C
i = 1 word.charAt(1) = A	reverse = A + C	= AC
i = 2 word.charAt(2) = T	reverse = T + AC	= TAC

Figure 17-2

Lines 7–11 test whether word and reverse are the same. The code uses a Boolean operator, the equivalence sign (==), to perform the test. You also use an if-then-else conditional to tell what happens if the Boolean equivalence is true (Palindrome!) or else it is false (Not a palindrome).

TECHNICAL STUFF

The equals sign (=) is used to assign a value. The Boolean equivalence operator (==) is used to test if two items are equal, resulting in true or false.

Line 12 completes the program by ending the onEvent function. The **Palindrome!** or **Not a palindrome** message is displayed onscreen.

WARNING

In text-based coding, punctuation matters! Type a semicolon at the end of each complete command. And check that the opening and closing curly braces, quotation marks, and parentheses are in the right places.

TIP

This code is shown in text mode instead of block mode. When using App Lab to write JavaScript code, it's easier to type for loop statements in text mode. It's also easier to set up your Boolean condition (word == reverse) in text mode!

TIP

The variables word and reverse and the loop variable, i, are all local variables. Their values are relevant only inside the onEvent function. The ultimate goal of the function is figuring out whether the user's input is a palindrome or not. After the function tells the user this information, there is no reason to store or use these three variables.

Save, Test, and Debug Your App

As you work, App Lab automatically saves your program in the cloud.

Test your program by trying different words and numbers to find out whether they are palindromes. Fix any bugs to ensure that your program works the way you want it to. In text-based code, errors in punctuation and spelling are common. For help with testing and debugging your App Lab program, refer to Chapter 3.

TIP

Every now and then, you'll find that your App Lab code appears not to work, even though you have debugged it carefully and are certain the code is correct. When this happens, try refreshing the page in your web browser. My students and I find that this solves the problem most of the time!

Share Your App with the World

After your app operates as you want it to, set the status of your program to Share. See Chapter 19 for details on sharing apps you create in App Lab.

Enhance Your App

Add the following cool new features to your app:

- **Sound effects for different results:** Add fun sound effects, with a different effect playing for each outcome. Place the sound commands inside the if–then–else conditional. Play a sound in the style of "cheers and applause" when a palindrome is found. Play a "womp" or a "crash" or a similar sound when a palindrome is not found.

- **Reversal function:** Instead of checking for palindromes, why not convert the app to a word reverser! Just ask the user for input and then use the for loop to complete the reversal. Replace the if–then–else conditional with code that displays the reverse of the input. For example, input the name STANLEY and the app outputs the word YELNATS! (Stanley Yelnats is the name of the main character in the book *Holes.* Note that this makes the first and last name together a palindrome!)

For Loops

Many loop types allow you to repeat code in your programs. Common commands for coding repetition (see Chapter 1) are repeat loops, forever loops, and repeat until loops (see Chapter 8). The Evil Olive project features a more difficult but important loop type: the for loop.

Use the for loop when you know the number of loop cycles before starting the loop. Unlike a simple repeat loop, a for loop lets you control how you move through the loop, for instance, counting by twos or counting backwards.

A for loop has a loop counter and a header made of three parts: the starting value of the loop counter, the ending value, and the increment. The statements inside the curly braces after the header are executed the number of cycles specified by the loop. For example, in this for loop:

```
for (var i = 0; i < 5; i++) {
  //commands ;
}
```

The loop counter starts at 0 and goes to 4, incrementing by 1 on each cycle. So the loop counter takes on the values 0, 1, 2, 3, and 4. The loop executes a total of five times.

Most beginning programmers don't run into for loops until they've gained a little bit of skill in writing code. But learning how to work with a simple for loop will open the door to writing more powerful programs — such as Evil Olive!

Searching Algorithms

Searching is a task that computer programs perform all the time. *Searching* means looking for an item in a larger group of items. Searching can be performed on items that are sorted or unsorted. (See Chapter 16 to learn more about sorting.) For example, you search for a topic in a book by flipping through the *index,* a list of topics sorted alphabetically. Your search probably involves an *algorithm* such as locating the first letter of your word in the alphabetized first letters of the words in the index, then moving on to locating the second letter, and so on until you find your target word.

If you were to search for a topic in a list that is not alphabetized, you can guess that it could be a quick search (if you accidentally stumble on the topic near the beginning of the list) or a long search (if you have to check every item in the list for a match). Searching is usually done on sorted groups – otherwise, you would simply have to resort to checking every item in the group, one at a time, until (by luck) you find the item you seek!

Several different programming techniques exist for searching a sorted list. In one type of search, called a *linear* search, the code runs through all the items in a list, in order, until the target item is reached. To reverse the letters in a word, the Evil Olive project uses a linear search to move letter-by-letter through the word input by the user.

Another search, called a *binary* search, cuts the group of search objects in half, and then eliminates the half where the target is not located. This process is repeated over and over until the target item is finally located. When playing the game, "I'm thinking of a number from 1 to 100. Guess my number!" the guesser's best winning strategy is using a binary search algorithm.

Unlike a sort algorithm, when working with a search algorithm you don't have to account for every item in a group of items. After you locate the target item, there is no reason to do anything with the other items in the group. Also, different search algorithms require different amounts of time to complete. The search algorithm a coder chooses is based on things such as the type of items and the size of the group of items being searched.

Sushi Matchup

Sushi Matchup is a fun toy where the goal is to get matching pieces of sushi. The user presses a button to get three reels of sushi pictures spinning, and then clicks the spacebar to stop the reels. The toy tells whether the reels match.

Shutterstock image 418466866 by Rimma Z

This project pulls together many coding concepts you've learned previously in this book. It also adds new ideas, including logical operators and broadcasting. Working in Scratch, you start this project by putting your graphic design skills in action to create a toy interface featuring any theme you want. Then you write your code.

Coding your matchup toy lets you apply your know-how of event handlers to make the action begin when the user clicks the Start button and end when the user clicks a key. It also requires you to write code that *broadcasts,* or sends messages, among sprites to coordinate the actions of all the sprites onscreen. You can also use your knowledge of loops, sounds, and animation to make the reels of images appear to spin. Finally, you can write a new block (also known as a *function*) to figure out whether the user got a match. This new block of code uses *logical operators* to tell the user whether she matched two characters, three characters, or none.

Brainstorm

Your matchup toy can feature any characters and theme you want. You can make it a sports matchup, a celebrity matchup, a car matchup — anything! You can also get creative with the styling of the characters and the interface. I chose sushi because the characters have creative and interesting shapes. Figure 18-1 shows how my completed matchup toy looks.

Shutterstock image 418466866 by Rimma Z

Figure 18-1

To get started, I searched the web and found a great set of sushi clip art characters in a library, and then I purchased the collection (see the figure on the chapter's first page). But you can easily find free character clip art in the Scratch Library or Google Images. Or you can draw your own characters.

Also, I drew the toy interface on the background by using the drawing tools in Scratch. But you can use any program you want to draw and save your interface, and then import it to Scratch. The choices are endless.

Start a New Project

Begin creating your Sushi Matchup program by starting a new project:

1. Open Scratch at `https://scratch.mit.edu`. If prompted, enable Flash to run Scratch. Log in to the account you created to use Scratch (see Chapter 2).

2. On the Scratch home page, select Create. Or if you're already working in Scratch, choose File ⇨ New from the menu bar.

3. Name your program by typing a name in the Project Name field at the top of the Scratch interface.

4. Cut (delete) Scratch Cat from the project by clicking or tapping the X in the Scratch Cat icon.

Draw a Toy Interface on the Backdrop

The *backdrop* is the background color or image that fills the screen of your app. Draw a backdrop for your matchup game as follows:

1. At the Stage, click the Backdrops tab. If you want, change the default costume name, which is `backdrop1`.

You won't be getting a costume out of the library for this project. Instead, you'll be using the Scratch drawing tools to create your own backdrop costume.

I created a name for this currently blank costume, typing `toyInterface` in the Name field.

2. Click or press the Convert to Vector button.

   Next, you'll draw a few rectangles and drag them to different parts of the screen to make the interface for your toy. Vector mode allows you to work with these shapes as individual objects that you can adjust as often as you need to during the design process.

3. Click the rectangle icon, and then click the empty backdrop and drag to draw a rectangle that fills the entire backdrop. Use the Fill tools to color the rectangle however you want.

   I used a gradient with shades of gray.

4. Click the rectangle icon again, then click and drag to draw a rectangle to create a black stripe across the top of the backdrop. Use the Fill tools to color the rectangle black.

5. Repeat Step 4 to create a black rectangle at the bottom of the backdrop.

6. Click the rectangle icon again, and then click and drag to draw a large rectangle in the middle of the backdrop. Fill any way you want and set the Outline thickness to something like `20`.

   This rectangle is the main viewing screen, which will house the reels where the sushi characters will be displayed.

7. Click the reshape icon (below the arrow icon), and then click the left edge of the rectangle to display a resizing dot. Drag the dot to stretch the edge of the rectangle, making it curve. Make as many dots as you want and stretch them to create the curve you want. Repeat this on the right side of the rectangle.

Figure 18-2 shows the backdrop with the filled in background rectangle, the top and bottom black stripes, and the rounded rectangle in the process of being curved at the edges.

TIP

If you want to adjust the position of any rectangle, click the Arrow key and then click the rectangle and drag it as needed.

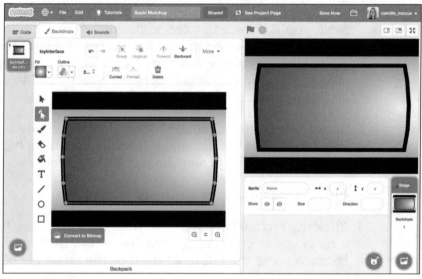

Figure 18-2

8. Add an inner edge to the rounded rectangle viewing screen as follows:

a. Click the Arrow key and then click the rounded rectangle you drew in Step 7.

b. Click the Copy button and then click the Paste button to create a copy of the rounded rectangle.

c. Click and drag a sizing dot at the corner of the copied rectangle to shrink it so that it fits just inside the original rectangle.

d. Set the outline color of the copy to gold and the fill color to transparent.

9. Create the windows for the reels where the sushi characters will be displayed. Click the rectangle icon, and then click and drag to draw a rectangle for the first reel. Use the Fill tools to color the rectangle white.

10. Copy and paste the rectangle you drew in Step 9 two more times to create rectangles for the windows of the second reel and the third reel. Drag the reel rectangles into the positions you want.

11. Click the text icon and then click the backdrop and type a title for your toy. (I typed **SUSHI MATCHUP**.) Click and drag a corner sizing dot of your text object to make it the size you want. Then click the center of the text object and drag it to the location you want.

12. While your text object title is still selected, click the Fill button to display the color selector pop-up. Adjust the sliders in the pop-up to make the title text the color you want, as shown in Figure 18-3.

Your toy interface is now complete!

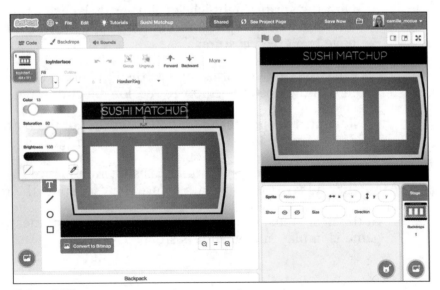

Figure 18-3

Add a Button Sprite

The button starts the action of the toy! The user presses the button to start the reels of images spinning. Add a button as follows:

1. In the sprite area of the Scratch interface, click the Choose a Sprite icon.

2. Click the Button1 sprite. Change the default sprite name (Button1) by typing button in the Sprite name field in the sprite attributes area.

3. Click the button sprite and drag to where you want it positioned on the background.

4. Change the size of your button sprite by typing a number in the Size field in the sprite attributes area.

   I used a size of 30, but you can use any size that makes sense for your game.

5. Click the Costumes tab to see the green costume that comes with the sprite. Right-click (Win) or Ctrl-click the Costume icon and select Duplicate from the pop-up menu. You now have two green costumes.

6. Click the first costume and use the Fill button and the Fill tool in the Costume editor to recolor the button red.

7. Rename the first costume (*not* the sprite) of the button sprite redbutton and rename the second costume greenbutton.

8. Click the redbutton costume, as shown in Figure 18-4, so that this costume appears before the user spins the reels.

In the next steps, you code button to change costumes when the game is in play and when it is stopped.

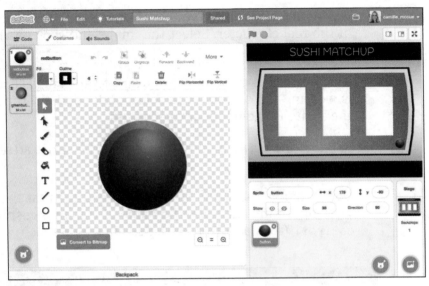

Figure 18-4

Add Reels Sprites

Your matchup toy features three reel sprites. Each reel has many character costumes that can appear during a spin. My game has three reel sprites and each reel has seven sushi costumes. The three reels are the same, with the same seven costumes.

During brainstorming, you found or drew images for the costumes and then saved the images on your computer.

TIP

Use thumbnail-sized images for sprite costumes. Smaller images result in better-looking sprites.

You may need to edit the images to remove background color. (See Chapter 2 for details on image editing.) Then follow these steps to add your reel sprites and multiple costume images to your toy:

1. In the Sprite area of the Scratch interface, hover over the Choose a Sprite button and choose Upload from the menu that appears.

2. Navigate to any image you previously saved for the costumes of the reel character. Select the image and click or tap the Choose button.

   A new sprite is created and appears on the stage. The sprite is wearing the costume you selected. By default, the name of the sprite is the name of the costume.

3. Rename the sprite by typing `reel1` in the sprite attributes area.

   Don't change the name of this first costume that the sprite is wearing. In my example, the name of this first costume is `caliroll` (for California roll). See Figure 18-5.

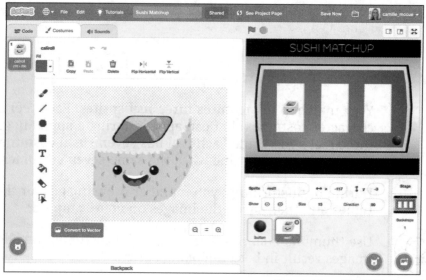

Shutterstock image 418466866 by Rimma Z

Figure 18-5

4. Add more costumes to the `reel1` sprite. Go to the Costumes tab for the `reel1` sprite, hover over the Choose a Costume button in the bottom-left corner, and then select Upload Costume from the pop-up menu. Navigate to the next

image you previously saved for the costumes of the reel character. Select the image and click or tap the Choose button.

The new costume is added to your collection of costumes for the `reel1` sprite.

5. Repeat Step 4 until you've added all the costumes you want for your `reel1` sprite.

My toy has a total of seven costumes. Note that the last costume you most recently uploaded is the one that the sprite is wearing. Each costume has a name and a number. For example, you can see in Figure 18-6 that `costume 4` is called `wasabi`. It doesn't matter what you name the costume because you'll be writing code for the costume number, not the name.

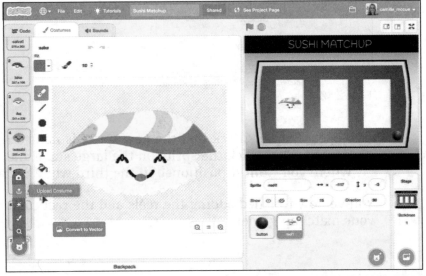

Shutterstock image 418466866 by Rimma Z

Figure 18-6

6. At the large stage, click the `reel1` sprite and drag it to where you want it positioned in the first white rectangle.

7. In the sprite attributes area, type a new size for the reel1 sprite.

   The size depends on how large you want the character to appear in the scene. I typed a size of 15.

8. Duplicate the reel1 sprite by Ctrl-clicking (Mac) or right-clicking (Win) the sprite icon and selecting Duplicate from the pop-up menu (see Figure 18-7). Check that the new sprite is named reel2 by default. Then click the sprite on the large stage and drag it to where you want it positioned in the second white rectangle.

Shutterstock image 418466866 by Rimma Z

Figure 18-7

9. Repeat Step 8. Check that the new sprite is named reel3 by default. Then click the sprite on the large stage and drag it to where you want it positioned in the third white rectangle.

You've now finished adding the reels and the reel costumes to your matchup game!

Add a Status Sprite

The last sprite you will make is a status sprite. After the user spins the reels, this sprite tells the user whether they have a match and what type of match. Follow these instructions:

1. In the sprite area of the Scratch interface, hover over the Choose a Sprite icon, and choose Paint from the menu that appears. See Figure 18-8.

   A new sprite appears in the sprite area, and the sprite Costume editor opens on the Costumes tab.

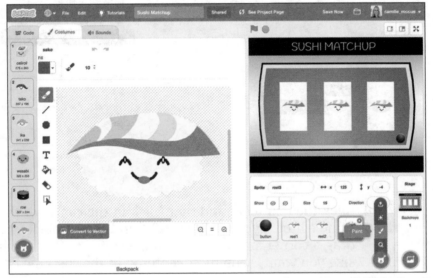

Shutterstock image 418466866 by Rimma Z

Figure 18-8

2. Change the default name for the sprite (Sprite1) to status. Change the default costume name for this sprite (costume1) to blank.

   Don't draw anything for this costume, just leave it blank. See Figure 18-9.

3. Add more costumes to the status sprite. Remain working in the Costumes tab for status. Hover over the Choose a Costume button in the bottom-left corner, and then select Paint from the pop-up menu. A new costume appears in the costume collection for the sprite. Name the new costume twoMatch.

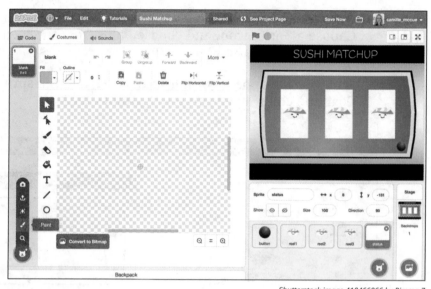

Figure 18-9

4. Click the text icon, and then click in the center of the costume editor. Type **MATCH TWO!** in the text object. Click and drag a corner sizing dot of your text object to make it the size you want, keeping it centered in the costume editor.

TIP

You can always reposition the object in the costume editor by clicking the Arrow tool and then clicking center of the text object and dragging it.

5. While your text object title is still selected, click the Fill button to display the color selector pop-up. Adjust the sliders in the pop-up to make the title text the color you want.

6. Repeat Steps 3–5 to create a third costume for the status sprite. Name this costume allMatch, and type **ALL MATCH!** in the text object.

7. Drag the status sprite to a position at the bottom of the stage, in the lower black rectangle.

See Figure 18-10. You've made all the sprites and their costumes for your matchup toy. Time to get coding!

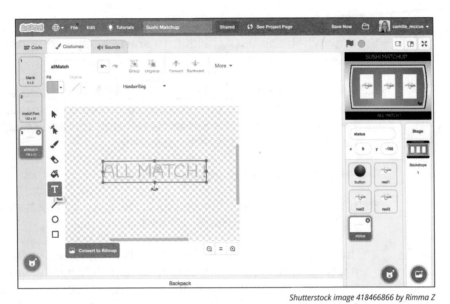

Figure 18-10

Code the Button to Trigger the Spin

You will write a when this sprite is clicked program for the button sprite. This program makes the button sprite broadcast to the reels the command to spin. It also tell the button sprite to wear its green costume when spinning the reels and its red costume the rest of the time. Lastly, the program for the button sprite calls a block, called checkMatch, which checks whether any of the characters on the reels match.

Write the program for the button sprite by following these steps:

1. Select the button sprite.

2. On the Code tab of the Scratch interface, select the Events icon. Drag a when this sprite clicked command to the Code workspace.

3. Select the Looks icon. Drag a switch costume to command to the Code workspace, and attach it to the previous command. Click the small arrow in the command and select greenbutton from the menu.

This command causes button to wear its greenbutton costume when the user clicks it to start the spinning of the
reels.

4. Select the Events icon. Drag a broadcast command to the
Code workspace and attach it to the previous command. Click
the small arrow in the broadcast command and select New
message from the drop-down menu.

The New Message dialog box appear.

5. In the New Message dialog box, type spin as the new message name (see Figure 18-11) and then click OK.

The broadcast command now reads broadcast spin. The
message spin will be broadcast to all other sprites and the
stage. Although you have not yet defined what spin means,
any object that is listening for a message will be able to
receive this broadcast.

New Message ✕

New message name:

spin

Cancel   OK

Figure 18-11

6. From the Control category, drag a wait until command and
attach it to the previous command. Then, from the Sensing
category, drag a key Space pressed? command and insert it
into the wait until command.

The completed command now looks like this:

The command just sits and waits until the user clicks the spacebar on the keyboard to stop the reels spinning. When the user clicks the space bar, it moves on to the next command.

7. Select the Looks icon. Drag a `switch costume to` command to the Code workspace, and attach it to the previous command. Click the small arrow in the command and select `redbutton` from the menu.

   This command causes `button` to wear its `redbutton` costume when the user clicks the spacebar to stop the spinning of the reels.

8. From the Control category, drag a `wait` command and attach it to the previous command. Type `0.5` in the empty field.

   The completed command reads `wait 0.5` seconds. It waits briefly before executing the next command. This makes sure that all the reels have had time to stop spinning before your program decides whether there are any matches.

9. Select the My Blocks icon. Click the Make a Block button to create a new code block. In the Make a Block dialog, name this new code block `checkMatch` and click OK.

   See Figure 18-12. The new block header is added to your workspace, and the new command tile, `checkMatch` is added to your commands in the My Blocks category. In the next section, you define what the `checkMatch` code block does.

10. From the My Blocks category, drag your new `checkMatch` command to the Code workspace, and attach it to the previous command.

   This command is the heart and soul of the Sushi Matchup program. It decides whether or not a match has occurred on the reels and then tells the user.

See Figure 18-13 for the complete `when this sprite clicked` code for the `button` sprite.

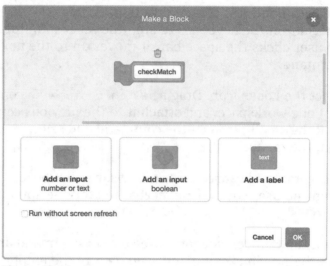

Figure 18-12

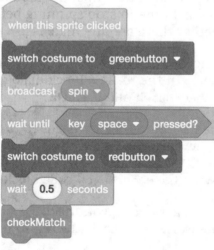

Figure 18-13

Create wear Variables

The wear variables identify which costume each reel is displaying. The value of each wear variable is assigned randomly during the spin, so that each reel displays a random costume. Then, when the spin is finished, the values of the wear variables are compared to see if any (or all) of them match.

Each reel has one wear variable. Follow these steps to create these variable for your matchup toy:

1. Click or tap the reel1 sprite to select it.

2. On the Code tab of the Scratch interface, select the Variables icon, and then click or tap the Make a Variable button.

   The New Variable dialog box opens, as shown in Figure 18-14.

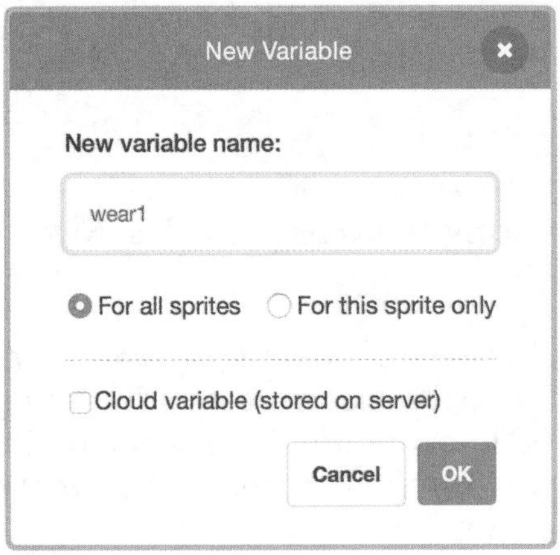

Figure 18-14

3. In the New Variable Name field, type wear1. Leave the For All Sprites radio button selected. Click or tap OK.

   The wear1 variable identifies the costume number of the reel1 sprite.

4. Repeat Step 3 to make two more variables, wear2 and wear3.

   You're making each variable available for all sprites, so it doesn't matter which sprite is selected when you create the wear variables. All three variables — wear1, wear2, and wear3 — are now listed with the Variables commands.

5. Click to deselect the check box in front of each variable name, as shown in Figure 18-15.

Now the variable names won't appear on the stage of your toy.

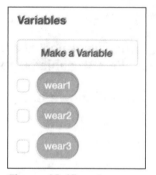

Variables

Make a Variable

wear1

wear2

wear3

Figure 18-15

You've now finished creating the wear variables. Next, we add sounds.

TECHNICAL STUFF

By selecting For All Sprites when creating the wear variables, you created variables that are *global* in scope. The value of each wear variable needs to be known outside the code on its reel so that the checkMatch algorithm (which you write later) can access and compare the values.

Add Sounds

The matchup toy needs a few sounds: a pop sound to make it sound like the reels are spinning, another sound to indicate when two reel match, and a third sound for when the user matches all the reels.

To add sounds to your sprites, do the following:

1. Select the button sprite.

2. On the Sounds tab of the Scratch interface, select the icon for the pop sound. Drag the sound onto the reel1 sprite in the sprites area.

(The pop sound came with the button sprite when you added it from the Scratch Library.) You've given a copy of pop to reel1.

3. Continue working on the Sounds tab for the button sprite. Delete the pop sound on button because you don't need it anymore.

4. Click the Choose a Sound icon at the bottom left of the Sounds tab and select Fairydust from the Choose a Sound library.

   Fairydust is added to the sounds available for the button sprite.

5. Click the Choose a Sound icon again (see Figure 18-16) and then select Cheer from the Choose a Sound library.

   Cheer is added to the sounds available for the button sprite. The icon for the Cheer sound is added below the icon for the Fairydust sound.

You've now completed adding the three sounds you need for your matchup toy.

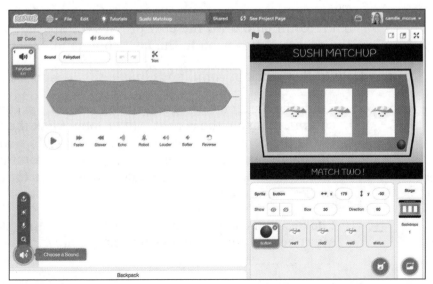

Shutterstock image 418466866 by Rimma Z

Figure 18-16

Code the Reels to Spin

This program makes each reel spin when it receives the spin broadcast message. It also tells each reel to stop spinning when the user clicks the spacebar. Lastly, for reel1 only, the code includes a command to play a pop sound so that the spin makes a spinning sound!

Follow these steps to write a when spin received program for the reels:

1. Select the reel1 sprite.

2. On the Code tab of the Scratch interface, select the Events icon. Drag a when I receive spin command to the Code workspace.

   Note that spin is already selected in the command because you've created only one broadcast so far.

3. From the Control category, drag a repeat until command and attach it to the previous command. Then, from the Sensing category, drag a key Space pressed? command and insert it into the wait until command.

   This completed command runs everything inside repeat until command until the user presses the spacebar. Then the program moves on to the next command.

4. Build this block of commands inside the repeat until:

   a. From the Variables category, drag a set my variable to command inside the repeat until loop. Click the arrow tab in the command to change my variable to wear1. From the Operators category, drag a pick random command into the set wear1 to command. Type values for the pick random command.

   I have seven costumes on each reel, so my range is 1 to 7. My complete command looks like the following:

b. Select the Looks icon. Drag a `switch costume to` command to the Code workspace, and attach it to the previous command, inside the `repeat until`. Select the Variables icon. Drag the `wear1` variable inside the `switch costume to` command.

This command now shows `switch costume to wear1`. This makes the `reel1` sprite display the costume number randomly chosen in the previous command.

c. From the Control category, drag a `wait` command and attach it to the previous command. Type `0.1` in the empty field.

This completed command now reads `wait 0.1 seconds`. The command waits briefly before executing the next command. This gives the user just enough time to see the costume before the program changes to the next randomly selected costume on the reel.

d. From the Sound category, drag a `start sound pop` command and attach it to the previous command.

Note that `pop` is already selected in the command because you have only one sound on the `reel1` sprite. The completed code for `reel1` is shown in Figure 18-17.

5. Add the code block from `reel1` to the other two reels. Click the top of the code block and drag it onto the sprite icon for `reel2` (in the sprite area). The entire block will be copied onto `reel2`. Repeat for `reel3`.

6. As shown in Figure 18-18, edit the `reel2` code by changing `wear1` to `wear 2` in the variable command. Change the `switch costume` command to `wear2`. Also, remove the `start sound pop` command from the `reel2` code block, because only one of the reels needs to play the sound.

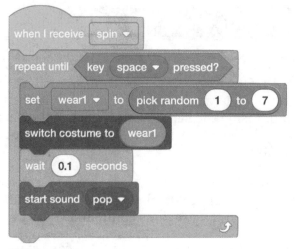

Figure 18-17

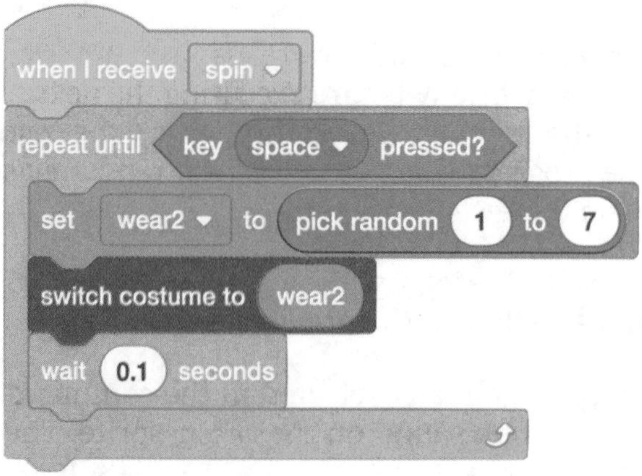

Figure 18-18

7. As shown in Figure 18-19, edit the reel3 code by changing wear1 to wear 3 in the variable command. Change the switch costume command to wear3. Also, remove the start sound pop command from the reel3 code block.

The reels now have the code they need to display randomly selected costumes that change quickly, one after another. This animation makes the reels appear to be spinning.

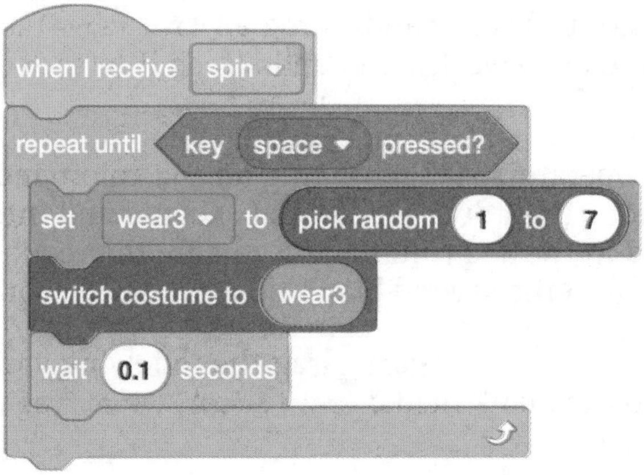

Figure 18-19

Code the checkMatch Block

You created a checkMatch code block header and command tile. Now write the code for that block. The checkMatch code block executes after the user has pressed the spacebar to stop spinning the reels.

This code block checks whether costumes on the reels match by comparing the values of the wear variables. It first checks the most restrictive condition: whether all three of the costumes match. If that fails, the block checks the second most restrictive condition: whether any two of the costumes match. If that fails, there is no match. The checkMatch condition then broadcasts the result to the status sprite.

You'll write the code for the checkMatch code block (shown in Figure 18-20) in several stages. Here you start by setting up the overall structure of the if-then-else command, and writing the code for the if part of this command. Remember, the if checks the most restrictive condition (a triple match):

1. Select the button sprite.

2. Work at the define checkMatch code block header in the workspace.

3. From the Control commands, drag an if—then—else command to the Code workspace, and attach it to the code block header.

4. From the Operators category, drag an and command into the if condition. Then drag an equals (=) command into the first blank field in the and command. Drag another equals (=) command into the second blank field in the and command.

5. From the Variables category, drag the following variables, in order, into the blank fields: wear1, wear2, wear2 again, and lastly, wear3.

The if—then—else command, and the condition in the if, should now look like this:

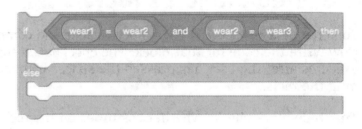

The if condition uses the and logical operator to test whether all three wear variables are the same value. If this occurs, the else command is ignored.

TIP

When using an and logical operator, every condition (all the items connected by and) must be true for the entire statement to be true.

If all three reel sprites are wearing the same costume, the then portion of the if—then—else executes. This makes the toy display **ALL MATCH!**

Now you write code to build the then consequence:

1. From the Events category, drag a broadcast command to the Code workspace and attach it inside the then command. Click the small arrow in the broadcast command and select New Message from the drop-down menu. In the New Message dialog

box, type status_allmatch as the new message name and then click OK.

The broadcast command now looks like this:

The status_allmatch message will be broadcast to all other sprites and the stage. Any object listening for a message will be able to receive this broadcast.

2. From the Sound category, drag a play sound until done command and attach it to the previous command. Press the small arrow in the command and select the Cheer sound.

The then consequence is now complete. This set of commands executes when the costumes on all three reels match. The broadcast will be heard by the status reel, which will display the **ALL MATCH!** message, and the most enthusiastic sound of the toy will play.

Next, you build the else consequence of the if-then-else command. The else executes when there is no triple match. And within that else, you build an if-then. This if-then checks whether a pair of the reels match.

1. From the Control commands, drag an if-then command to the Code workspace, and attach it inside the else.

2. From the Operators category, drag an or command into the if condition. Then drag another or command into the first blank field of the or. Then drag an equals (=) command into each of the three blank fields. The command should look like this:

3. From the Variable category, drag the following variables, in order, into the open fields: wear1, wear2, wear2, wear3, wear1, and lastly, wear3. The condition of the if-then command should now read like this:

This if condition uses the or logical operator to test the costumes on the reels in pairs. If any pair is a match, the toy produces a **MATCH TWO!**

TIP

When using an or logical operator, as long as *any* condition (any of the items connected by or) is true, the entire statement will be true.

TECHNICAL
STUFF

When using logical operators, test the most strict condition first. Then drop down to less strict conditions. In the matchup game, the most strict condition is matching all three reels. If the triple match occurs, you don't continue testing for matched pairs. There's no need to report a matched pair when the player has already won the triple match!

Finally, you build the then consequence of the if-then command, which is inside the else:

1. From the Events category, drag a broadcast command to the Code workspace and attach it inside the then. Click the small arrow in the broadcast command and select New Message from the drop-down menu. In the New Message dialog box, type status_matchTwo as the new message name and then click OK.

The broadcast command should now look like this:

broadcast status_matchtwo ▼

The status_matchtwo message will be broadcast to all other sprites and the stage. Any object that is listening for a message will be able to receive this broadcast.

2. From the Sound category, drag a play sound until done command and attach it to the previous command. Press the small arrow in the command and select the Fairydust sound.

This then consequence occurs when the costumes on only two of reels match, but not all three. The broadcast will be heard by the status reel, which will display the **MATCH TWO!** message, and the Fairydust sound will play.

That's the end of the code for the checkMatch block. Note that if a match does not occur, no message is broadcast to the status sprite, so it continues to wears the blank costume, which it was commanded to do when the button sprite was pressed. Coding the checkMatch block involved a lot of steps, so you might want to check your code against the completed code block in Figure 18-20.

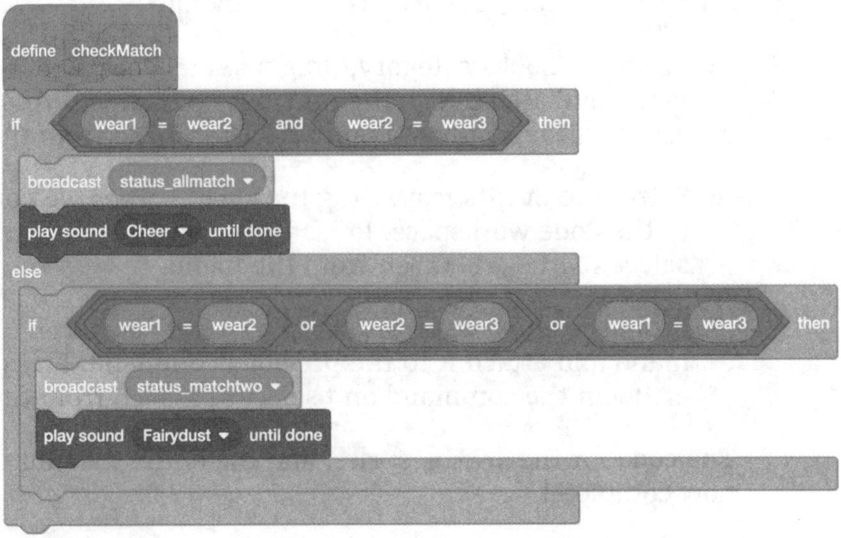

Figure 18-20

Code the status Sprite

You will write code so that when the status sprite receives a broadcast message from checkMatch, it knows what status to display to the user. Refer to Figure 18-21 and follow these steps:

1. Select the status sprite.

2. On the Code tab of the Scratch interface, select the Events icon. Drag the when I receive command to the Code workspace. Click the arrow in the command and select spin from the menu (it may already be the default).

3. From the Looks category, drag a switch costume to command and attach it to the previous command. Press the arrow in the command and select blank from the menu (it may already be the default).

4. Select the Events icon. Drag the when I receive command to the Code workspace. Press the arrow in the command and select status_matchtwo from the menu.

5. From the Looks category, drag a switch costume to command and attach it to the previous command. Press the arrow in the command and select matchTwo from the menu.

6. Select the Events icon. Drag the when I receive command to the Code workspace. Press the arrow in the command and select status_allmatch from the menu.

7. From the Looks category, drag a switch costume to command and attach it to the previous command. Press the arrow in the command and select allMatch from the menu.

The code for the status sprite, and the entire matchup toy is now complete!

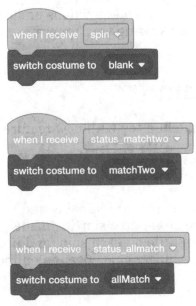

Figure 18-21

Save, Test, and Debug Your Program

As you work, Scratch saves your program in the cloud, so you don't have to take any special actions to save your work.

Test your program and fix any bugs to ensure that the program works the way you want it to. Run the program many times to make sure that all reel costumes appear. If you don't, check that the random number range is set correctly. Also, make sure the timing works well, and adjust the wait times if needed. Lastly, check that the program is displaying the correct status when you get a triple match or a pairwise match. If you have a bug here, you'll need to examine your checkMatch block for accuracy. (See Chapter 3 for help in debugging Scratch programs.)

Share Your Program with the World

After your program operates perfectly, it's time to share it. Set the status of your program to Share, and then add to your project page a description of your program and directions on how to run it. See Chapter 19 for details on sharing your programs.

Enhance Your Program

Consider enhancing your matchup toy with new features:

- **More character costumes on the reels:** Add new character costumes to make it more challenging to get a match!

- **Tokens:** Add tokens! Create a `tokens` variable and write green flag code that sets `tokens` to a starting value (such as 100). Decrement `tokens` a little on each spin, and increment `tokens` for matches. For a bigger challenge, go online and research `expected value` to figure out the best decrement and increment values for `tokens`.

Broadcasting

Broadcasting is a method of allowing sprites in Scratch (or, more generally, objects in other languages) to communicate with each other. Broadcasting consists of a sender, a message, and one or more receivers. For example, in the matchup toy, you wanted the button press to cause the reels to spin (display different character costumes). To make this happen, you have to code a message (`spin`) and make the `button` sprite broadcast this message when clicked.

The reels are "listening" at all times, ready to receive this message. Only when they receive the broadcast message do they execute the commands attached to `spin`. Broadcasting also keeps sprites operating on a "need to know basis." Each sprite broadcasts and receives only the information it needs to know.

More advanced programming languages such as JavaScript have other related ways to send information between objects. To learn more, research function parameters and function returns. (Scratch has function parameters, which you can use when creating a block.)

Logical Operators

You use *logical operators* when you need your program to make a decision based on multiple conditions. Logical operators include and, or, and not. Scratch uses the actual words for these operators, but JavaScript uses && for and, || for or, and ! for not.

The and operator means that *all* conditions must be true to return a true value. The or operator means that when *any* condition (one or more) is true, the statement returns a true value. The not operator makes a true condition false, and a false condition true.

In the matchup toy, you use the logical operator and to check for a triple match. To find out whether all three costumes on the reels match, you must check wear1 = wear 2 and wear2 = wear3. Both equalities must be true for a triple match.

The logical operator or is used to check for a matched pair. As long as any pair of costume numbers is equal — wear1 = wear2 or wear2 = wear3 or wear1 = wear3 — the statement is true. Only one of these equalities needs to be true for a matched pair.

Because the triple match condition is tested first, the pairwise match is tested only if the triple match is false — so at best, only a pair can match! However, if there are no pairwise matches, the or operator returns a false value. The false value means each reel sprite displayed a different costume, so there is no match of any type.

Part 6

Onwards and Upwards

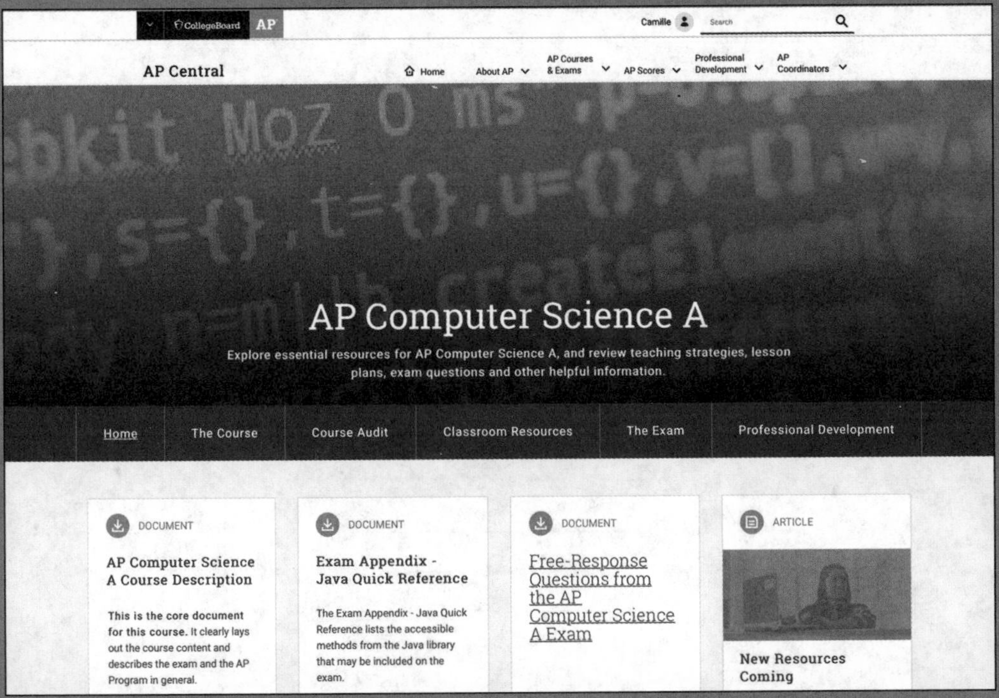

In this part you'll . . .

- Find inspiration for coding new apps

- Learn ways to get social by sharing your programs

- Explore your next steps in leveling up as a coder

Creating and Sharing

You've tackled a lot of fun projects in this book, but how do you bring your own ideas to life? How do you spark those ideas in the first place?

Unlike what many people think, coding is not a solo activity conducted in a dark room surrounded by caffeinated drinks. Coding is a highly creative — and highly social — process, one that solves real problems. The process of developing a new app, website, or control program for a gadget often brings together programmers, graphic designers, animators, musicians, data scientists, engineers, and advertising professionals. It's not just you and your computer; it's you and a lot of your peers working together towards a common goal!

For now, you don't need an army of people to code cool projects, but you do need a little inspiration to get started. This chapter will help you get your creative juices flowing, as well as get your completed projects out in front of an audience. Sharing your work and engaging in a larger community of coders is one of the best ways to build your skills — and your positive reputation.

Programming Your Own Ideas

You may find it tough to think up something you want to create with code. Or you might have a great idea but then discover that someone else beat you to it. Or maybe you have a cool, revolutionary idea but don't know how to turn something so complicated into code. Every coder on Earth has felt these same feelings and thought these same thoughts — you're not alone!

The key to pushing past these roadblocks is to take concrete action: Design and code something small. Getting a project underway will provide you with something that you can expand and evolve, or use as a springboard for bouncing in a new direction. In this section, you discover some techniques you can use to get creative and get going.

Remixing apps you like

What apps do you enjoy? Arcade games? Tamagotchi pets? Reaction time games? Why do you like them? Can you find something similar in the Scratch or App Lab or MakeCode libraries? In other words, can you find a kid-friendly example of the type of coding you want to do?

If you can find a project that appeals to you, you can *remix* it — start with the existing project and then change it to create your own version, adding new graphics and code however you want. Having a basic project as a starting point can help relieve some of the pressure of trying to create something from the nothing of a blank screen.

Figure 19-1 shows a Scratch project called Scrolling Slopeformer, by im_feeling_itchy. Scratchers are invited to remix the game and add new levels. To remix a project, click the Remix button at the top right of the project page. Your My Stuff folder now contains a copy of the project, for you to modify however you want. An *attribution* — a thank-you noting the original maker of the project — is added to your copy.

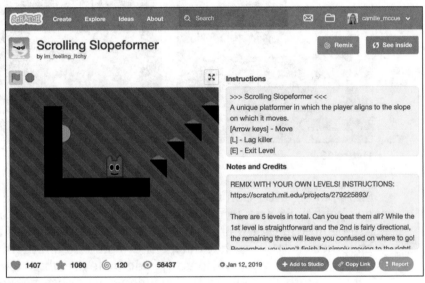

Figure 19-1

Observing daily human challenges

As you go through your day, pay attention to some of the little things that could be improved, and then think about how you could put your coding skills to work to fix them.

Do you want to build a simple website to help your brother with his dog-walking business? Or a Scratch game to quiz you on your French vocabulary? Maybe a simple geolocation app that helps your mom find where she parked her car? (This project is easy to do using a Google Maps API and another simple programming language called App Inventor.)

Or do you want to build a micro:bit temperature gadget that messages you in your room when the dessert you're refrigerating has reached the desired temperature? (I built the one shown in Figure 19-2. You can see the degrees Celsius reported from the micro:bit to the tablet, with the temperature reading dropping the moment the gadget is put into the fridge.)

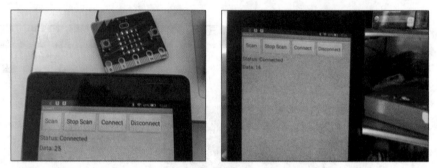

Figure 19-2

Start paying attention to the ways in which people of all ages go about their days, and jot down what you observe in a journal. Are people doing things that cost them time, money, effort, or happiness — things that maybe they could do another way? Reflect on your observations and add little drawings and notes about how to fix some of the challenges you observe. You might be able to transform some of your ideas into apps that could make big differences in people's lives!

Entering some contests

One way to spark ideas is to answer a design challenge in a competition. Contests such as the annual Congressional App Challenge (www.congressionalappchallenge.us/) invite students to work individually or in teams to prototype any app concept that will be useful to people in their community. For example, one student team came up with an app to help local veterans find support resources close to their homes. By thinking about and researching a specific audience and their needs, you begin empathizing with that group, and you can better *ideate* (come up with ideas for) new technology products to help them.

Other contests are hosted by a variety of organizations, sometimes leading up to a special event or limited to specific regions
or student audiences. For example, the Games for Change Student
Challenge (www.gamesforchange.org/studentchallenge/) hosts
competitions in major metropolitan areas, inviting students
to create and submit games that make a difference. Entrants can
create games about one of the challenge themes, such as endan-
gered species, disrupting aging, and automated communities
2050. New contest sponsors and events appear online with
varying frequencies — just Google *student app development*
competitions every so often to see what's out there!

haring and Showcasing Your Work

A great way to engage fully in the world of coding is to share
your work, making it publicly viewable. Doing so allows others
to use your app and provide feedback. Here's how to share your
work in each of the three IDEs used in this book.

Sharing a Scratch project

Scratch provides an exciting set of tools for sharing your work
with the world. After you've completed a project, follow these
steps to share it:

1. At the top of the workspace, click the See Project Page
   button.

2. At the project page, click the Share button.

   The project page appears, as shown in Figure 19-3.

3. In the empty Instructions box, type information about how
   to use your app. In the Notes and Credits box, type any additional information you want to provide.

4. If you want to add your project to a Scratch studio, click the
   Add to Studio button.

   See the next section for help on creating a Scratch studio.

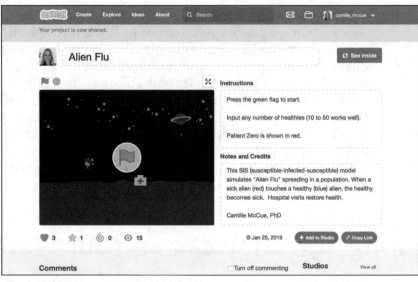

Figure 19-3

5. To copy the link to your shared project, click the Copy Link button.

   You can distribute this link by email or on any social media platform you want.

Working with Scratch studios

Scratch studios are collections of Scratch projects. When you create a studio, you are the manager of the studio and can add your projects and other people's shared projects to the studio. You can also invite one or more friends to serve as *curators* for your studio, which means they can also add projects. Here's a quick how-to on using Scratch Studios:

1. At the top of the Scratch workspace, click the My Stuff icon.

   The My Stuff page appears, as shown in Figure 19-4.

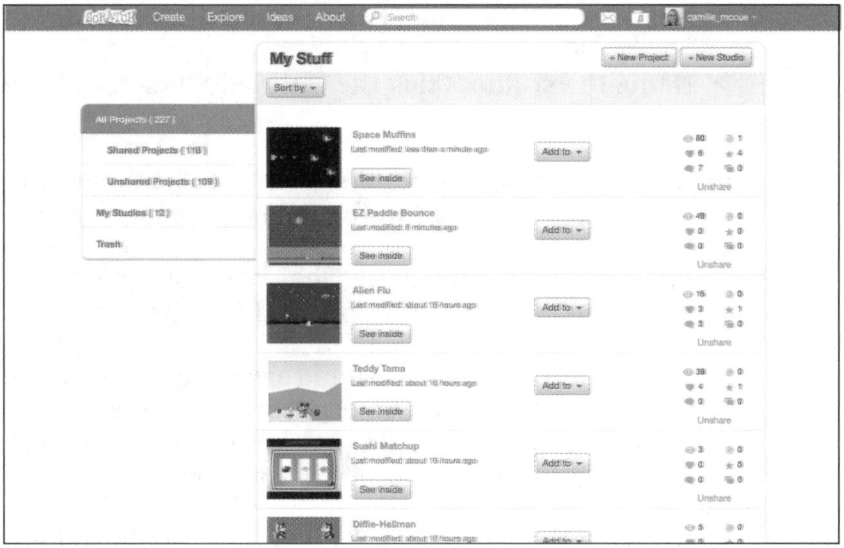

Figure 19-4

2. Add a new studio by clicking the New Studio button (top
right).

A new studio is created, as shown in Figure 19-5, with you
as the manager — the person in charge of the studio.

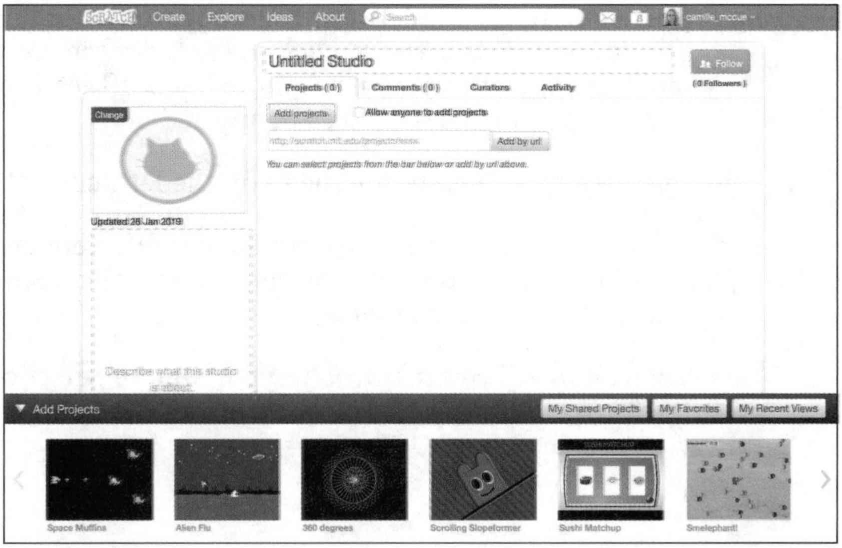

Figure 19-5

Here are some things you can do in your new studio:

- **Name the studio.** Click the Untitled Studio field and type a new name.

- **Add an icon for the studio.** Click the Change button near the Scratch Cat shadow (on the left) and upload your own image.

- **Describe the studio.** Note what types of projects it features by typing in the description field (on the left).

- **Add projects.** Click the Add Projects button and type the URL (web address) of the projects you want to add. You can also click the Add Projects drop-down list at the bottom of the screen and select the projects you want to add.

- **Let others add projects:** To let other people add projects, select the Allow Anyone to Add Projects check box.

- **Add curators.** Click the Curators tab and then click the Invite Curators button to add curators — friends who serve as co-managers — to your studio.

- **Follow.** Click the Follow button to follow the activity of the studio. Other people can also click the Follow button when they're in your studio to see the latest activity, such as the posting of new comments and the addition of projects. To view a log of this activity, click the Activity tab. Your Scratch mailbox (the letter icon next to the My Stuff icon) also receives and displays notices of any activity.

- **Open your studios.** In the menu on the left, click My Studios.

Whether you're looking at your studio or a different studio, or just checking out individual projects, you can also read or add comments to projects as follows:

- **Turn on or off commenting in your studio.** Select or deselect the Turn Off Commenting check box on the Comments tab in your studio.

✔ **See and post comments on a studio.** Click the Comments tab in the studio.

✔ **See and post comments on a project.** On the project page (not the See Inside page where the code is located), scroll down and type a comment in the empty box and then click Post. Figure 19-6 shows some of the comments left by Scratch users on my Space Muffins game.

REMEMBER

Your comments should be kind, helpful, and respectful — if you're trolling, Scratch will delete your comment.

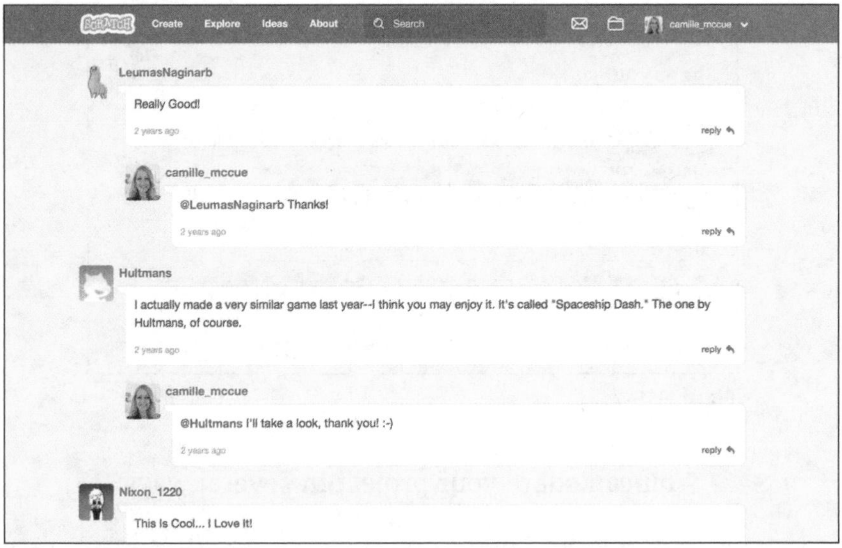

Figure 19-6

TIP

See the vast assortment of studios in Scratch! At your My Stuff Page, click Explore (in the upper-left corner) and then select Studios on the page that appears.

TIP

Besides commenting on a project, you can engage in other ways. At any project page, click the heart icon to love the project, click the star icon to make it a favorite, or click the spiral icon to remix it. The eyeball icon shows the number of views for the project.

Sharing an App Lab project

App Lab makes it easy to share your work, both online and to mobile devices! After you have completed a project, follow these steps to share it:

1. When you have a project open, click the Share button at the top of the App Lab workspace.

   A Share Your Project dialog box opens. Figure 19-7 shows the dialog box for my Get the Biscuit app. (Our Corgi, Pepper, loves to get biscuits!)

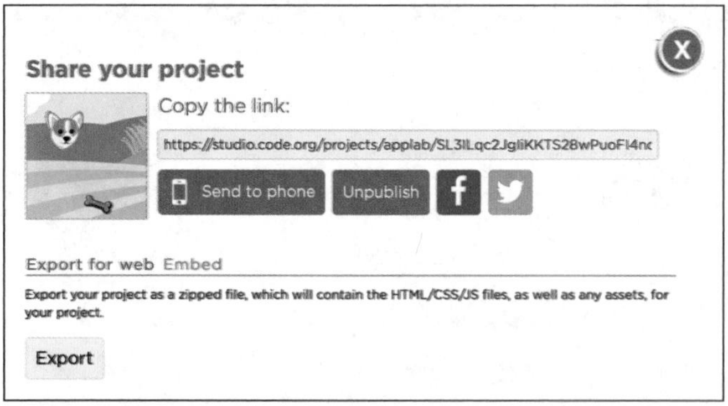

Share your project

Copy the link:

https://studio.code.org/projects/applab/SL3ILqc2JgliKKTS28wPuoFl4n

☐ Send to phone   Unpublish   f 🐦

Export for web Embed

Export your project as a zipped file, which will contain the HTML/CSS/JS files, as well as any assets, for your project.

Export

Figure 19-7

2. You can share your project in several ways:

   • **Copy the Link:** Copy the link, or URL address, and send it to someone in an email or instant message.

   • **Send to Phone:** Send the app's link to any phone number you enter. When recipients click the link, they can play with your app on their phones. Cool!

   • **Facebook and Twitter:** Create a post and include the link to your project. You can confirm the post before making it live.

   • **Export for Web or Embed:** Add your project to a web page on a website you operate. (You must click Advanced Options for this option to be available.)

If you decide that you no longer want to share a project, click the Unpublish button. (Note that this button is labeled Publish if you haven't published a project yet.)

Playing with shared App Lab projects

Code.org displays a huge collection (millions!) of projects shared by its users. You can see an organized list of your own projects by clicking My Projects in the App Lab IDE. To see the entire public collection of projects in Code.org (shown in Figure 19-8), go to https://studio.code.org/projects/public. This Projects page has many different collections, including App Lab projects. (You might have to scroll down the page to see these.)

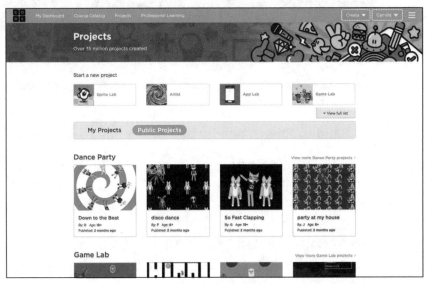

Figure 19-8

When you click a public project, a web page opens where you can use the app onscreen. For example, Figure 19-9 shows my Mystic Sheep toy as displayed by Code.org.

This page has three useful buttons in the upper-right corner:

- **View Code:** Open the project page from the creator of the project to see the code. From this page, you can also remix the code to make a copy for yourself.

Figure 19-9

▶ **Make My Own:** Go to App Lab, where you can begin creating your own project.

▶ **Send to Phone:** Send a link to the app to a mobile phone.

The sheer enormity of Code.org's shared projects should provide plenty of inspiration and guidance for endless hours of app creation!

Sharing a MakeCode project

To share a MakeCode project, you share a link to the project. Here's how to share your work:

1. At the top of the MakeCode workspace, click the Share button.

   The Share Project dialog box opens, as shown in Figure 19-10.

2. Click Publish project.

   A message appears, letting you know your project has been shared. Figure 19-11 shows the message I received when sharing my Sword Snake Shield project.

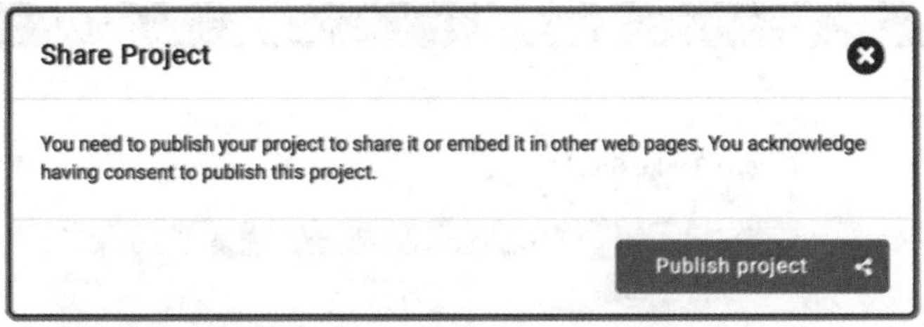

Figure 19-10

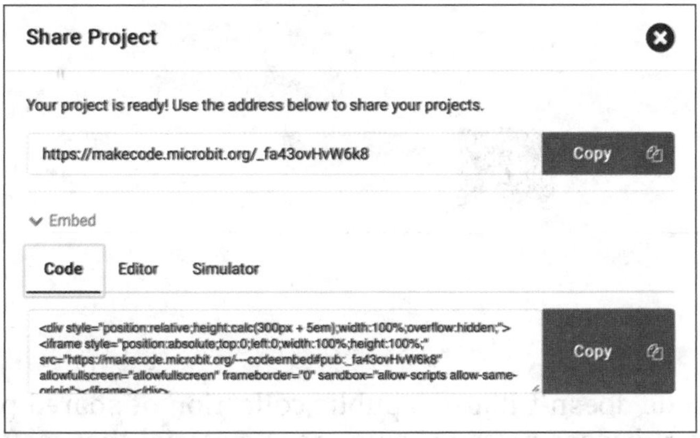

Figure 19-11

3. To share your project as a link, click the Copy button next to the URL address provided (the one that starts with `https://makecode.microbit.org/`) and then paste it into an email message, a social media post, or another distribution method.

Alternatively, you can share your project by embedding it in a web page you manage. Just click the Copy button next to the HTML code and then paste it into the source code for your web page.

4. Test the URL for the shared project by pasting it into the address bar of a web browser page to see what your user will see.

Figure 19-12 shows how the MakeCode project appears to users. Note that they can play with the simulator (in the lower-left corner of the web page), and they can download the code to tinker with it themselves.

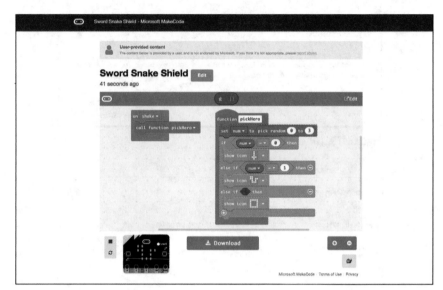

Figure 19-12

Exploring other MakeCode projects online

MakeCode doesn't house a public collection of shared projects. However, it does provide some great material that may spark your creativity at the MakeCode Ideas page located at https:// microbit.org/ideas/.

Another good place to get a variety of tutorials and example projects online is the MakeCode home page at https://makecode. microbit.org. You can reach the home page also by clicking the Home button at the top left of the workspace when working on any of your MakeCode projects.

Figure 19-13 shows the MakeCode home page. It lists your projects, followed by an extensive set of tutorials, followed lots of other resources, including mini-courses and hardware help.

TIP

MakeCode provides resources in many different programming languages, both block and text-based, for creating control code to construct micro:bit gadgets! Tinkering with the MakeCode files is a good way to get started with a new language such as Python.

TIP

MakeCode doesn't use a login system, so the files you create reside with your browser on your computer. If you want to use another browser or computer to work on a file, you must create and share the link to it (see the "Sharing a MakeCode project" section).

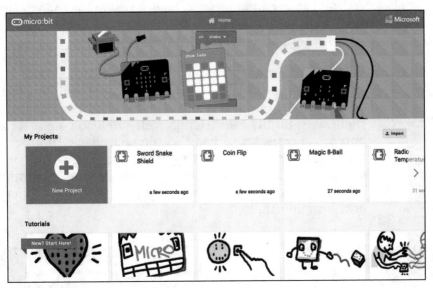

Figure 19-13

Where to Go from Here

Now that you have a handle on the basics of coding, I hope that you want to do even more coding! As you've seen, coding is a creative process that lets you take ideas and turn them into real, functional technology products. So what's next? Where do you go from here?

You can take many different routes to advance your coding skills. You can continue using the Scratch and JavaScript skills you've learned, building more complex programs and sharing them with family and friends. You can also construct apps to enter into contests or gadgets to use in hackathons or science and engineering fairs. With the two languages you've learned so far, you have a head start on AP (advanced placement) courses you can take in high school — and earn college credit at the same time!

Maybe you want to pair your new JavaScript skills with a bit of work in HTML and CSS — the languages of web pages — to build interactive websites. Or perhaps you want to go full throttle and learn a new computer programming language with increased complexity, such as Python or Java.

No matter what you set as your goal, resources and courses are available to help you level up. Keep reading to find out more!

Upping Your Game

You have several options for learning more about programming and computer science. This section describes some ways you can kick it up a notch and increase your coding mojo.

Online learning

Online courses give you the opportunity to learn at home, usually with background information, video, code examples, and *code runners*, places that let you build and run code and then check the code for functionality. Many online courses are free, and some higher-level for-pay options may be worthwhile. This section lists some popular providers.

For kids and tweens:

- **Kodable** (www.kodable.com/) provides fun, step-by-step, online and unplugged lessons that build a solid foundation in computational thinking and progress kids through JavaScript. Subscriptions range from $5 to $7 per month.

- **Tynker** (www.tynker.com/) offers coding experiences structured as interactives stories. Kids and tweens can build skills in game design, AR (augmented reality), Minecraft modding, and more. Subscriptions range from $10 to $20 per month, or you can purchase a lifetime subscription for $180.

For tweens and teens:

- ✔ **Code.org** (https://code.org/) created the App Lab IDE used in this book and offers great, free curriculum, targeting K–12 audiences, with modern, fun videos (many with celebrities) and cool projects. The highest level of content is the AP Computer Science Principles course, featuring JavaScript.

- ✔ **CodeHS** (https://codehs.com/) offers a fabulous collection of free courses, support videos, engaging projects, and a coderunner. CodeHS offers both AP Computer Science Principles and AP Computer Science A (Java). It also offers courses in website development, mobile apps, Python, and virtual reality programming (using A–Frame).

For teens who want to turn pro:

- ✔ **Codeacademy** (www.codeacademy.com/) provides professional–grade courses at introductory levels in web development, programming, and data science. Instruction, authentic coding projects, and human assistance can help you gain skills in HTML, CSS, Python, JavaScript, Java, SQL, Ruby, C++, and others. A monthly fee of $20 to $40 is based on the subscription you choose.

- ✔ **Coursera** (www.coursera.org/) provides affordable, professional–level courses, certificates and degrees from universities and tech entities worldwide. Examples include Algorithms, offered by Stanford, and Developing Applications with Google Cloud, offered by Google. Many courses are free, others have a one–time fee (under $100), and others offer monthly subscriptions ranging from $40 to $80.

- ✔ **Udemy** (www.udemy.com/) delivers a wide range of courses, developed by practitioner experts in fields including machine learning, pixel art, motion graphics, and 3D game development. Courses consist of user–paced instructional videos and range in cost from a few dollars to a few hundred dollars. (Higher–priced courses are frequently on sale for under $20.)

✓ **Udacity** (www.udacity.com/) offers courses and nanodegrees in cutting-edge fields in conjunction with elite providers. Expect to see progressive offerings including a Self-Driving Car Engineer Nanodegree with Nvidia, Uber, and McLaren. Udacity also focuses on helping learners get jobs following the completion of their coursework. Subscriptions can run about $200 per month.

Camps

If you seek all-day coding instruction surrounded by peers who share your enthusiasm for coding, consider attending a camp:

✓ **iD Tech** (www.idtech.com/) offers day and sleepaway summer camps held at university campuses nationwide. Camps feature coding, game design, digital media and robotics. The cost of a week-long day camp ranges from $750 to $1000.

✓ **Digital Media Academy** (www.digitalmediaacademy.org/) provides day and sleepaway summer camps, focusing on tech (coding and robotics) and media (photography, animation, and film production). Hosted onsite at major universities, day camps are in the $1000 to $1200 range.

✓ **University-hosted programs,** local to institutions across the country, provide a wide range of coding and general STEM (science, technology, engineering, and mathematics) camps. These camps are often funded through grants and may be offered for free. Check the websites of universities near you to discover the availability of these programs. Be sure to check by spring break before the summer of interest to ensure that you complete the admissions documents on time!

Books

For Dummies for Kids books — like the one you're reading now — are excellent and inexpensive guides for learning how to code in new languages. Each of the following books features a different language and provides several fun and instructional coding projects in that language, tailored for kids and tweens:

- *JavaScript For Kids For Dummies* by Chris Minnick and Eva Holland

- *Minecraft Modding For Kids For Dummies* by Sarah Guthals, PhD, Stephen Foster, PhD, and Lindsey Handley, PhD

- *Python For Kids For Dummies* by Brendan Scott

- *Raspberry Pi For Kids For Dummies* by Richard Wentk

- *Ruby For Kids For Dummies* by Christopher Haupt

- *Scratch For Kids For Dummies* by Derek Breen

And for parents and caregivers who want to ramp up their skills to help and support kids in their coding endeavors, take a look at *Helping Kids with Coding For Dummies* by Camille McCue, PhD (me!) and Sarah Guthals, PhD.

Next Steps

Fast-forward to five, ten, and fifteen years down the road, you may be thinking about how far you can take your passion for coding. Here's a glimpse of your possible future.

AP computer science courses

Many schools offer computer science courses beginning in middle school and progressing in difficulty through high school. An organization called the College Board — they administer the SAT exam — offers two Advanced Placement courses at the high school level: AP Computer Science Principles (AP CSP) and AP Computer Science A — Java (AP CSA). AP CSP gives you broad coverage of Internet architecture, programming fundamentals (taught in a variety of languages), cybersecurity, data basics, and the social impact of computing. AP CSA provides thorough introductory coverage of Java programming. Students earn AP scores for their performance in these courses and sufficiently high scores can translate into college credit.

Students who want to take these AP computer science courses but don't have access to them at their schools should check out a few excellent online providers. Code.org (https://code. org/) and CodeHS (https://codehs.com/) offer free courses. Others, including Johns Hopkins University — Center for Talented Youth (https://cty.jhu.edu), Edhesive (https:// edhesive.com), and International Connections Academy (www. internationalconnectionsacademy.com/) offer teacher-led credit-bearing courses for a fee. If you take one of these online courses, you'll have to find a local high school that will allow you to submit the AP performance task artifacts online (applies to only the AP CSP) as well as sit for the AP exam in May (applies to both courses).

College degrees for the budding coder

More and more universities are offering degree programs in coding and associated fields in computer science. Some of the most prestigious programs are offered at big-name, four-year institutions such as MIT, Stanford, Carnegie Mellon, Cornell, the University of Washington, Georgia Tech, the University of Texas at Austin (my alma mater!), Princeton, UPenn, CalTech, University of Southern California, University of Illinois — Urban Champaign, and many schools in the University of California system. You may also want to consider a more progressive path, such as attending Make School or Full Sail — these schools offer less traditional and more industry-targeted degrees, often with completion times of around two years.

Each school has a different focus, such as programming, human-computer interaction, robotics, data analytics, artificial intelligence, and virtual reality. Every university has its own entry requirements, acceptance rates, and costs, so researching your options early (during your freshman year of high school) can help ensure that you get on a path that leads you to your college destination.

TIP

Building your coding skills even before you apply to a university is critical to being admitted to a competitive school if you plan to major in computer science. You should start creating a portfolio of websites and apps — and control code for electronic and robotic devices if you plan to pursue computer engineering — so you can showcase your work and rise to the top of the pile of students applying for admission.

Cool coding careers

The proportion of careers that require a knowledge of coding is on the rise. By the time you enter the job market, that proportion will be even higher! Pursuing a career in coding means different things, and the available options are surprisingly diverse. You might choose an entrepreneurial path, building apps you sell in the App Store and the Google Play Store. You might choose to construct and maintain websites for companies, large and small. You might work in marketing or government as a social media guru.

Or maybe you'll be part of a team harvesting and analyzing data for any number of purposes, from sales to sports to medicine to politics. You could work in the arts, coding a range of creative experiences from virtual museums to 4D roller coaster rides to Cirque du Soleil–style productions. You could get involved in architecture and city planning, designing and coding smart cities and homes of the future.

Perhaps you'll work in personal electronics, creating cool new wearables for fashion, fitness, or health monitoring. Or perhaps you want to work at a university or a corporate research facility, inventing new languages and applications.

Whatever path you choose, you've made a smart choice in learning to code. And whether you pursue a coding career or not, your new coding abilities will elevate and enhance your education and career options in the years to come. Congratulations, you've reached the end — and it's only the beginning!

Index

About the Author

Camille Moody McCue, PhD is a STEM teacher and author who has worked for companies including IBM, NASA, and PBS. Always energized by her daily connection with students, Camille teaches everyone from kindergarteners to graduate students, and everything from Scratch to AP Computer Science (Java). Most recently, Camille helmed the development of a new, 5000-square-feet, state-of-the-art startup incubator — the largest K-12 facility of its kind — at the Adelson Educational Campus in Las Vegas.

Camille earned her Bachelor of Arts degree in mathematics (University of Texas at Austin) and her advanced degrees in curriculum and instruction; her doctoral research at University of Nevada, Las Vegas focused on tween coding. A longtime Dummies author, *Coding For Kids For Dummies*, 2nd Edition is Camille's tenth technology book for Wiley.

Camille and her awesome husband Michael are the proud parents of two absolutely incredible sons, Ian and Carson. Everyone in the household is remarkably tech-savvy with the exception of the beagles, Rocky and Lucy, and the Corgi, Pepper, who actively rebels against technology by growling at the television and chewing all available remote control devices.

Dedication

I dedicate this book to those I teach — my students — and those who taught me when I was a kid — my teachers and my parents. It takes a village.

Author's Acknowledgments

Thanks again to the amazing team members at Wiley for their dedicated work in supporting technology instruction through the *For Kids For Dummies* series! None of this would be possible without the talent and commitment of Executive Editor Steve Hayes, whom I've had the pleasure of working with for more than two decades. For this revised title, I am especially indebted to my fabulous project editor, Susan Pink, for her excellence in managing both the big picture and the small details with such aplomb. I'd also like to express my gratitude to technical editor, Michelle Krazniak, for ensuring that all those steps in all those projects work start-to-finish. And finally, thank you to Production Editor Siddique Shaik for laying everything out so beautifully and putting up with my endless revisions.

As always, I feel fortunate to have a wonderful family who champions my efforts to promote technology education among youth. Michael, Ian, Carson, and Beverly (my mom!) — your collective drive, intelligence, and love keeps me fired up, curious, learning, and motivated 24-7.

My last big thank you goes to all of my students, including those who allowed me to share photos of them in this book: Demetria, Zoe, Tal, Annelissa, and Owen; and Hailey, who let me feature her very first coding project.

Publisher's Acknowledgments

Executive Editor: Steve Hayes

Project Editor: Susan Pink

Copy Editor: Susan Pink

Technical Editor: Michelle Krazniak

Editorial Assistant: Matt Lowe

Sr. Editorial Assistant: Cherie Case

Production Editor: Siddique Shaik